THE MAKING OF MODERN THEOLOGY

19TH AND 20TH CENTURY THEOLOGICAL TEXTS

This series of theological texts is designed to introduce a new generation of readers — theological students, students of religion, ordained ministers and the interested general reader — to the writings of some of those Christian theologians who, since the beginning of the 19th century, have had a formative influence on the development of Christian theology. Each volume in the series is intended to introduce the theologian, to trace the emergence of key or seminal ideas and insights, particularly within their social and historical context, and to show how they have contributed to the making of modern theology. The primary way in which this is done is by allowing the theologians chosen to address us in their own words.

There are three sections to each volume. The Introduction includes a short biography of the theologian, and an overview of his or her theology in relation to the texts which have been selected for study. The Selected Texts, the bulk of each volume, consisted largely of substantial edited selections from the theologian's writings. Each text is also introduced with information about its origin and its significance. The guiding rule in making the selection of texts has been the question: in what way has this particular theologian contributed to the shaping of contemporary theology? A Select Bibliography provides guidance for those who wish to read further both in the primary literature and in secondary sources.

Friedrich Schleiermacher 1768-1834

THE MAKING OF MODERN THEOLOGY

19TH AND 20TH CENTURY THEOLOGICAL TEXTS

General Editor: John de Gruchy

FRIEDRICH SCHLEIERMACHER

Pioneer of Modern Theology

KEITH CLEMENTS

COLLINS

Collins Liturgical Publications
8 Grafton Street, London W1X 3LA

Collins Liturgical in USA
Icehouse One — 401
151 Union Street, San Francisco, CA 94111-1299

Collins Liturgical in Canada
Novalis, Box 9700, Terminal,
375 Rideau St, Ottawa, Ontario K1G 4B4

Distributed in Ireland by
Educational Company of Ireland
21 Talbot Street, Dublin 1

Collins Liturgical Australia
PO Box 316, Blackburn, Victoria 3130

Collins Liturgical New Zealand
PO Box 1, Auckland

Library of Congress Cataloging-in-Publication Data

Clements, K. W. (Keith W.)
    Friedrich Schleiermacher: pioneer of modern theology.

    (The Making of modern theology)
    Bibliography: p.
    Includes index.
    1. Schleiermacher, Friedrich, 1768-1834.   I. Title.   II. Series.
BX4827.S3C54 1987   230′.044′0924   87-18268
ISBN 0-00-599060-2
ISBN 0-00-599980-4 (pbk.)

ACKNOWLEDGEMENTS

The publishers acknowledge with thanks permission to quote from the following copyright translations:

Christmas Eve: Dialogue on the Incarnation, by permission of Terrence N. Tice; *Hermeneutics: The Handwritten Manuscripts*, by permission of The Scholars Press, Decatur, Ga; *The Life of Jesus*, by permission of Fortress Press, Philadelphia, Penn.

ISBN 0 00 599980 4

First published 1987

Typographical design Colin Reed
Typeset by John Swain & Son Limited
Printed in Great Britain by
Richard Clay Ltd, Bungay, Suffolk

CONTENTS

LIST OF SELECTED TEXTS

INTRODUCTION

1

SCHLEIERMACHER IN
HIS CONTEXT

Friedrich Schleiermacher (1768-1834) merits the title 'Pioneer of Modern Theology' in more than one sense. Acknowledged debts to his thought, and evidence of his influence, can be found in leading Protestant theologians, biblical scholars and philosophers of religion until well into the twentieth century. Moreover, the student who takes the trouble to read Schleiermacher at first hand is likely again and again to be prompted to remark 'How like Bultmann!' or 'Just so, Tillich!' Over a whole range of issues Schleiermacher foreshadows approaches which we recognize as distinctively 'modern' or, as some may prefer, 'liberal'.

On the other hand, as often happens in the history of ideas, direct historical determination of one thinker by a particular predecessor is not always explicitly demonstrable. The 'modern' note in Schleiermacher's work sounds familiar to us across nearly two centuries, regardless of how it may have been mediated by more recent theologians, because Schleiermacher to a remarkable extent articulated both questions and ideas which struggle towards the surface whenever and wherever theology resolutely faces the questions posed to traditional belief by modern western thought and culture: questions of historical knowledge of the past, of the scientific explanation of nature, of the nature of 'authority' in religion, of the validity of any claim to a special revelation in a multi-religious world, and, most fundamentally, the question of what place is left for belief in 'God', in an age which trusts more in immediate experience and empirical observation than in metaphysical speculation about any reality existing 'beyond' human experience in this world. Whether as progenitor or prototype, Schleiermacher was the first Protestant theologian to be acutely aware of these issues and to attempt a systematic answer to them. With him, modern Protestant theology effectively begins.

Not that one is likely to find many actual disciples of Schleiermacher today. But there has been renewed and increasingly sympathetic interest in his work over the past thirty years, by scholars who have felt that it was time for him to be given a fairer hearing than obtained during the ascendency of 'neo-orthodox' theology under Karl Barth (1886-1968) and Emil Brunner (1889-1966) — the period, roughly, 1920-60. This theology, returning to the Reformed emphasis upon the unknowability of God apart from his self-revelation through his Word, and underlining the utter distinction between God and the world, regarded Schleiermacher as leading the great defection in modern Protestant theology. Thanks to him, it was alleged, the interest of theology centred on the human phenomenon of 'religion' instead of its real subject, God's own glory and self-revelation to man. The issues here are indeed fundamental and serious, but one result of Barth's unrelenting polemic against Schleiermacher was that generations of students became much more familiar with Barth's criticisms than with Schleiermacher himself, who was dismissed at second-hand. That is still at least partly the case today. For this reason, we shall hardly refer to Barth's critique again until the end of this introductory section. It is important that some acquaintance should be made with Schleiermacher without the feeling that Barth is breathing down one's neck. In any case, Barth's own rejection of Schleiermacher grew out of a ceaseless dialogue with one whom he respected even in profound disagreement. In 1946, the University of Bonn, like so much else in Germany, lay in the ruins of war. It was Barth himself, spending the summer semester there, who discovered the bust of Schleiermacher lying amid the rubble and restored it to a position of appropriate honour!

Schleiermacher must be allowed to speak for himself, and from his own context. He desired to be, not a name for posterity, but a servant of his own generation, church and people, and as such he first deserves to be known and assessed. We need therefore to appreciate the intellectual, social and cultural context in which his life and thought were shaped, and the critical significance of that context for Christianity in the whole modern era.

SCHLEIERMACHER'S CONTEXT: THE ENLIGHTENMENT AND ITS AFTERMATH

Schleiermacher was born into the world of the Enlightenment (German *Aufklärung*), that period of European thought and culture occupying roughly the whole of the eighteenth century and, with the latter half of the preceding century, comprising what is often called the 'Age of Reason'. As that name implies, it was the period when the innate and universal endowments of human thought were adjudged to be capable of providing man with whatever knowledge of nature, morality and religion was necessary for his welfare. It marked the beginnings in Europe of the exile of orthodox Christian theology towards the periphery of intellectual and social life, as both the credibility of, and necessity for, supernaturally inspired doctrines were challenged by rational, anti-dogmatic modes of thought.

The Enlightenment has been described as being English in origin and French in style. Certainly a main English ingredient was the new picture of the natural universe based on the physics of Isaac Newton (1642-1727), a grand cosmic machine of interacting causes and effects, precisely measurable and predictable according to mathematical laws. And it was another Englishman, Lord Herbert of Cherbury (1583-1648) who was among the first to give a cogent statement of the beliefs later to be popularly known as *Deism:* the common notions inherent in the human mind constituted 'the only truly Catholic Church which does not err'. These notions were, essentially, belief in a supreme Being who exercised government over all things, who was to be worshipped by the practice of virtue, and who in the life to come would mete out just rewards and punishments. These beliefs could be known quite apart from special divine revelations, and in any case claims to such supernatural disclosures or miraculous interventions were highly dubious. In part, this aversion to the traditional claims of religious authority was a legacy of the Wars of Religion which had devastated Europe earlier in the seventeenth century. When the pressing of the truth-claims of Catholics and Protestants had such dire results, commonsense was bound to ask whether any party actually had any distinctive truth that was worth knowing. The 'natural religion' that could be discerned by unaided reason seemed more than enough for human needs.

The Enlightenment was certainly French in style in that it was critical of much that was traditional or appealed to the authority of tradition as such, and it was in France that the critical temper became most virulent in the atheist, materialist and anti-clerical *philosophes,* of whom Voltaire was the ablest spokesman. In Germany, however, the Enlightenment found particular expression in *historical* study. A new interest in the ancient civilizations, coupled with exact study of the classical languages, arose. This began to have uncomfortable implications for orthodox religion when rationalistic scholars insisted that the biblical texts, too, could and should be studied as purely human documents, regardless of any veneration of them by the Church as media of divine revelation. A radical exponent of this line was H.S. Reimarus (1694-1768) who argued that the New Testament, even in its most supernaturalistic passages, could be explained in wholly naturalistic terms. He thus eliminated all elements of the miraculous from the ministry of Jesus and the early Church. Less extreme, and remaining much more within the context of orthodox Lutheranism, was J.S. Semler (1725-91) of Halle, who was nevertheless prepared to allow a far greater human factor in the biblical narratives than had hitherto been recognized. But the rationalistic attack on the historical basis of orthodox Christianity had a peculiarly double-edged irony as seen in one of the greatest figures of the German Enlightenment, the popularizer of Reimarus, G.E. Lessing (1729-81). According to Lessing, quite apart from the dubiety of the historicity of much of the biblical record, necessary truths of revelation could not in any case depend on accidental truths (i.e. particular events) of history. Historical happenings can do no more than exemplify or illustrate the general, universal principles of truth and virtue which reason can attain. Once again, special revelation is rendered superfluous, indeed offensive, to human capacity. It was Lessing, also, who articulated most clearly the Enlightenment idea of the progressive education of the human race through successive historical epochs. The very term 'Enlightenment' itself, of course, as a self-description indicated the consciousness of an age confident of a burgeoning maturity.

No one emphasized 'maturity' more than did Immanuel Kant (1724-1804), the philosopher of Königsberg whom history has shown to be the pivotal intellectual figure of the age. The distinctively moral element in man, says Kant, requires man to be an *autonomous* agent, that is, one who acts according to what he sees to be intrinsically true and good, and not in tutelage to some external authority. For Kant, the Enlightenment was itself a decisive step towards the emancipation of man from the 'tutelage' of mediaeval times. Man needed, and was reaching, his 'coming of age'. In one sense, then, Kant represented the summation of the Enlightenment. In another sense he pointed beyond it and opened up the whole question of human knowledge in a new way, which was to be pursued throughout the nineteenth century and into the present. For, while Kant believed with the Enlightenment in human reason as the key to knowledge, he radically redefined the scope and role of reason. Human reason, he maintained, is capable of dealing only with the sensible, empirical world. It does so, moreover, by applying to the 'phenomena' perceived by the senses the innate or *a priori* categories with which the mind is endowed ('programmed' we might say in today's computer-jargon). 'Space' and 'time', for instance, are not entities which the mind perceives in the world, but basic principles by which the mind organizes its perceptions into a coherent pattern. Human knowledge is thus a synthetic creation of the mind working upon external data, and contains an irreducibly 'subjective' element. There is no completely 'objective' knowledge of 'things-in-themselves', that is, totally independent of the activity of the knowing mind.

Along with much else, the traditional metaphysical systems in which the doctrine of God, and the proofs of God's existence, had been framed, were casualties of the Kantian revolution. Such systems had presupposed that the human mind could comprehend realities beyond the spatio-temporal world, to the extent even of being able to deduce their existence, whereas on the Kantian view reason was limited to this finite world — and even then was confined within the perspective of our own subjectivity. Not that Kant wished to demolish belief in God. In fact he claimed that he was removing an untenable *knowledge* of God in order to make room for *faith*. The real basis of faith, he maintained, lay in man's moral sense, the 'practical' as distinct from 'pure' reason. We are endowed with awareness of a 'categorical imperative', the voice within of moral obligation, which, when obeyed, signifies our acknowledgment of a moral lawgiver. God is thus an inference from the moral sense, not a conclusion to an abstract argument of 'pure' reason. From Kant onwards, human awareness, subjectivity and feeling would be central in western thought.

The Enlightenment was not just the prerogative of refined philosophy. It articulated the spirit of the age, which was one of relative indifference to religion among the educated classes, who were casually grateful to the philosophers for conveniently adducing intellectual grounds for their scepticism. It was the age of form. Human behaviour should, ideally, conform to the patterns of what could most universally be demonstrated to be prudent. This cool rationality in manners and social convention was reflected in the clean-limbed, classical architecture of the time, not to mention the elegant, formal garden where every shrub had its place. Indeed everything had its rationally assigned place, even God who was located at a safe distance from the physical world of natural causes and effects, and the realm of human decisions.

But the mainstream of an age often generates its counter-currents. Eighteenth century Germany was home not only to the Enlightenment but to *Pietism* also. This revival of personal religion was, admittedly, more of a reaction against the arid, lifeless orthodoxy prevailing among the Protestant churches since the later seventeenth century, than a protest against rationalistic philosophy at large. Worship had become a dull formality; sermons displayed an abstruse irrelevance; Christian living seemed little different from social convention. Against all this, P.J. Spener (1635-1705) and others launched a campaign for a renewed fervour in preaching, prayer and pastoral life, centred on Bible teaching and programmes of charity among the poor in the parishes. So began one of the most significant religious movements in modern Germany, which was to have far-reaching social and cultural consequences as well. The greatest figure of eighteenth century Pietism was Nicolas von Zinzendorf (1700-60), an aristocrat who underwent an intensely emotional experience of personal conversion and dedication to Jesus, and who ever after evinced a simple, fervid faith in the atoning blood of the Lamb. Herrnhut, on one of his estates, became a centre for Moravian refugees, and Zinzendorf himself eventually became leader of the Moravian Brethren. 'Pietism' today often denotes a highly individualistic brand of Christianity, but the Moravians, as well as burning with personal devotion to the Saviour, were emphatically communal in practice. As well as living in close-knit communities they founded schools, orphanages and other charitable institutions, and were the Protestant pioneers of overseas missions. Their influence upon John Wesley (1703-91), founder of English Methodism, is well known. While conservative in theology, their emphasis upon personal, inward experience as against formal conformity to external doctrinal norms, was to be an important ingredient in that loosening of intellectualism which, on the philosophical and cultural level, was to mark the end of the Enlightenment.

On that level, the later eighteenth century saw the growth of the *Romantic* movement in art and literature — and philosophy too. In its infancy as the *Sturm und Drang* (storm and stress) movement, it was expressive of a cheerful impatience with the essentially conformist ethos of the Enlightenment, and a desire to allow the *individual's* feelings, however apparently irrational and unconventional, to have their way against the generalized notions of prudence, rationality and even morality. Full-grown Romanticism, which by the turn of the century had effectively replaced the Enlightenment as the dominant cultural ethos, was at once a view of art and human creativity, an attitude to human behaviour, and a philosophical vision embracing all reality, human, natural and divine.

The term Romanticism is, notoriously, as hard to define as it is frequently used. Indeed, one of the Romantic characteristics is to cross boundaries and to soften distinctions. German Romanticist philosophy had as its motif 'the idea of the infinite in the finite . . . in which nature and human history alike are conceived synoptically as forms or manifest-ations of one infinite Life'.[1]* It thus has a more religious or mystical ring than the naturalistic Enlightenment view of the world. J.W. von Goethe (1749-1832) the greatest of the Romantic poets and writers, conveys its essence in his lines:

> So, waiting, I have won from you the end:
> God's presence in each element.

The undertone could, of course, be taken to be pantheistic. Romanticism was above all a journey into the inner feelings and passions which consti-tuted the soul and which were to be regarded, ultimately, as a microcosm of the infinite life with which they were in continuity. 'The way to all mys-teries lies inwards,' stated the young Novalis, another of the most distinc-tive Romantic poets. English-speaking readers will be more familiar with the closely parallel sentiments of a poet like Wordsworth, especially his *Lines Composed a Few Miles Above Tintern Abbey,* and the works of Keats and Shelley. This inward journey — which was simultaneously a passage to the infinite — carried an emphasis upon the individual as opposed to abstractions about 'man', and on *feeling* as against intellectu-alized concepts and external norms.

Towards the end of the eighteenth century, then, Enlightenment rationality and Romantic passion were vying to be the order of the day. Both, however, had reason to be excited by *the* great event of the age, with which on the political level the modern age emerges: the French Revolu-tion of 1789. Intellectually and emotionally it convulsed the whole of Europe. Rationalists hailed its necessity; Romantics celebrated its accomplishment as the triumph of human will over despotism, at least in its first idealistic phase. It was the great, signal demonstration, that what had been, need no longer be, despite the obscurantist dogma (religious as well as political) which had supported so powerfully the status quo. It represented a breakthrough in emancipation, a further release from tutelage.

The intellectual and cultural scene of the latter eighteenth century was not, however, a comfortable context for Christian theology. The initia-tive had moved to the advocates of, successively, rationality and feeling. Both rejected religious dogma with its appeal to authority, whether of an infallible Bible or an infallible Church. Instead, both acknowledged

* Numbered notes are on pp. 279ff.

some inherent human capacity to discern whatever truth there was to learn. Dogmatic orthodoxy in the churches survived, of course, but by degrees it was ever in retreat, especially in the face of the advancing historical criticism. It might insist on the miraculous as testimony to the supernatural origin and the truth of Christianity, but the miraculous was itself slipping away like an ebb tide from the world of everyday experience. Pietism survived attractively, but at the price of keeping itself well insulated from the newer intellectual movements. What options remained for theology? It could of course accede to the demands of rationalism and move in a deistic direction, resulting in a decidedly attenuated form of belief, a vague providence and an unexceptionable moralism. Such capitulation to the spirit of the age would have cost Christianity its identity completely.

There was another option, however. The Enlightenment and its successor Romanticism alike regarded themselves as the champions of human interests in opposition to all obscurantism, dogmatism, and subjection to a 'God' conceived of as a limit or threat to human freedom and fulfilment. The age claimed to speak on behalf of man, and the traditional religious orthodoxy seemed a tedious, quarrelsome exercise in outworn creeds which served no human interest whatever. A daring but highly creative option for theology, faced with such assumptions, would be to challenge the age at the core of its citadel-belief: humanity. Suppose that theology was to agree with Enlightened and Romantic alike that man's real business is to be true to his own nature, to be truly and fully human, and yet to claim that the age has not yet properly discerned what it is to be human? Suppose that religion was to be re-defined as something that was unique, yet the heart and source from which all that is worthy in humanity arises? In other words, religion as the core and essence of being human? And suppose further that 'God' was to be viewed not as a doubtful or speculative 'extra' to the natural world and the realm of human experience, but as the ineluctable object of every moment of human consciousness? Suppose all this, and a whole new vista of theological possibilities arises. This is precisely what happened with Friedrich Schleiermacher. 'This is my vocation,' he once wrote, 'to represent more clearly that which dwells in all true human beings, and to bring it home to their consciences.'[2]

Though the Enlightenment has gone, and likewise Romanticism, the fruits of those movements are still with us, and the central question around which theology and contemporary thought meet is still 'What is man?' That in itself is a valid reason for continually paying attention to

Schleiermacher, who pioneered the approach to God as an experience essential to true humanity.

SCHLEIERMACHER: A LIFE IN OUTLINE

Friedrich Daniel Ernst Schleiermacher was born on 21 November, 1768, in the Silesian town of Breslau (today's Wroclaw in what is now the south of Poland). His father, Gottlieb Schleiermacher, was a Reformed pastor, a chaplain in the Prussian army. Both the 'Prussian' and 'Reformed' sides to his heritage were to be deeply significant to the future theologian. Germany at that time was not a single state but a conglomerate of principalities of which Prussia, occupying several territories to the north and east, and Austria in the south-east, were by far the most powerful. By 'Reformed' is meant those Protestant churches which in historical origin and in doctrine and order were Calvinist rather than Lutheran. It was both as a Prussian patriot and as an expositor of the Reformed faith that Friedrich was to make his name in his own time.

Gottlieb Schleiermacher had in younger days contented himself with a rationalist Enlightenment theology, but through some Moravian contacts he experienced a devotional renewal. He and his wife determined to entrust their children to a Moravian upbringing, and so in 1783 Friedrich, with his sister and brother, joined the Moravian boarding school at Niesky. Friedrich was never to see his parents again. His mother died a few weeks after his entry to the school, and his father's journeys with the regiment prevented any further contact beyond their frequent correspondence.

The community of the Brethren effectively became Friedrich's new family home in his formative and adolescent years. In 1785 he transferred to the Moravian theological seminary at Barby. The warm-hearted devotion to Jesus, with the shared life of rigorous study, vital worship and close personal relationships gave him his primary religious experience and its influence never left him, even though he was to leave the Moravians. Many years later, after a return visit to Barby one Easter, he wrote to his sister:

Verily, dear Charlotte, there is not throughout Christendom, in our day, a form of public worship which expresses more worthily, and awakens more thoroughly the spirit of true Christian piety, than does that of the Herrnhut brotherhood! And while absorbed in heavenly faith and love, I could not but feel deeply how far behind them we are in our church, where the poor sermon is everything, and even this is hampered by meaningless restrictions, while, on the other hand, it is subject to every change in the times, and is rarely animated by a true and living spirit.[3]

The heart of religion as an inward, highly personal experience of the influence of Jesus, not in an 'individualistic' sense but always in community, was to be the core of both Schleiermacher's theology and spirituality. That is why, in later life, again after revisiting the Brethren he could say:

> There is no other place which could call forth such lively reminiscences of the entire onward movement of my mind, from its first awakening to a higher life, up to the point which I have at present attained. Here it was for the first time that I awoke to the consciousness of the relations of man to a higher world. . . . Here it was that that mystic tendency developed itself, which has been of so much importance to me, and has supported and carried me through all the storms of scepticism. Then it was only germinating, now it has attained its full development, and I may say, that after all I have passed through, *I have become a Herrnhuter again, only of a higher order.* (Emphases mine)[4]

A Herrnhuter *again:* the seminarian at Barby felt led, eventually, to break with the community which had spiritually nurtured him. At the heart of Moravian piety was the belief in the atoning sacrifice of Christ for sin. Acceptance of this doctrine in grateful, humble submission would bring a liberating, peace-bearing bliss to the soul. Friedrich felt unsure of the doctrine in its customary formulation, and finally summoned up the nerve to admit to these doubts in a moving letter to his father, which was as sensitive to the pain which it would cause his parent, as it was honest in stating his intellectual and spiritual difficulties. We can only imagine Friedrich's feelings on reading his father's angry and anguished reply, modelled on St Paul's address to the Galatians — 'Oh, thou insensate son! Who has deluded thee, that thou no longer obeyest the truth, thou, before whose eyes Christ was pictured. . . .' Friedrich responded eloquently and characteristically:

> You say that the glorification of God is the end of our being, and I say the glorification of the creature; is not this in the end the same thing? Is not the Creator more and more glorified the happier and the more perfect his creatures are? I also consider the glorification of God, the endeavour to become ever more pleasant in his sight, the first of duties; I also would regard myself as the most unfeeling, the most miserable of men, did I not feel the most sincere love and filial gratitude towards the all-good God, who, even in the midst of the painful circumstances that

are now besetting me, lets me experience such far preponderating good. Why do you say, dearest father, that I no longer worship your God, but that I desire to serve stranger gods? Is it not one and the same God who has created you and me, and whom we both reverence?[5]

Already in this letter we detect a distinction which was to be crucial in Schleiermacher's thought, between religion as that which is felt inwardly and doctrinal statement as that which is an outward formulation and secondary in importance to feeling.

But it was no wonder that Gottlieb felt betrayed. He had placed his son with the Brethren as an insurance against the corruption of the Enlightenment — and now those acids of scepticism were apparently eroding even these walls of piety. He showed scant sympathy when Friedrich lamented the sudden coldness of the Moravian teachers towards him — 'it is their duty to take care that one mangy sheep do not contaminate the whole flock'. In fact, paradoxically, it was the very isolation of Barby, cultural and intellectual, which was the root cause of Friedrich's disquiet. There had been no attempt to face squarely the rationalist questions. The views of critical scholars like Semler were filtered to the students only via the pejorative comments of the teachers. To the independent-minded, such virtual censorship could only increase curiosity for the wider intellectual world. Friedrich and a small circle of friends had begun to read Goethe surreptiously. He came to the conclusion that a resolution of his uncertainties could only be found in an atmosphere of free inquiry such as Barby could not provide, and eventually his father grudgingly agreed to his going to the University of Halle, on condition that he lodged with an uncle, Samuel Stubenrauch, who taught theology there. The Enlightenment certainly made its presence felt at Halle, where Semler, though now advanced in years, was a member of the faculty.

Schleiermacher matriculated at Halle in 1787. Particularly under the guidance of August Eberhard he made an intensive study of Kant, whose *Critique of Pure Reason* had appeared in 1781, and *Critique of Practical Reason* in 1788, Schleiermacher's second year at Halle. (Schleiermacher did in fact meet Kant at Königsberg a few years later in 1791.) But we do not get a picture of an especially exciting university experience. In fact after only two years Schleiermacher followed Samuel Stubenrauch to Drossen, near Frankfurt-on-Oder, where his uncle had taken a country parish with a parsonage offering suitable accommodation for private study. Nor does Schleiermacher at this period appear to have been a very exciting person. Kant continued to be a major interest, and he began to flex his intellectual muscles with some essays on moral good and freedom. But the Christianity which these propounded was attenuated even by Kantian standards, man's goal being simply to fulfil his moral duty here and now without reference either to God or a hereafter. His physical health was poor, his mind suffering from a degree of rationalistic aridity, his spirit depressed. It seemed a far cry from both the warmth at Barby and the hopes with which he had left the Brethren.

Subsequent events showed that one of the main reasons for this trough in his thought and spirits was simply lack of congenial company. In 1790 he successfully took the theological examination in Berlin to qualify as a minister in the Reformed Church, and soon after became private tutor to the family of a nobleman, Count Wilhelm Dohna, at Schlobitten in East Prussia. Here was a warm, pious, refined and intellectually lively domestic circle in which Schleiermacher began to flourish again both personally and intellectually. He wrote to his father (now reconciled with his son): 'My heart is properly cultivated here, and is not left to wither under the burden of cold erudition, and my religious feelings are not deadened by theological enquiries. Here also I enjoy that domestic life for which, after all, man was created, and that warms my feelings . . . I learn to know myself and others.'[6] Not least of the attractions were the charms of one of the young countesses, Frederike, who was but first of a series of women for whom Schleiermacher was to cherish an ardent, inward admiration. Intellectually, he continued to study Kant and to develop his own concept of the importance of *individuality*, the seed for which had already been sown in the Moravian ethos.

The Schlobitten idyll ended in 1794, when differences of opinion between the Count and Schleiermacher as to the best methods of educating the children became so acute that, in a friendly spirit, both sides agreed to terminate their relationship. Schleiermacher returned to Berlin to take the second theological examination, taught briefly at a classical seminary in the city, and then took the post of assistant pastor to the Reformed congregation at Landsberg in Brandenburg, where he ministered until 1796. His pen was active in translating a number of English sermons (he learned the language with the Moravians, whose schools were attended by many English pupils). Here too he began his study of Spinoza (1632-77) whose philosophy of the 'World Spirit' was widely regarded as pantheist in approach. Then, in 1796 came his first appointment to a post of mature responsibility, that of Reformed preacher to Berlin's principal hospital, the Charité. In itself this chaplaincy was a relatively inconspicuous position, but it was a secure niche in the Prussian capital, where Schleiermacher was to make his first major impact on the religious and intellectual scene of his day, and his first decisive contribution to the story of modern theology.

Educated Berlin at this time was falling under the spell of Goethe, and fast becoming the vanguard of Romanticism. Schleiermacher quickly found an entrée into some of the liveliest salons and circles of artists and thinkers. Especially important for him were those who gathered at the home of a Jewish couple, Marcus and Henriette Herz. There in turn he met a young poet and writer, Friedrich Schlegel (1772-1829), an encounter which was a turning point in his life. Schlegel's lively imagination and restless, penetrating mind quickly captured Schleiermacher's soul. He poured out his excitement to his sister:

> Wherever he be, his wit and his simplicity make him the most delightful companion; but to me he is more than that, he is of the greatest and most essential benefit. I have never, it is true, been deprived of intellectual society here, and I have always known some man with whom I could talk about each individual science that interests me. Nevertheless, I always felt the want of a companion to whom I could freely impart my philosophical ideas, and who would enter with me into the deepest abstractions. This great void he has filled up most gloriously. To him I can not only pour out what is already in me, but by means of the exhaustless stream of new views and new ideas which is ever flowing into him, much that has been lying dormant in me, is likewise set in motion.[7]

The very terms in which Schleiermacher describes this relationship and the creativity it induced in himself are Romantic indeed. Value is placed on inward feeling and vision, and above all on the *growth* of individuality. But by the same token, if we describe Schleiermacher as a 'Romantic' at this stage, the term must be carefully qualified. As we have seen, its meaning is inherently elusive. It is certainly misleading to see Schleiermacher, under the sway of the Berlin poets and artists, being swept into an irrational subjectivity, of which his theology was merely a religious version. True, for a time the relationship with Schlegel was close. For some months they lodged together. They undertook one of the most important literary ventures of the time, the translation of the works of Plato. But Schleiermacher himself, while having a certain susceptibility to poetry and music, was not in any sense an artist, nor did he make any pretensions to being one. Moreover, the particular friendship with Schlegel did not last more than a few years, and the Plato translation was, eventually, to be left to Schleiermacher alone.

The deepest importance of the Berlin Romantic circles to Schleiermacher lay less in Romanticism as such, than in the personal friendships they opened to him. This side of Schleiermacher's life is not incidental to his theology: his personal relationships with others formed the most pressing and immediate context to his theology, and between his understanding of human friendship and his theology there are the most intimate connexions and parallels. When, as we shall see, Schleiermacher speaks of the essence of religion as being the 'feeling of dependence', his emphasis on 'dependence' cannot be fully grasped except in the light of the intricate dependencies between humans, as wrought out of his own experience. To Henriette Herz, his most intimate confidante over the years, he once wrote:

> Ah, dear Jette, be generous and write often to me; that alone can keep me alive, for I cannot thrive in solitude. In truth, I am the least independent and least self-sufficing of mortals; indeed, I sometimes doubt whether I be really an individual. I stretch out all my roots and leaves in search of affection; it is necessary for me to feel myself in immediate contact with it, and when I am unable to drink in full draughts of it, I at once dry up and wither. Such is my nature; there is no remedy for it; *and, if there were, I should not wish to employ it.* (Emphases mine)[8]

Not that Schleiermacher was the morbid, self-pitying individual who drains others of their concern to the point of exhaustion. He was eminently sociable and highly popular in company. To his friends he clearly gave as much as he received, and he was loved by many for his animation, his gentle wit and sincere interest in others' concerns. He would have understood, and heartily endorsed, Martin Buber's dictum over a century later, that 'All real living is meeting'. Again, to Henriette Herz he could write while away from Berlin:

> Yes: let us confess with pride and joy, that there are not many such united circles of love and friendship as ours, which has been brought together in such a wonderful way from almost all the extremities of the moral world. All who belong to it are at this moment present to my soul. May they all draw closer and closer around you, each in his own way and with such gifts of mind and heart as he may possess.[9]

To belong to such a 'circle' was for Schleiermacher an almost mystical reality, yet not one in which any particular member lost his or her individuality to that of the group as a whole. Rather, the individual contributed something utterly unique to the group, and at the same time the whole circle was somehow present and active through each member of the group. Another such circle was that of the family of Ernst von Willich, a pastor whom Schleiermacher first met in 1801, and whose wedded joy

Schleiermacher felt as if it was his own. 'With you, in you, and for you, and all our other dear ones, then I live, and the world must be content with what I can do for it in the way of my vocation', he wrote to Willich and his bride on their wedding.

This is perhaps the point at which to deal with Schleiermacher's relations with women, a matter which has by turns embarrassed and intrigued his biographers and commentators. Even in his own lifetime his friendship with Henriette Herz caused a certain amount of gossip in the Berlin salons. Neither Henriette nor Schleiermacher made any pretence to hide their genuine admiration for each other. They contented themselves with asserting that their ties were purely those of intellectual and spiritual friendship, which indeed they were. Marcus Herz was no less equable. More fraught was Schleiermacher's love for Eleonore Grunow, the wife of a Berlin pastor, and unhappily so. Schleiermacher desperately wanted Eleonore to dissolve her miserable, childless marriage, in his eyes no real marriage at all, so as to enable their union. The attachment was mutual — virtually a secret betrothal — and Schleiermacher nursed hopes of a positive decision about the divorce as late as 1804, when she finally decided to continue in her present state. Schleiermacher later returned to a more conventional attitude to the indissolubility of marriage. But in these years he had certainly been a Romantic in the sense of allowing passion its rights over convention. His literary response to a work of Schlegel, *Confidential Letter on Lucinde* was written in this mood and aroused some controversy. Schleiermacher's own attainment of marital bliss came, ironically, through the tragically early death of Ernst von Willich, whose wedding had enthused Schleiermacher so much. What had already been an admiring friendship with Willich's bride, Henriette von Kathen, blossomed into a love for his widow and they married in 1809. 'Except in domestic life, all that we enjoy and all that we attempt, is but vain illusion,' said Schleiermacher to his sister Charlotte.

Schleiermacher enjoyed close friendships and intellectual discourse with both men and women. But there were aspects of his feelings and thought which he could evidently trust to a woman more than to a man, whether the woman was his sister Charlotte, or Eleonore Grunow, or his bride-to-be, or her sister Charlotte von Kathen, or of course his chief partner in dialogue Henriette Herz. Writing to Eleonore in 1802, he confessed that his high regard for women was awakened first by the young Countess Frederike — who had since tragically died — and that awakening, he said, was a meritorious work, 'for it is through the knowledge of the feminine heart and mind that I have learnt to know what real human worth is'. But it was to Charlotte von Kathen that he made one of his most revealing admissions — 'if ever I find myself sportively indulging in an impossible wish, it is, that I were a woman'.[10] This confession has provoked wry smiles or raised eyebrows from later commentators who are inclined to commend Schleiermacher to a psychiatrist without further ado. The reason Schleiermacher gives for this fantasy, however, should be noted. It is the opportunity, as he sees it, for women to retain inner feelings of love and imagination as compared with men who are so quickly lost and occupied in activity. Protestant *machismo* ('Rise up, O men of God!') has long been embarrassed by feminine humanity, and perhaps Schleiermacher has an important speech to deliver in this direction as well. Maybe feminist theology will offer yet another new perspective on Schleiermacher.

Schleiermacher was a diligent and effective preacher at the Charité, where he alternated with his Lutheran colleague in ministering to the congregation of patients and visitors on Sundays. But the most important 'addresses' of this Berlin period were never delivered orally. *On Religion. Speeches to its Cultured Despisers* appeared in 1799, an auspicious date for a work which, as well as giving its young author a reputation overnight, bid farewell to the Enlightenment of the eighteenth century and opened up one of the most important highways of Christian thought in the nineteenth century. The 'cultured despisers' were the educated, artistic and philosophical habitués of the Berlin salons who, if they gave religious belief any consideration, did so only to dismiss it as an obsolete stage of human development. But, through them, it was a whole age, moving from rationalism towards Romanticism, which was addressed. It was, therefore, a work of apologetics, and rarely can such a work have been cast in such a direct form of speech, attacking the sceptics as ruthlessly as it defended the faith. 'There was a time when you held it a mark of special courage to cast off partially the restraints of inherited dogma. You were still ready to discuss particular subjects, though it were only to efface one of these notions. . . . But that time is long past. Piety is now no more to be spoken of, and even the Graces, with most unwomanly hardness, destroy the tenderest blossoms of the human heart, and I can link the interest I require from you to nothing but your contempt. I will ask you therefore, just to be well-informed and thorough-going in this contempt.'[11] The irony, the wit, the person-to-person style is sustained unflinchingly throughout all five chapters.

Such assurance was based in part upon a deep conviction that the cultured dismissal of religion stemmed from an ignorance of what actually constituted religion. Not the outwardly observable practices, not the written dogmatic formulae, about which so much could be argued for and against, formed the essence of religion, but the *inward disposition* of piety — 'You must transport yourselves into the interior of a pious soul and seek to understand its inspiration.' There, argued Schleiermacher, religion would be seen to be quite distinct from *knowledge* of the world (the sphere of science) and from *activity* in the world (the sphere of art and ethics). Religion was *feeling*, a basic or primal awareness of the self in its relation to 'the Universe', by which Schleiermacher does not mean just the space-time cosmos, but rather the world as mediating the presence of the Infinite, or God. It should be noted that while Schleiermacher distinguished feeling from knowing and doing, equally he insisted that feeling always accompanies these other two elements, and therefore it is 'impossible to be moral or scientific without being religious'. The cultured despisers, by rejecting religion, were depriving themselves of the vital energies necessary to those selfsame activities which they affected to value so highly. 'Consequently, you have no living insight into any of these activities.'

Now the cultured despisers did not constitute a homogeneous group, and in the *Speeches* Schleiermacher was fighting on several fronts at once for the distinctness and fundamental human significance of religion. The Enlightenment had greatly elevated the stature of natural science as a form of knowledge. Religion was not to be rejected on scientific grounds, according to Schleiermacher, as if religion claimed to be a theory about the causal structure of the world in competition with the scientific view. Religion took no such analytical view, being instead a direct, intuitive feeling for the Infinite in and through the finite world. Nor, however much Romanticist aesthetics appealed to Schleiermacher via Schlegel and others, was religion a matter of artistic taste or activity. Perhaps most significantly of all, it was to be distinguished from moral activity. Schleiermacher probably saw the chief threat here as coming from idealistic philosophy in the wake of Kant, especially in the work of J.G. Fichte (1762-1814) who in a speculative way interpreted 'God' as meaning the supreme idea of moral duty. For one thing, this wholly subsumed religion under morality, which for Schleiermacher ignored the nature of religion as a *sui generis* 'sense and taste for the Infinite' (though to be sure it did not exist *apart from* morality). For another, 'the highest utterance of the speculation of our days, complete rounded idealism', as was found in Fichte and most grandly in the system of G.W.F. Hegel (1770-1831), claimed just too much for the human mind. It was a proud, arrogant attempt at a complete, immediate apprehension of ultimate truth which 'annihilates the Universe, while it seems to aim at constructing it'. In other words, it claims to enable man to think like God. Finally, throughout his identification of religion with feeling there ran a resolution to distinguish religion from *doctrine*, which is a conceptual, descriptive reflection upon religious feeling, and not itself the essence of religion. Brian Gerrish is right to identify here one of the main poles of Schleiermacher's thought, namely, the distinction between 'feeling and intellect, intuitive piety and reflective belief'. In part, it was a distinction which he received from the Moravians with their insistence on personal piety, but it was only by intensifying the distinction that he was able to leave the Moravians and maintain his own Christian identity, when the one doctrine which the Brethren did emphasize proved unacceptable to him in its current formulation.

Dogmatic orthodoxy, no less than Enlightenment rationalism or speculative idealism, is therefore rejected as not touching the heart of religion, by the author of the *Speeches*. With the *Speeches* there was born what is aptly described as 'liberal evangelicalism',[12] that is, that resilient tendency in modern Protestantism to underline the personal nature of faith as an immediate relation to the living God, as distinct from submission to doctrinal or credal propositions about God.

The *Speeches* excited immediate attention in Germany just because so many issues of the day were dealt with at once, by means of a single, compelling insight into the nature of religion. It spoke from, and to, a particular generation's experience. Many Romantics welcomed it, including Goethe himself — until he came to the fourth chapter which cogently argues for the necessity of a community, or church, for the cultivation of religion. From the rationalist side were those who saw it as pious sentimentality. In some orthodox eyes it manifested a dangerous, free-thinking pantheistic tendency and some church officials in Berlin were alarmed. But to many the *Speeches* came as a revelation, indeed a liberation. 'They killed rationalism for me', said Claus Harms, a younger contemporary whose mature theology was to be of a very different stamp to Schleiermacher's. It could now be seen that religion need not be edged out of human interests as obsolete and irrelevant. It had an integrity and a role of its own, and it belonged to essential humanity. Schleiermacher had therefore reclaimed the centre of the intellectual and cultural stage for religion, to the extent that it could question rationalism, Romanticism or any human science or cultural stance, not from without, as Pietism and dogmatic orthodoxy felt inclined to do, but from within the arena of debate.

Schleiermacher moved on from, but never disowned, the *Speeches*. He brought out a revised edition, with copious explanatory notes and shorn of much of the quasi-pantheistic language, in 1806 and a final edition in 1822. In later years, as will be seen, he was to define the religious or pious 'feeling' more precisely. But the feeling, the 'pious self-consciousness', as such remained fundamental to his thought. Soon after the *Speeches* of 1799 came the *Soliloquies*, which explored further the importance of individuality and the relation between self-consciousness and intuition of the Universe.

In 1802 Schleiermacher left Berlin once again for the east, to become minister of the Court-Church in Stolpe, Pomerania — actually several Reformed congregations in the area. His intellectual development continued as he worked on a book examining the history of ethical theories, with particular reference to Kant and Fichte. Two years later he was appointed by the Prussian government to a professorship at the University of Halle, and to the post of University Preacher there. Halle was at that time being formed into the foremost Prussian University, and Schleiermacher's own Prussian loyalty was evident in accepting the post, since he had already turned down a more lucrative offer at Würzburg in Bavaria. The theological faculty at Halle, hitherto entirely Lutheran in composition, contained a wide variety of theological stances, from Pietists and orthodox to rationalists. In this, his first academic appointment, Schleiermacher lectured on a wide variety of subjects (as was usual at that time before the age of specialization) — philosophy, systematic theology, ethics and New Testament exegesis. In addition, a quite new subject appeared on the new professor's list of classes: hermeneutics. Preparation for these excited him considerably, for he was aware that he was breaking quite new ground in proposing that the study and interpretation of historical texts required a strictly scientific discipline of its own. This field was to form one of Schleiermacher's most signal contributions to nineteenth century thought, and not just in its theological application either. An historical-critical essay on 1 Timothy demonstrated his ability in the biblical field as in others, arguing against its Pauline authorship on internal grounds.

Schleiermacher's five years at Halle were a period of development, marking his transition from being a youthful genius with Romantic leanings, to being a mature theologian capable of dealing expansively and authoritatively with his Protestant tradition in relation to the culture and thought of his time. This process of maturation was assisted by changes in his personal circumstances, and by the impact of social and political events in Germany. For both the man and his country it proved to be a most critical time.

On the personal level, it was during this time that Eleonore Grunow finally declined to separate from her husband. Passion, then, did not always have the last word in the face of social convention. Some have seen in her refusal one of the stimuli behind the relatively short *Christmas Eve. Dialogue on the Incarnation* of 1806. Intended as a Christmas gift to his friends, this is a theological discussion of the credibility and historicity of the orthodox person of Christ, in relation to the immediate joy experienced in the Christmas festival. The 'dialogue', however, is not set in the form of abstract dialectics, but in the drawing-room of a middle-class circle of family and friends keeping Christmas together, and who each in turn serve as the mouthpieces of theological viewpoints varying from conventional Pietism to rationalist scepticism. It may be, as Gerrish suggests, that in this charming vignette of the cultured German Christmas, the picture of the hostess radiating warmth and love among the family and their guests, Schleiermacher was grieving over the domestic bliss that was eluding him in Eleonore's refusal. But from a theological point of view it is more interesting to ask which of the interlocutors is speaking for Schleiermacher himself. Probably none of them exactly reproduces his thoughts at that time, and indeed his mind was very likely still in a process of internal debate with itself. In one sense, the whole group is Schleiermacherian in acknowledging as a genuine experience the feelings of peaceful joy as the Christmas festival diffuses benevolence far and near. Differences emerge over what, if anything, is the historical source of these feelings. Two characters in particular probably echo Schleiermacher's views most nearly. The first is Ernst, who against the rationalist Leonhardt argues that 'Something inward must lie at its basis, otherwise it could neither be effective nor endure. This inner something, however, can be nothing else than the ground of all joy itself.' That is, the universal joy of Christmas bespeaks a restoration of our original, primal or archetypal humanity, something that could not emerge from our present divided humanity as it is. There is therefore a *historical necessity* for a redeemer, to account for this experience, and in answer to Enlightenment scepticism the slightest historical traces are sufficient as actual 'evidence'. Second, the character Eduard expounds the meaning of Christmas along the lines of the Fourth Gospel — Schleiermacher's own favourite New Testament source of christology — wherein salvation is depicted as the realization by an individual that his life is grounded in the eternal Being which has united himself with man. This realization, in turn, is historically mediated to the individual through the actual community of the Church, the community of true self-consciousness.

Much interest has been devoted to *Christmas Eve* in recent years. Not only does it show Schleiermacher still holding to religious *feeling* (in this case Christmas joy and peace) as the keystone of Christianity, but it also reveals Schleiermacher moving rapidly towards the features of his mature theology: the question of the relation of this emotion to history, on the one hand the present church community which acts as the bearer of this consciousness, and on the other hand the historical *origin* of this consciousness in the figure of the Redeemer himself. The early Schleiermacher had never been a wholly 'subjective' individualist, as the passages in the *Speeches* dealing with Christian community demonstrate, and likewise those passages rejecting any notion of a general 'natural religion' over and above the 'positive' historical religions of the world. But *Christmas Eve* manifests a markedly increased historical awareness, and this can be connected not only to his current concerns in New Testament history and exegesis, and hermeneutics, but also to the *contemporary* history of Prussia which was rapidly approaching a crisis.

Germany at the turn of the century was a paradox to the world. It was breathtaking in its cultural advance — and in its political backwardness. A people who could produce a Lessing, a Kant, a Goethe, a Schiller and a Beethoven still could not produce a constitution anywhere near resembling a form of representative government. It was still a conglomerate of separate principalities, many of them tiny city-states and princedoms. But size was no guarantee of progress, as even relatively powerful Prussia showed. Germany was still an agrarian society, indeed in many areas still a feudalistic one especially on the huge estates in the east of Prussia where serfdom still effectively operated. The intellectual acumen of the Enlightenment and the imaginative genius of Romanticism had in Germany barely engaged with major social and political issues, as compared with the French *philosophes* who, intellectually, helped to prepare the way for the Revolution. That revolution was — until the Reign of Terror — heart-stirring for many in Germany (including the youthful Schleiermacher) but relatively ineffective in creating a new political consciousness. Social prejudice and snobbery were often ridiculed by the German dramatists, but criticism of social attitudes is not criticism of social and political structure. Eventually in Prussia some reforms of the feudalistic order were set in train, under the resolute statesman Freiherr vom Stein. But the body politic seemed destined to be archaic for a long time.

Then came the fateful year of 1806. Prussia had watched with a degree of detachment the rise of Napoleon's European empire. In August 1806 Berlin learnt that Napoleon was secretly offering Hanover back to the English throne. Prussia issued an ultimatum to Napoleon, who promptly dispatched his army. In October, at Auerstadt and Jena the Prussian forces were routed. The Prussian state, for all its vaunted claims to tradition and culture, collapsed. The hour of reality had cruelly struck.

With his own eyes Schleiermacher saw Halle fall to the French invaders, bewailing what he judged to be the military incompetence of the Prussian commander. His own house was plundered and occupied by French troops. He therefore felt in an acutely personal way the humiliation brought upon the Prussians as a whole. The university was dissolved. Even his university church was commandeered by the French as a grain store. Schleiermacher's professional career seemed to have gone too, but he vowed to stay on in Halle as long as he had 'potatoes and salt'. Now, what had always been latent in the child of the Prussian army chaplain burst forth with no holds barred — his patriotism. The old Prussia had been crushed, but the new Prussia would arise. But it was a patriotism within a sense of the divine purpose. 'The rod of wrath must fall upon every German land,' he wrote to Henriette Herz in November 1806, 'only on this condition can a strong and happy future bloom forth. Happy they who live to see it; but those who die, let them die in faith. . . .' From this point on, Schleiermacher's perceived context in which theology and ethics were worked out, widened decidedly from that of the domestic hearth and cultured salon to that of the nation, in its struggle for identity and in its relations with other nations. The nation became, for Schleiermacher, the widest human circle to which the individual belonged, to which the individual contributed uniquely in moral service and thereby found his or her fulfilment, and equally the nation's individuality with its unique heritage and purpose was to be mirrored in the life of each and every one of its citizens. Schleiermacher now made himself one with the movement for reform of the Prussian political and educational system, widely held to be responsible for the inefficiency which led to the disaster of 1806. The longer-term goal would be liberation from Napoleonic imperialism, and, connected with that, the wish which was beginning to dawn in the breasts of liberally-inclined Germans, for German unification. A fragmented Germany, such as existed then, would always be a prey to external domination.

Under the partial dismemberment inflicted on Prussia by the French conquerors, Halle was detached from Prussia and granted to Westphalia. If Schleiermacher was to serve the cause of Prussian rebirth he obviously could do so no longer in Halle. In 1807 he returned to Berlin where he found some opportunity for teaching. In 1809 he married Henriette von Willich (see above p. 21) and became minister of the Trinity Church, whose pulpit he occupied for the rest of his days and made famous through his preaching, both in Germany and beyond. For the rest of his life, the Prussian capital was to be the scene of all his activities and concerns. These activities can be seen as occupying at least three dimensions, any of which by itself would have ensured his place in the story of German, indeed European, life and thought. We may call these dimensions respectively the academic, the political and the ecclesiastical. Each of them needs to be understood within the context of the Prussian capital which, under King Friedrich Wilhelm III, was aspiring towards a new order for a new Prussia.

On the *academic* level, Schleiermacher was closely involved in the formation of the new University of Berlin, a vital part of the programme for Prussian renewal. With Halle and the other Prussian universities having been lost from Prussia, it was imperative for a new seat of learning to be established in the geographical and political centre if, as Friedrich Wilhelm III was reported as saying, Prussia was to make up for physical loss through intellectual gain. Schleiermacher publicized his own views in *Thoughts on German Universities from a German Viewpoint* in 1808, and was appointed to the commission led by Wilhelm von Humboldt, which laid down the basic pattern to be followed. The University which opened in 1810 reflected several of Schleiermacher's deepest convictions about higher learning: a broad, coherent understanding of learning, philosophically based, in which individual disciplines could be pursued on their own but with equal scientific rigour; a combination of research and teaching (there were those who wanted a purely 'technical' centre purely for teaching); and a guarantee by the state of freedom in research and teaching. Schleiermacher was appointed to the chair of theology, and became first Dean of the theological faculty in 1810. He was Rector of the University in 1815.

As a teacher Schleiermacher's industry was prodigious, covering almost every branch of theology except Old Testament — dogmatics, ethics, church history, New Testament history and exegesis, hermeneutics and practical theology — and also many subjects in philosophy. For Schleiermacher these 'areas' of study were not just self-contained specialisms but were all parts of one organic whole. He set out this detailed yet unified view of the disciplines in his *Brief Outline of the Study of Theology* (1811). It was the usual practice of professors to issue outlines of the subject-matter they intended to cover in their courses, and in origin the *Brief Outline* was simply Schleiermacher's own intended syllabus which had been taking shape as early as his Halle period. But it became a manifesto and it was unique for its time, for never before had so much breadth and detail in theology been comprehended within a single vision. 'Only a few sheets, but a whole world of new thoughts!' exclaimed his disciple Lücke. Schleiermacher, after an introduction, set out three main divisions in theology: Philosophical Theology, Historical Theology (under which dogmatics as well as church history was included) and Practical Theology — the last-named so placed not because it was least in importance but quite the opposite. Practical Theology was to be the summit of the whole theological enterprise, for theology as an overall discipline was, for Schleiermacher, to be in the service of the Church's preaching and pastoral responsibility. The *Brief Outline* was deeply significant, in centres elsewhere as well as in Berlin, in encouraging Protestant Theology to develop a distinct sense of its own identity and purpose, to be pursued with scientific rigour and integrity, as would enable it to stand alongside the other sciences of a post-Enlightenment university. In a university such as Berlin, where the leading philosopher Fichte had doubted whether theology had any right whatsoever to a department of its own, such rigour was highly necessary.

Schleiermacher's personal academic stature beyond the narrowly theological realm was put beyond all doubt, first by his translation of the works of Plato, begun with Schlegel years before but virtually all his own work, and published in series during 1804-28, and second by his outstanding work for the Philosophical Division of the Berlin Academy of Sciences. Adolf von Harnack (1851-1930), the eminent church historian and leading Liberal Protestant theologian at the end of the nineteenth century, recorded in his famous history of the Academy his view of Schleiermacher as one of the most seminal and formative influences upon this, the most prestigious body of higher learning and research in Germany.

On the *political* level, Schleiermacher's activities were both official and unofficial. In 1810 he was appointed to an advisory post on education in the Ministry of the Interior, and so had a further significant role in the rebuilding of education in Prussia. But he was under suspicion by the more conservative authorities on account of his somewhat 'subversive' patriotic tendencies. In fact two years previously he had been involved in some circles of patriots agitating for a popular uprising against Napoleon, to the extent of making a clandestine journey through East

Prussia, contacting high-level diplomats and even members of the royal family.

In 1813 the king promised Prussia a new constitution including a parliament. Such a potential liberalization of the state, together with the reforms being worked by Stein, aroused deep anxiety among conservatives. For the liberal patriot who wanted to see Prussia strengthened through reform, such policies were the only hope for the future. For a time he edited the *Prussische Zeitung,* a newspaper pressing this political opinion and criticizing any thought of compromise with Napoleon. For several months there were battles with the censor, and on one occasion there came an order (not actually enforced) for Schleiermacher to leave Berlin and Prussian soil at once. In July 1813 he received a government reprimand accusing him of advocating in his columns the violent overthrow of the Prussian government, and therefore treason. Schleiermacher cheerfully ignored such reactionary officialdom, but there were other quarrels and reprimands, and the *Prussische Zeitung* disappeared from the scene at the end of 1814. If some of the most worthy names in later theology, in Germany and elsewhere, have dared to out-face the state, then in this respect as well Schleiermacher may lay a certain claim to parentage!

Schleiermacher may have lost his newspaper, but he kept his pulpit and had no inhibitions about using it for the proclamation of his Protestant, Prussian patriotism. In 1813, with Napoleon in humiliating retreat from Russia, Prussia joined in the onslaught on the tyrant. Hundreds of Berlin students enlisted as volunteers and departed for Breslau — but not before crowding into the Trinity Church. An eyewitness records:

After having pronounced a short prayer, full of unction, Schleiermacher went up into the pulpit. . . . There, in this holy place and at this solemn hour, stood the physically so small and insignificant man, his noble countenance beaming with intellect, and his clear, sonorous, penetrating voice ringing through the overflowing church. Speaking from his heart with pious enthusiasm, his every word penetrated to the heart, and the clear, full, mighty stream of his eloquence carried everyone along with it. His bold, frank declaration of the causes of our deep fall, his severe denunciation of our actual defects, as evinced in the narrow-hearted spirit of caste, of proud aristocratism, and in the dead forms of bureaucratism, struck down like thunder and lightning, and the subsequent elevation of the heart to God on the wings of solemn devotion was like harp-tones from a higher world. And when, at last, with the full fire of enthusiasm, he addressed the noble youths already

31

equipped for battle, and next, turning to their mothers, the greater number of whom were present, he concluded with the words: 'Blessed is the womb that has borne such a son, blessed the breast that has nourished such a babe,' — a thrill of deep emotion ran through the assembly, and amid loud sobs and weeping, Schleiermacher pronounced the conclusive Amen.[13]

Rapturous maybe, but that report of a particularly emotional occasion also conveys well the impact Schleiermacher made through his primary *ecclesiastical* activity, his preaching ministry at the Trinity Church week by week. In the pulpit, despite his slight, and slightly deformed, figure, he had a charismatic ability to sway a whole congregation through fervent delivery and profound wrestling with many of the most vital religious questions troubling people of the day. Generations of Berlin students, as well as educated citizens, drank in deeply from Schleiermacher's sermons which consequently must be reckoned as among the chief influences he wrought on his time — the more so as many of them found their way into print. Many young people passed through his confirmation classes, among them a youth by the name of Bismarck, later to be virtually synonymous with the creation and consolidation of the Prussian Empire. But he was intricately involved at 'higher' levels of ecclesiastical affairs as well, which at times brought him into conflict with the throne. Friedrich Wilhelm III desired a union of the Reformed and Lutheran Churches in Prussia, and at least partly at his instigation a joint Reformed-Lutheran celebration of communion took place in Berlin in 1817, in commemoration of the tercentenary of the Reformation. Schleiermacher welcomed such unity in terms of worship and brotherly acceptance, and strongly objected to Lutheran demands for exact doctrinal and liturgical agreement before 'union' could occur. This was of course simply an expression of his belief that theological or doctrinal formulae were secondary to the essential nature of religion as immediate feeling for the redemptive work of God.

Much more complicated, indeed many might think tedious, was the protracted controversy over the liturgy, embroiled as it was with the prerogatives, if any, of the sovereign in such matters. King Friedrich Wilhelm III, despite his later disclaimers, did have decided views on the matter. Schleiermacher was committed, first, to the essential independence of the Church from the state (and here the Reformed theologian, finding himself in Berlin rather than Geneva, was prepared to invoke the Lutheran doctrine of the 'two kingdoms'); and second, to the desirability (as a Reformed theologian) of a synodal-presbyterial form of church-government. In his eyes, the question of the liturgy should wait upon the decision regarding the form of church government, since it was the Church itself, not royal fiat or state decree, which should determine the pattern of divine worship.

Schleiermacher, then, led a life of immense richness and wholeness, personally and publicly, theologically and politically. It is important to note these involvements of a theologian who, because the history of theology is so often viewed merely as a succession of ideas, is seen simply as the originator of the emphasis upon 'religious feeling', and hence as a somewhat remote and ineffectual purveyor of an intellectually refined Pietism, far removed from the exigencies of life in this world. Of course by the later standards of 'political theology' he is open to the accusation of being thought-bound within the horizons of bourgeois society for whom the cultivation of inner 'feelings' was but a necessary concomitant of a social order afraid of change. It has to be remembered that not only was Schleiermacher pre-Marx in context but Germany as such was still pre-industrial. The sense of a proletariat was hardly on the horizon, in an agrarian society where the serfs were still being set free. The just way to assess Schleiermacher is not to judge his context solely, but rather to enquire whether, within that historical setting, he had perceptions into the nature of human relationships which are of more than passing significance, and can be extrapolated to social situations nearer our own. National feeling, personal relationships, the relation of religion to both science and artistic activity are in any case still part of our landscape.

It is fitting to end this biographical outline with a description of the culminating masterpiece of Schleiermacher's Berlin years, and his whole life, the mammoth *Christian Faith* which appeared in 1821-22 and again in a revised version in 1830. This, the outcome of his lectures on dogmatic theology, was given the extended title 'Connected Exhibition of the Christian Faith, according to the Principles of the Evangelical Church' which indicates one of its underlying motives, that of providing a coherent, unifying theology for the new united Church of Prussia. Nothing on such a scale, and so systematic, had appeared in Protestantism since John Calvin's *Institutes of the Christian Religion* nearly three centuries earlier. Nothing had appeared which matched its tightness of argument, its austerity of expression, while seeking to be true to the facts of the 'pious consciousness'. The 'religious emotion' is now given a more precise definition, the 'feeling of absolute dependence'. Beginning here, the work moves on to the nature of distinctively *Christian* religion — the referral of everything to the experience of redemption wrought by Christ

— and thence to the great traditional doctrines of creation, salvatión, sanctification, the Church, the last things and, finally, the Holy Trinity. At every point, the meaning of the doctrine in question is located in the nature of the religious feeling which, as ever, is the immediate reality at issue. Nothing claiming to be of Schleiermacher in his mature range can be afforded recognition unless it can be shown to be consistent with, if not explicitly stated in, this work which amounts to his *summa theologica*. It set a quite new standard for Protestant theology. The twentieth century systematic works of giants like Barth and Tillich were the products of theologians who had been prompted to emulate, as well as originate, even in disagreement.

The wholeness and many-sidedness of Schleiermacher's life and thought authenticate, for himself, what he states in his *Brief Outline of the Study of Theology:* 'If we conceive of an interest in religion and a scientific spirit, existing in a state of union, in the highest degree and in the greatest possible equilibrium, and with a view both to theory and practice — we have the idea of a *Prince of the Church*.'[14] Despite his sometimes stormy relations with those in authority, he was decorated by the king for his services to the Church and the state. When he died of pneumonia in February 1834, thousands lined the streets of Berlin as his cortège passed, a testimony to the place he held in religion and in society at large, in and for his time.

2

MAIN THEMES IN SCHLEIERMACHER'S THEOLOGY

Our selection of themes from Schleiermacher's work and the corresponding texts chosen to exemplify his treatment of these do not pretend to be an exhaustive survey of his theology. They do, however, bring into relief the particular contribution which Schleiermacher made to the renewing of theology in his own day, and the ways in which subsequent theology and philosophy of religion have felt indebted to him. This does mean omission of certain areas of considerable interest in their own right, such as Schleiermacher's ethics and more general philosophy — not to mention his New Testament studies, in addition to the gospel material relating to his understanding of the person of Jesus, only a small amount of which we are able to deal with here.

The obvious starting-point in any treatment of Schleiermacher's theology is his analysis of religious 'feeling'. We then move on to his criterion for the distinctiveness of the Christian religion, seen in christocentric terms. Only then is it appropriate to take up Schleiermacher's view of the nature and role of theology, even though in strictly logical terms it might be assumed that this should be the starting-point for a discussion of any theologian's thought. In Schleiermacher, however, religion as feeling is emphatically primary, and theology secondary. We shall then look at an element of particular importance in Schleiermacher's theological method, namely, the understanding of religion and theology as *historically* conditioned, and therewith the importance of a method of understanding historical documents (hermeneutics). The doctrine of God's action in the world, and the central doctrine of the person and work of Christ, then follow naturally. Next, the matter of Schleiermacher's Protestant patriotism, and his view of the relations of church and state, must be considered, since not only were these of utmost importance in his theological development but point to issues of continuing urgency in an age of ideology and nationalism. Finally, we shall examine briefly how Schleiermacher anticipated much of the ground to be debated in the field of the study of religions, and the place of Christianity in relation to other faiths.

1. RELIGION AS FEELING AND RELATIONSHIP*

'The contemplation of the pious is the *immediate consciousness* of the universal existence of all finite things, in and through the Infinite, and of all temporal things in and through the Eternal.'[15] 'True religion is *sense and taste* for the Infinite.'[16] Schleiermacher's ascription of religion to the realm of *feeling* marked the start of modern Protestantism's habitual emphasis on the knowledge of God as inward and experiential. It is an emphasis seen variously in a succession of figures as diverse as Søren Kierkegaard (1813-55), Albrecht Ritschl (1822-89), Adolf von Harnack (1851-1931), Ernst Troeltsch (1855-1923), Rudolf Bultmann (1884-1976), Rudolf Otto (1869-1937), John Oman (1860-1939), H.H. Farmer (1892-1981) and John Baillie (1886-1960). However vulnerable the historicity of the biblical witness may appear to be, however problematical the traditional doctrinal formulae may sound in the light of modern thought, actual religious 'experience' as a fact of the believer's life cannot be gainsaid. Post-Enlightenment theology not only allows but often insists upon the place of 'subjectivity' in belief.

Schleiermacher's emphasis upon religion as feeling, though it owed much both to his Moravian nurture and his Romantic leanings at the turn of the century, was not the automatic expression of a past education and a present influence. It was a deliberately sustained emphasis, because Schleiermacher saw that in the face of rationalism and post-Christian Romanticism, there was a crucial need to state the unique and essential nature of religion as an indelible aspect of human existence, not an antique and superfluous adornment. His emphasis upon the 'emotions' or 'consciousness' was not an attempt to find a safe sanctuary for religion in the inner life, beyond the reach of rationalism and scientific materialism. True, in the *Speeches* Schleiermacher is at pains to distinguish religion as feeling, from activity (artistic or moral) on the one hand, and from knowledge (scientific or metaphysical) on the other. Quantity of knowledge is not quantity of piety. Schleiermacher was particularly anxious that religion should not enter the wrong competition with natural science, for religion could never win a contest on supplying information about the world. But the 'feeling' or 'sense' of God as the Infinite in which all finite things exist, does not subsist in isolation as some self-contained element of the human consciousness. It does not live *apart from* artistic or

* For texts, see below pp. 66ff.

ethical activity, or from scientific or speculative knowledge. In turn, none of these activities can flourish without the 'pious consciousness'. Schleiermacher's notion of religion as pertaining to feeling was thus part of a whole new anthropology of human existence. His *Speeches* are more than just a rescue-operation for the beleaguered 'religious' aspect of life. They comprise a positive, new vision of what it is to be truly human, in a wholeness, richness and freedom not known by the passing wisdom of the age.

The passages from the *Speeches* and *The Christian Faith* given below should therefore be studied very carefully in order to ascertain exactly what Schleiermacher understood by 'feeling' as the mode of religious apprehension. In *The Christian Faith*, it will be seen, the 'pious consciousness' is more precisely defined as 'the feeling of *absolute dependence*' *(schlechtin abhängig)*. But it is in the second of the *Speeches* that the most intricate account of this 'emotion' is given. Here, while Schleiermacher speaks of the religious feeling as a self-consciousness, it is clear that this cannot mean simply a 'consciousness of oneself' without reference to any reality other than oneself. The self-consciousness of which Schleiermacher speaks is a consciousness of the self as determined by, or acted upon by, what is other than the self, as well as its own inwardly motivated actions. It is the self-in-relation which is the object of consciousness. This must be stated in view of the frequency with which, especially under the neo-orthodox attack, Schleiermacher has been accused of indulging in a concentration on the self's own feelings and emotions, resulting in an entirely subjectivist, individualist occupation with 'religion' instead of attending to the true 'object' of faith, namely God himself. This is to ignore the depth and subtlety of Schleiermacher's analysis, which sets forth not the self *per se*, but the self in relationship. It is the self grounded in a realm of what is other than the self, of other persons, the realm of nature and society, the whole finite realm grounded in the Infinite, which Schleiermacher is concerned with. The human consciousness is thus never entirely *self-* awareness, for the self can never be extracted from the realm of otherness.

We have then in Schleiermacher an intensely *relational* view of humanity. Emotions are significant not simply because they are 'felt', but because they are inward witnesses and responses to realities other than the self. In the second of the *Speeches* Schleiermacher with great delicacy uncovers how in every perception of an object external to ourselves, there is a primary moment of encounter of which we are barely conscious because it is so fleeting, when we are virtually one with that object in consciousness. In this sense Schleiermacher can dare to say that all true consciousness is religious, in that it relates us to what is other than ourselves, and takes us out of ourselves into an awareness of the total realm of the finite which in turn lives in the Infinite; and it is, ultimately, our consciousness of the world as the medium through which the infinite God is acting upon us, which is the heart of religious awareness. Schleiermacher's 'feeling of absolute dependence', it may be noted at this point, does not correspond to what are sometimes considered to be the typically 'religious' emotions of awe and wonder in face of the 'numinous', to use the famous terminology of Rudolf Otto (1869-1937). Like Schleiermacher, Otto sought to identify a specifically religious element in human experience, and located it in the sense of the mystery which is both fearful and attractive, the *mysterium tremendens et fascinans*. Such a 'numinous' encounter comes as a strange irruption into the world of normal experience. But for Schleiermacher it is precisely the world of 'normal' experience which mediates the 'religious experience'. The sense of being utterly dependent is given in and with this experienced world of relatedness. It is a world in which we feel partly, but never wholly, free as personal agents. It is a world, in which we feel partly dependent in relation to many objects (other persons, family, nation, nature and so on). But further, in and with all this, in our openness to what is other to us, we have a sense of ourselves and all else being *utterly* dependent on — what? There is no item in the finite world to which such feeling is appropriate. It can only refer to the Infinite. God is the correlate of this religious consciousness. This of course is in a way parallel to Kant's argument for God as the inferred lawgiver behind the moral imperative.

Because Schleiermacher's understanding of 'feeling' or 'self-consciousness' is so thoroughly relational, it is not surprising that he expounds 'religious emotion' as incapable of surviving within the isolated individual. The individual, as was stated in the biographical section, is always seen by Schleiermacher in relation to the group of which it is a member, and which it mirrors in its unique, particular way. Schleiermacher continually sees the human self in relation to other selves in the actual world of space and time. His view of religion is therefore fundamentally communal — 'If there is religion at all, it must be social, for that is the nature of man, and it is quite peculiarly the nature of religion.'[17] The feeling of absolute dependence can only be communicated and cultivated by human fellowship, one to another. Here is one point where in Schleiermacher's case theology and life converge most conspicuously, for as has been seen Schleiermacher himself could not bear solitude. For him, to be an authentic individual, both in theory and practice, meant to belong to a circle, to which the individual could contribute something of himself or herself; and in turn it meant to mediate in one's own unique existence the characteristic life of the group to which one belonged. For Schleiermacher the friend and intimate of so many, the one who regarded the domestic scene and family happiness as the chief human goal, Schleiermacher the Prussian patriot, the relatedness of human existence was axiomatic in life as well as in theology. Closely parallel to this view of human interdependence was Schleiermacher's interest in language, the medium through which human communality is effected. Language exhibits in another way the relation between the individual and the community. The individual only learns the language by participating in the community. The language has its general, technical features transcending any one individual's use of them. But equally, the individual can give a unique and possibly highly creative and original use of the common language.

Relatedness, community, language: these features of human existence in space and time are comprehended within Schleiermacher's acute *historical* sense. The religious consciousness, especially, is drawn into a fascination with how the Spirit has affected selves in other times and contexts, and in this way the self becomes part of a still wider communion, educative and enriching, in a fellowship where communication takes place even across the centuries. We shall meet this again in Section 4 where we shall examine Schleiermacher's understanding of hermeneutics as a 'conventional' discipline (pp. 46ff.).

It was said earlier that Schleiermacher's emphasis upon the inward has become the stamp of much modern Protestant theology. His emphasis upon relatedness, on human interdependence, on community in history, has not always been followed so conspicuously. The existentialist theology of Rudolf Bultmann, for example, has an affinity with that of Schleiermacher in speaking of God only in terms of human existence as affected by encounter with God. But such theology has tended to detach the self from the concrete relations of society and church. The believer is set free to face *his* future in freedom, rather than to enter into new relations with others.

Finally, it should be recognized that in opening up the inner world of religious experience to precise description, Schleiermacher was anticipating a good deal of that philosophical method which has come to be known as *phenomenology*. This is the discipline which enquires into the fundamental structures of reality not by detached observation of the world, or by abstract reasoning or speculation, but by exploration of human consciousness as the experience of this reality. It is essentially a descriptive analysis of what is felt and experienced in common human awareness, and has been developed in distinctive ways by such figures as M. Scheler (1874-1928), E. Husserl (1859-1938) and M. Heidegger (1889-1976) in the twentieth century.[18]

2. THE DISTINCTIVENESS OF CHRISTIANITY: REDEMPTION THROUGH JESUS CHRIST*

The relationship between 'religion' in general and Christianity as a particular faith has been one of the most keenly debated areas of theology for the past two hundred years. In Section 8 pp. 61ff., we shall consider how Schleiermacher conceived this relationship. For the moment it suffices to say that while he began his theological career with an exploration of 'religion' in an unqualified sense, and opened *The Christian Faith* with a developed account of the 'religious consciousness' (the feeling of absolute dependence), he emphatically asserted the distinctiveness of Christianity as an historical religion. Just how he saw this distinctiveness was to be both typical and formative of much subsequent Protestant thought. It is summed up in one of the most important theses in *The Christian Faith*: 'Christianity is a monotheistic faith belonging to the teleological type of religion, and is essentially distinguished from other such faiths by the fact that in it *everything is related to the redemption accomplished by Jesus of Nazareth*.'[19] This relatively simple-sounding statement is laden with vast implications. First, Christianity is a religion of *redemption*, by which Schleiermacher means a passage out of evil, enabled by some other agent than the self which is redeemed. In the case of a 'teleological' religion, that is, one where a moral rather than an aesthetic task predominates, this redemption must mean the passage from God-forgetfulness to God-consciousness, so that the latter awareness predominates in all the states and activities of life. Redemption is thus an inward, experiential change, and the essence of Christianity is, first, that this redemption is accepted as the work of Jesus, and second, that everything else in the scheme of belief is seen in relationship to this redemption.

With a new and peculiar intensity, Schleiermacher thereby focuses Christian identity and thought onto the figure of Jesus. The inward experience of redemption — the impartation of a God-consciousness or sense of absolute dependence as the key element of awareness — is given

* For texts, see below pp. 108ff.

in the encounter between Jesus and the person concerned. Of course, Jesus and his redemptive work have always been constitutive of Christianity, and it can be argued that Schleiermacher was simply forwarding in more contemporary terms the classic Protestant terminology of the saving knowledge of God as stated by Martin Luther — by faith alone, by grace alone, by Christ alone. But Schleiermacher is making the redemptive experience of Jesus determinative on a new scale. For now, a doctrine or aspect of belief is properly Christian *only* as it is seen as somehow stemming from that Jesus-induced redemptive experience. A particular element has been made the hub of all thinking and activity, and a quite new understanding of the corpus of doctrine results. The various doctrines — creation, redemption, sanctification, church and so forth — are no longer self-contained items touching each other at their edges. Each of them, now, has to be seen as in some way a reflection upon the new consciousness given by Jesus to the believer within the believing community. The doctrine of creation, for example, is now not concerned with questions about the 'origin' of the world. Rather, it explicates those features of the absolute dependence of the world upon God *as known through the feeling of such dependence*, and that feeling is adequately given only by relationship with Jesus. (For exposition of the redemptive relationship with Christ, see Section 6, pp. 53ff.) Similarly, the divine attributes of omnipotence, omnipresence and omniscience are not to be taken as referring to 'special' qualities within God himself, independent of the world, 'but only something special in the manner in which the feeling of absolute dependence is to be related to him.'[20] The religious self-consciousness given by Jesus has become the centre and connexion for everything else in Christianity.

The *christocentricity* of Protestant theology from Schleiermacher onwards has been most marked. Jesus, to use the language of contemporary fashion, provides the definition of God. This increasing emphasis upon the primacy of Jesus Christ for all comprehension of God was in part a compensation for the collapse of the traditional metaphysics which for centuries had appeared to fill with substance the talk about God existing in his own reality beyond the finite and temporal realm. After that collapse, God as an *experience* became more crucial than ever, and this could be located in the experience of the influence of Jesus. Towards the end of the nineteenth century this emphasis appeared as one of the foremost features of the Liberal Protestant theology of Albrecht Ritschl, Adolf von Harnack and Wilhelm Herrmann.[21] Nor did it end there. Albeit on a different plane, the intense christocentricity of Karl Barth's theology of revelation can be seen as marking one of the elements of his Liberal Protestant nurture which he retained and transposed, while revolting against so much else in that ethos. There is redemptive christocentricity too in Rudolf Bultmann's existential view of grace. It is in the message of the crucified Christ that God's word comes and creates a new trust in the forgiving grace of God, freeing man from false attachment to this world. In more Anglo-Saxon vein, the emphasis appears in much of the person- alist theology of the mid-twentieth century which was especially a feature of liberal Reformed theologians like John Baillie, who wrote: 'It is not as the result of an inference of any kind . . . that the knowledge of God's activity comes to us. It comes through our direct personal encounter with him in the Person of Jesus Christ his Son our Lord.'[22]

Baillie's statement conveys well that typical modern claim that the personal, liberating encounter with Jesus is a self-authenticating experi- ence of God. It need not and cannot be 'proved' by anything outside itself. No one expounded such a view more cogently than Schleiermacher him- self in *The Christian Faith* where it became clear just how radically chris- tocentric, in the context of the times, was his understanding of faith. The redemptive experience of Jesus is not substantiated by miracles, or pro- phetic fulfilments, or by claims to 'inspiration'. In the biblical witness, according to Schleiermacher, such elements are rather the expression or predisposition of a faith in Jesus *which is already held*, than arguments or supports for that faith, a faith which has its own origin purely in the direct, personal communion with Jesus. Schleiermacher was thus detaching faith in Jesus from a generalized 'belief in miracles' or 'belief in the Bible' or 'faith in the supernatural'. The one miracle is Jesus himself and his redemptive influence. All else has significance only if illustrative of that. In this way, Schleiermacher was anticipating much in the modern appro- ach to the Bible which attempts to distinguish between essential truth and peripheral, symbolic expressions of that truth — for example Bult- mann's attempt at demythologizing the 'kerygma' by distinguishing it from the 'mythological' expression in which it is cast. Schleiermacher himself would probably have said that he was merely applying again Luther's discriminating approach to the Scripture which, being 'the crib wherein Christ lieth', contains elements of greater and lesser spiritual significance.

3. THEOLOGY AS REFLECTION AND COMMUNICATION*

Over the past two hundred years no greater question has faced theology than the issue of its own nature as an intellectual discipline. Is it in any way a 'science' comparable to those other branches of learning which have made such spectacular advances, and enjoy such great prestige, in the modern era — most obviously the 'natural sciences'? Or can it claim to rival the refinement of philosophy, whether analytical or speculative, empiricist or idealist? Every student of theology soon learns that *theologia* literally means God-talk, speech or discourse about God. But 'God' has become problematical since the Enlightenment, so it is not surprising that the discipline has been questioned from within as well as without on what its status, purpose and methods should be. That uncertainty is reflected at a practical level within the policies of the modern university. What place does theology have in a modern, public centre of free enquiry and learning? At the most, it might be thought that the phenomenon of theology within the history of ideas should be allowed some attention, just as religion as a sociological phenomenon could lie on the syllabus within the social sciences. But does discussion of the content of theology, in such a way as assumes that issues of serious moment are at stake, have any place in the university as distinct from the seminary?

Friedrich Schleiermacher provided the first clearly articulated and thoroughly organized exposition of what Protestant theology should be in the nineteenth century. At first sight it is surprising that he should have taken so seriously the intellectual expression of Christian faith, for in the *Speeches* the young writer with Romanticist leanings emphasized religion as *feeling*, as distinct from doing and *knowing*. 'Quantity of knowledge is not quantity of piety'.[23] Religion was defensible insofar as it was distinguishable from 'this miserable love of system', the principles, dogmas and creeds which appeared to make orthodoxy a laughing stock to the educated of the day. Yet twenty years later the author of *The Christian Faith* produced the first truly systematic account of Protestant theology since Calvin's *Institutes*. There had not been a change of mind, but a shift in priorities.

The author of the *Speeches* was anxious to defend religion from charges arising out of mistaken identity. The cultured despisers assumed that

* For texts, see below pp. 124ff.

43

Christianity comprised the worn-out dogmas, the discredited beliefs in providence, miracles and immortality, the contradictory or competing systems of this school and that. Such contempt, Schleiermacher acknowledged, was understandable; but it did not touch religion as religion, which is not theology or doctrine, but the inner, immediate consciousness of the Infinite in the finite, and is not attributable to either knowledge or action though it always accompanies both.

Schleiermacher makes clear that on one level piety and theology have no intrinsic connexion with each other. The very pious may be totally untutored in doctrine, the doctrinally erudite may be very short on piety. In religion, feeling is primary, and religious 'knowledge' is simply reflection upon that feeling. When the mature Schleiermacher comes to define the nature of theology, it is that 'Christian doctrines are accounts of the Christian religious affections set forth in speech'.[24] They are not direct, literal statements about God in himself in the way that, for instance, the natural scientist gives 'factual' information about some aspect of the finite world in his purview. More was at stake for Schleiermacher here than an escape from an embarrassingly naive doctrinal orthodoxy. His sharp differentiation of piety from knowledge was, equally, a counter to the rationalistic assumptions of the philosophical idealism, first of Fichte and then of Hegel (from 1818 also teaching at Berlin, and dismissive of Schleiermacher). For the speculative idealists the human mind was in some way continuous with Absolute mind or spirit, and therefore able to comprehend the rationality of ultimate reality. For Schleiermacher, such speculation was presumptuous and was the antithesis to religion as the consciousness not of continuity with the divine, but of the absolute dependence of the finite on the Infinite (albeit an Infinite present in and with the finite).

For Schleiermacher, then, any 'knowledge' in religion, in an intellectual sense, could only be a reflection upon the conscious feelings of relationship to the divine, not a description or analysis directly of the divine *per se* (but, as we saw in Section 1, pp. 36ff., neither were the feelings those of the self *per se*, in isolation from what is other). Schleiermacher was among the first to realize that theology defeats its own purpose if it speaks of God as if he were simply another 'object', distinguished from other 'objects' only by being 'greater' and 'removed from' the finite world. Such a 'God' is less than the truly Infinite One present in and to the whole universe. Such a view of God, says Schleiermacher, 'as one single being outside of the world and behind the world is not the beginning and the end of religion'. True religion is not this — or any other — *idea* but 'immediate

44

consciousness of the Deity as he is found in ourselves and in the world'.[25] It is the immediate consciousness which is the material upon which theology works directly. This is the basic tenet of Schleiermacher which has drawn the later neo-orthodox fire, charging that he has substituted human feelings, human religiosity, human psychology and subjectivity for the proper subject-matter of theology, namely God's divinity and purpose as self-revealed in his Word. Again, the charge must be set against the evidence that Schleiermacher was interested in the 'emotions' precisely because they did point beyond themselves to the reality which had stimulated them.

But why should anyone bother with intellectual reflection upon the religious consciousness which, originating independently of knowledge, would appear to be capable of managing itself? Why does piety need doctrine or theology? For Schleiermacher the answer lies in his wider anthropology of knowing, doing and feeling. Notice that his basic thesis on doctrines states that they are accounts of the Christian religious feelings *set forth in speech*. We are back with Schleiermacher's historical, communal, relational view of humanity, the concrete manifestation of which is language, utterance. Feeling of any sort, he maintains, once it reaches a certain intensity manifests itself outwardly in voice and gesture, a communication of inner self-consciousness to others. This is so pre-eminently in religion and above all in Christianity: 'The whole work of the Redeemer himself was conditioned by the communicability of his self-consciousness by means of speech, and similarly Christianity has always and everywhere spread itself solely by preaching. Every proposition which can be an element of the Christian preaching *(kerygma)* is also a doctrine, because it bears witness to the determination of the religious self-consciousness as inward certainty.'[26]

Hence the necessity for theology, which is a concomitant of the necessity for *speech* in the religious self-consciousness, the paradigm and historical origin of which is Jesus Christ. Theology and doctrine are therefore essentially statements of what can and should be the content of Christian preaching. Theology is thus fundamentally a *Church* discipline, or at least one which exists to serve the Church. In Richard Niebuhr's apt phrases, theology for Schleiermacher is the 'countervoice of the Church', or 'preaching-faith's descriptive science of itself'.[27] It is a sheer necessity for a communal religion. Further, there is an even deeper reason for theology — a theological (!) reason. Schleiermacher has already defined Christianity as the religion which refers everything to the redemption accomplished by Jesus (see Section 2, pp. 40ff.), and the heart of that redemptive activity lies in Jesus' self-communication (by speech) of his own self-consciousness. Theology has a christological rationale in Schleiermacher.

Schleiermacher's *Brief Outline of the Study of Theology* (1810) has already been mentioned (see above pp. 29f.), with its comprehensive yet succinct survey of how all the various sub-disciplines — from philology to dogmatics, from Church history to philosophy of religion — can be drawn into a coherent whole with a single overriding aim: that of serving 'Church-guidance'. Its three-fold division into Philosophical Theology (considering what type of religion is Christianity), Historical Theology and Practical Theology was designed to make clear that, culminating in Practical Theology (worship, preaching, pastoral leadership etc.), it was indeed the service as 'counter-voice' of the Church that was intended.

Schleiermacher's scheme, notably, does not exalt dogmatics to a division on its own, but accords it a place within Historical Theology. Dogmatics describes the leading doctrines and their interconnexions in the Church of the present. As such, it is a descriptive discipline not essentially different from that which uncovers the structure of leading ideas at earlier stages of history. Nor does it attempt an apologetic or a demonstration of the truth of the content of doctrine. It simply sets out to expound these doctrines and their interrelationships as clearly as possible. The best illustration of what Schleiermacher intended and advocated is of course his own *The Christian Faith*, so tightly argued, with a masterly architectonic character, proceeding step by step in numbered theses, yet never forgetting the one basic principle of the religious consciousness, and always seeking to do justice both to the classic Protestant heritage and to the current intellectual and cultural scene. Quite apart from the contents of *The Christian Faith* themselves, Schleiermacher in constructing this edifice rid Protestant theology, in one mighty blow, of that piecemeal, fragmentary method of the scholastics who had dominated the scene through the seventeenth and eighteenth centuries, and who had reduced dogmatics to a disjointed series of commentaries on classical or disputed texts, the *loci communes*. With Schleiermacher, theology began again to think big and to think whole.

4. HERMENEUTICS: CONVERSATION WITH HISTORY*

'. . . Schleiermacher's idea of theology is imbued with a deep historical

* For texts, see below pp. 157ff.

sense which, more than any other single feature of his thought, obtains for him the position of father of modern Protestantism.'[28] That historical sense, we have seen in the preceding section, included even his understanding of dogmatics, which is not for him an attempt to state 'timeless' truths, but an uncovering of the present consciousness of the Church in its specific, contemporary historical situation. Theology becomes thoroughly historicized once it is realized that the sources and traditions from which it draws its main statements of belief and doctrine speak from contexts and in terms very different from those of the present. The *interpretation of written texts* then assumes enormous significance and *hermeneutics,* the discipline of such interpretation, becomes crucial for theology. The subject has provoked vigorous debate in twentieth century theology in a number of areas. The existentialist and demythologizing programme of Rudolf Bultmann and Friedrich Gogarten (1887-1967),[29] for instance, required a specific hermeneutical approach to the New Testament. They argued that if the gospel message of the New Testament, the *kerygma* of the saving power of Jesus Christ, was to become intelligible to contemporary people then it had to be distinguished from the obsolete, time-conditioned cosmology of first century Palestine in which it was expressed in the New Testament. The 'mythology', however, has not so much to be dropped, as re-interpreted. For instance, the language of 'heaven' being somehow literally spatially removed from earth 'above' the sky is, as it stands, nonsense in the light of modern astronomy. But it is not on that account meaningless, provided that the meaning it had for first century people is appreciated. But how do we penetrate to that meaning? Its meaning then, said Bultmann, had less to do with cosmology than with human self-understanding. It was a particular, time-conditioned cultural expression of the fact that man is conscious of being a finite creature living in space and time, but limited also by an invisible, transcendent realm on which alone he can ultimately rely for security. The text has therefore to be examined with a view to the human, existential significance of the concepts used, and only then will they be able to communicate with us today. Such a hermeneutic, in the view of its critics, effectively forced the bible to give a pre-determined existentialist message, but Bultmann and his allies at least question whether it is possible *not* to approach the bible with a 'prior understanding' of what it is about, and argue that a responsible hermeneutic will reflect carefully on any presuppositions it brings to the reading. A very different, though parallel, case is that of contemporary liberation theology[30] which argues that no reading of the scripture is adequate which does not reflect on the socio-political context and involvement of both the reader and the original writer. For both the existentialist and the liberation (or political) theologian, what is at stake in both text and reader is a specific human situation and interest, which must be brought to light if there is to be authentic communication between past and present.

It is Schleiermacher who stands at the beginning of the whole hermeneutical concern in modern theology. He began lecturing on the subject at Halle, in his own words 'endeavouring to raise that which has hitherto been nothing more than a series of disconnected and unsatisfactory observations into the dignity of a science, which shall embrace the whole language as an object of intellectual discernment, and penetrate from without into its innermost depths.'[31] The issue was wider than theology alone, for classical studies and law also required the interpretation of documents from the past, and Schleiermacher sought the establishment of hermeneutics in the most comprehensive way as a discipline which could invoke principles whenever texts of any kind required interpretation. But further, Schleiermacher saw that the interpretation of writings (and other human artefacts such as monuments, architecture etc.) was an aspect of the still more fundamental human activity of *understanding* between persons. Communication requires that we should be able to discern what another person is thinking and feeling, and this we do by interpreting not only the spoken words we hear but also the facial expressions, gestures and total impression made upon us by the other person. We interpret the outward, physical sounds and movements by analogy with our own feelings and thoughts which produce such effects in ourselves, and thereby reach some understanding of the other person's consciousness and emotions. This of course is what every conversation involves, and for Schleiermacher the interpretation of a text and a conversation with another person *are* fundamentally the same operation. Both aim to know inner feelings, thoughts and motives via outward representations. So Schleiermacher says tersely: 'The success of the art of interpretation depends on one's linguistic competence and on one's ability to know people.'[32]

Schleiermacher's own linguistic competence was outstanding, as shown in one of his greatest achievements, his translation of Plato into German. There is an interesting reference, in an autobiographical fragment, to his own early difficulties in the learning of Latin:

Here I saw nothing but darkness; for although I learnt to translate the words mechanically into my mother tongue, I could not penetrate into the sense, and my mother, who directed my German readings with much judgment, had taught me not to read without understanding.[33] Perhaps it was exactly those early problems with his Latin which prompted his lifelong interest in the nature of translation and interpretation. But the reference to his mother's influence on his style of reading is suggestive also. As an adult he confessed to being a 'slow reader', often having to read a single passage many times over. This too bears on his hermeneutical teaching, which implies that, metaphorically if not actually, more than one reading of a text is necessary to discern its meaning. A *part* of the text — an incident in a play for instance — is seen in its significance only in the light of the whole plot, drama or argument. Equally, of course, the whole can only be appreciated in terms of its various elements. This is the basis of the famous *hermeneutical circle*, a continual reciprocity between whole and parts, which Schleiermacher envisaged as essential in the art of interpretation. The implication is clear, also, that interpretation can never be fixed and final. But above all, it was Schleiermacher's own 'ability to know people' which illuminated for him the art of interpretation, as he had come to know it as conversationalist, letter-writer and friend to so many. In hermeneutics, then, Schleiermacher's literary concerns and abilities, his historical sense, his anthropology of human relations and his own personal existence, all converged.

Schleiermacher's thinking on hermeneutics was first taken up in a major way by his biographer Wilhelm Dilthey (1833-1911), the philosopher of history.[34] Dilthey recognized the crucial significance for all historiography of Schleiermacher's insight that there is no direct way to the author's meaning in any given text, other than by the capacity of the reader or historian to discern analogies to his or her own inner experience, as suggested by the text. Historiography therefore contains an irreducibly subjective element, as is appropriate for what is a specifically *human* science, as distinct from a physical science. History is not primarily about bare 'events' in space and time, but about the human decisions, motives and feelings within those events. The historian reconstructs the past inwardly 're-living' the events in imaginative sympathy. Dilthey in turn became highly important for German understanding of history as a human science, greatly influencing such philosophers of religion as Ernst Troeltsch and, later, existentialist philosophers such as Martin Heidegger (1889-1976)[35] with his depiction of human concern with the past as a resource in facing the future, and of the way immediate human awareness shapes the way the past is viewed. There is also a close parallel between Dilthey's concept of 're-living' the past and the distinction made by the Oxford philosopher R.G. Collingwood (1889-1943) between the 'inside' and the 'outside' of an event — and the historian's concern with the former.[36]

In more recent years in the thought of such as H.-G. Gadamer,[37] there has been increasing criticism of the subjectivist emphasis in historical interpretation. What cannot be denied is the place of Schleiermacher as a prime mover in hermeneutics, with his dual recognition that the art requires the combination of the most exact philology, and the most sensitive human awareness in order 'To understand the text at first as well as and then even better than its author.'[38]

5. GOD AND THE WORLD*

What does it mean to speak of God acting in the world, whether in nature or in human history? Are there special, extraordinary events which are to be ascribed to divine agency and labelled 'supernatural' or 'miraculous'? Or does God somehow 'direct, control, suggest' everything that happens? Such questions became acute in the modern world, and still remain so, once the whole course of events in space and time was seen as an interconnecting whole, explicable in purely natural terms. There seems little need or room for 'divine agency' to explain happenings great or small.

Friedrich Schleiermacher was among the very first to deal with this question in the wake of the Enlightenment. Two developments in the eighteenth century had crucially changed the western way of regarding the world, at least for the educated. First, the Newtonian view of the physical universe as an uninterrupted system of cause and effect had become the standard and accepted picture. Second, Kant's theory of knowledge had argued that the concept of 'causality', as understood by natural science, could *only* apply to happenings within the finite realm of space and time; and outside the categories of space and time, reason cannot venture. To speak of *God* causing a particular thing to happen, in contradistinction to any spatio-temporal cause of that event, was meaningless. The remark of the astronomer Laplace to Napoleon, on being asked by the Emperor where God came into his system, is justly famous: 'Sire, I have no need of that hypothesis.'

In this situation at the close of the Enlightenment, theology seemed faced with three main options. One was to let scientific rationalism have its say and banish all talk of God's activity from the world. This was the

* For texts, see below pp. 172ff.

Deistic path, to a view of God apart from and outside the natural world of cause and effect, and who functioned as little more than a final moral arbiter over the universe. Another option, at the opposite extreme, was virtually to equate God and the natural order, so that all that happens is directly the doing of God, because everything is essentially part of the divine. This was the pantheistic way, greatly indebted to Spinoza. A third option, favoured among many orthodox theologians, was to allow a natural causation for the generality of events, but to posit specific events as special 'acts of God', manifested by miraculous occurrences testified to in Scripture. A general providence through the natural order was supplemented by an interventionalist special providence.

Schleiermacher rejected all three alternatives. The Deistic view was as far removed as could be imagined from his own conviction of the believer's communion with God in and through the world. 'Your feeling is piety', he states in the *Speeches*, 'in so far as it is the result of the operation of God in you by means of the operation of the world upon you.'[39] But neither, despite his critics' accusations, did he even in the early *Speeches* lapse into pantheism. His account of religion as the consciousness of 'all finite things, in and through the Infinite, and of all temporal things in and through the Eternal', to be sought 'in all that lives and moves, in all growth and change, in all doing and suffering', and to know in immediate feeling 'only such an existence in the Infinite and Eternal'[40] — this is not an equation of 'all that is' with God. It is rather a recognition of the existence of all things *in* God — in current parlance panentheism, not pantheism. Still less was Schleiermacher impressed with the orthodox rearguard action to defend the sporadic intervention of the supernatural (a term he rejected) in the world. In his view this amounted to a reduced view of the divine omnipotence. Schleiermacher at heart wished to remain true to the Reformed tradition of the universal sovereignty of God, his decree governing all things.

It was this inclusive doctrine which Schleiermacher sought to reconstruct. His treatment of God's preservative, directive activity in the world is contained in two relatively brief but brilliant passages in *The Christian Faith* (see texts, pp. 172-184) expounding the two theses: (1) 'The religious self-consciousness, by means of which we place all that affects or influences us in absolute dependence upon God, coincides entirely with the view that all such things are conditioned and determined by the interdependence of Nature'[41]; (2) 'It can never be necessary in the interest of religion so to interpret a fact that its dependence on God absolutely excludes its being conditioned by the system of Nature.'[42]

Schleiermacher entirely accepts the scientific picture of natural causation and interdependency as a seamless robe. The divine activity is not to be sought by attempts to find inexplicable rifts in the fabric, into which 'supernatural' explanations can be inserted. The religious sense is not dependent on those events which cannot, apparently, be explained by natural conditioning in the light of the present state of knowledge. Natural knowledge does not subvert the truly religious sense of dependence upon God, says Schleiermacher, which in fact is increased precisely in accordance with the extent of that knowledge — 'it can only be a false wisdom which would put religion aside, and a misconceived religion for love of which the progress of knowledge is to be arrested.'[43] Schleiermacher's perception was not always heeded, or known, in the nineteenth century, least of all in the English-speaking world with its battles of 'science versus religion'. Even today, the argument against the 'God of the gaps' needs rehearsing in face of religious supernaturalism, and Schleiermacher's version of it still reads more eloquently than most.

The clue to the whole concept of God's governance and preservation of all things lies for Schleiermacher, as with everything else, with the nature of the religious consciousness. This is a sense of *absolute* dependence, which is of a different order from that partial dependence, or interdependence, of items within the natural order as such. It is an immediate awareness, not deduced from or inferred from our knowledge of the world. It is therefore in one sense quite independent of the natural conditioned order of finite causes. But in another sense it relates closely to this order — as a whole, not to certain parts of it. Crucial, if implicit, here is Schleiermacher's understanding of individuality (see above, pp. 20, 38f.). The role of the individual, we have seen, is to reflect in a particular way the character of the whole of which it is a member. For the human self this means, ultimately, to be a kind of microcosm of the whole universe. One could therefore say, that my religious consciousness is not only the sense that *I* am absolutely dependent upon the Infinite, but, because I belong to that whole finite realm which I perceive as a unity, my consciousness is also an awareness that that universe, too, is absolutely dependent. All that is, I perceive through my sense of dependence, is absolutely dependent upon God. It is *both* an order of natural causation *and* willed by God. Neither contradicts the other.

God is in all and active in all things, therefore, for through all that happens his will is being expressed. He is to be sought in all that occurs and not just in the 'miraculous'. It should be noted that Schleiermacher did not dispute the *historicity* of the biblical miracles as such. What he did was to query how, faced with events however 'unusual' we could ever categorically deny a 'natural' explanation to them. The false distinction between 'natural' and 'supernatural' is to be abolished.

Schleiermacher was thus a pioneer in moving towards that modern distinction between a 'scientific' explanation of the natural relations between events and the 'theological' understanding that everything that affects us is grounded in God. The aim is to safeguard both the integrity of science as it explores a unified natural order, and the reality of God who, being unconditionally related to this whole natural realm, cannot be viewed as merely part of the series, or another item within it. With Schleiermacher we are on the way to the modern refusal to speak of God as an object within the world, a being among beings, but rather as the ground of all being, an approach which found its most impressive statement in the theology of Paul Tillich.

Schleiermacher's view of the whole finite order as ordained by God did not induce fatalism or passive resignation. Prayer and action are the means of man's free response to the operations of God through the world. 'To be a religious man and to pray are really one and the same thing,' he begins by saying in his sermon *The Power of Prayer in Relation to Outward Circumstances*. Man has the freedom to petition God, and the still more important freedom of being able to accept that which God disposes, and, in such acceptance, to find the highest good. 'He who prays must remember that everything that befalls us has its end in ourselves, and is intended for our improvement and the increase of good in us.'[44] For Schleiermacher himself, it is likely that the critical year of 1806, the year of Prussia's downfall and the collapse of his own professional career in Halle, marked a turning-point in his advance from a predominantly passive piety, to a view of faith as involving a concerted commitment, a positive alignment of oneself with the shaping forces of history, as he gave himself to the cause of Prussia's rebirth.

6. THE PERSON AND WORK OF CHRIST*

Christology formed the heart of the whole theological system of the mature Schleiermacher. One of his later critics, D.F. Strauss (1808-74) went so far as to suggest that *The Christian Faith* has only one dogma, that of the person of Christ.[45] It would be truer to say that the person *and work* of Christ constitute that core. Christology and soteriology were insepar-

* For texts, see below pp. 195ff.

able for Schleiermacher, and in both doctrines he exerted a dynamic influence on Protestant thought.

The fundamental reference point for Schleiermacher was always, we have seen, the consciousness of God, and the distinguishing feature of Christianity was the reference of everything to the redemption accomplished by Jesus of Nazareth, a redemption conceived as participation in the *perfect* God-consciousness of Jesus himself. It should again be recalled that for Schleiermacher the Christian life was never individualistic but a corporate existence in the Church, and 'Christian experience' is that of an historic community. The new corporate God-consciousness of the community originates in Jesus Christ himself. Schleiermacher's critics have sometimes concluded that the historic Christ on this basis is merely a postulate to account for the existence of the contemporary religious emotions. Such is not the case. There is a continual reciprocity between the contemporary experience and the historical figure who is its originator. Nor does Schleiermacher warrant the caricature that he makes Jesus simply the perfect Christian. The Christian is dependent upon Jesus for his religious consciousness, and the 'perfect Christian' in Schleiermacher's eyes would not be independent and self-sufficient in relation to Jesus.

Nor does Schleiermacher lose the historicity of Jesus to view, even though in the *Christmas Eve* dialogue of 1806 he seems prepared to allow the view that the present religious consciousness is of itself a sufficient pointer to an historical originator of such emotions, regardless of the degree of certainty of 'hard' historical evidence. But the God-consciousness of contemporary Christians is always filled out in terms of the historical Jesus. The believer is related to a recognizable historical figure in an immediate, living communion. Alongside the tightly argued christology in *The Christian Faith*, therefore, we have also Schleiermacher's Berlin lectures *The Life of Jesus*, one of the earliest in the great series of nineteenth century 'lives' which were to typify liberal theology.

Protestant liberalism has often been charged with reducing the historical Jesus to a moral and spiritual example or hero, in contrast to the one who saves lost mankind by his sacrifice. Schleiermacher's Christ, however, does not just serve as a spur to moral endeavour. His opening christological thesis runs: 'If the spontaneity of the new corporate life is original in the Redeemer and proceeds from him alone, then as an historical individual he must have been at the same time ideal (i.e. the ideal must have been completely historical in him), and each historical moment of his experience must at the same time have borne within it the ideal.'[46]

The new life is not generated by the believer, or by the community itself, but is actually imparted through communion with the Jesus in whom it has its source and who is its 'ideal' realization. It must be noted, however, that when Schleiermacher speaks of 'ideality' *(Urbildlichkeit)* he does not mean an abstract model of perfection, but something nearer the Platonic 'form', that which actually imparts reality to a particular object which participates in it. Also, while Schleiermacher speaks of the 'exemplary' status of Jesus *(Vorbildlichkeit)* he does not mean a kind of model to be copied, but rather the way in which Jesus himself exemplified the human race by solidarity with it in the fullness of humanity.

Schleiermacher fully recognized, and faced, the demands of a christology which was aware that if Jesus was 'truly man' this meant *historical* man, that is, not just a figure who 'really existed once upon a time', but one who was subject to all the exigencies of historical life. This meant, first, a full recognition of the development of the human Jesus 'in a certain similarity with his surroundings, that is, in general after the manner of his people'. Jesus was born into, lived in and became part of a specific social and cultural context. Schleiermacher's *Life of Jesus* is one of the first 'lives' to appreciate fully the need to see the figure being studied as set in that context. But also, with that appreciation comes awareness of a difficulty specific to christology:

> If we are not permitted to tear any man loose from the general condi-
> tion of his individual existence, therefore not from his rootage in the
> life of his people and not from his age, then this appears again to put an
> end to that application which we postulate is to be made of the knowl-
> edge of Christ, for we are in another age and belong to another culture.
> If therefore we cannot extract Christ from his historical setting in order
> to think of him within that of our people and our age, it follows again
> that the knowledge of him has no practical value, for he ceases to have
> exemplary character. But we can raise the question from another
> angle. If we are to think of him under the conditions of a definite age
> and a definite setting in the life of his people, does not this imply a
> greater diminution of the specific dignity of Christ?[47]

Liberal theology was not always so sensitive to the issues surrounding the quest of the historical Jesus. But how can a person, rooted in one specific historical context, have significance for all contexts? Or, in Schleier-macher's own terminology, how can the 'ideality' of the Redeemer be conceived *in* 'the perfectly natural historicity of his career'? Schleier-macher's answer lies in his conception of the unique God-consciousness of Jesus: 'The Redeemer, then, is like all men in virtue of the identity of human nature, but distinguished from them all by the constant potency of his God-consciousness, which was a veritable existence of God in him.'[48]

Here we have reached the crux of Schleiermacher's whole theology, and certainly the most vigorously contested element. Is Schleiermacher's Jesus Christ simply another man who is conscious of God to a higher degree than other men are? Is he in any way qualitatively different from the rest of the race, with which, as human, he is in solidarity? Schleiermacher is far from naive on this issue, and is fully aware that he is positing a peculiarity in Christ's activity which yet 'belongs to a general aspect of human nature' — but this by no means detracts from his dignity as Redeemer. For 'to ascribe to Christ an absolutely powerful God-consciousness, and to attribute to him an existence of God in him, are exactly the same thing'. Before rushing to shut the orthodox doors against Schleiermacher, the reader is advised to weigh carefully every word in that sentence — and every sentence in section 94 of *The Christian Faith* (below, pp. 385-9). What Schleiermacher is seeking is a christological statement which expresses the belief that Christ is human and divine, but in the language and anthropology which he considered to be valid for his day, as distinct from that of the classical metaphysics of the first Christian centuries.

God's existence, says Schleiermacher, can only be apprehended as 'pure activity', for God is one who *acts upon* what is not himself, but is not himself acted upon (or, 'passive'). God's existence in an individual requires not only that the individual be purely 'passive' in relation to God, but positively open to God through 'vital receptivity' which in turn 'confronts the totality of finite existence'. This could only take place through an intelligent, conscious individual. However, the general level of God-consciousness among people is *not* an existence of God in human nature, for it is not allowed to predominate, being subjected to sensuous emotions at every point. Christ himself 'is the only "other" in which there is an existence of God in the proper sense, so far, that is, as we posit the God-consciousness as continually and exclusively determining every moment, and consequently also this perfect indwelling of the Supreme Being as his peculiar being and his inmost self.'[49]

Christ, one might paraphrase Schleiermacher as saying, is the one human being whose life, as human as ours, is at the same time, and in every moment, the activity of God in the world. The God-consciousness in him was fully potent and determinative in all that he was and did. This is more than a 'psychologizing' of the divinity of Christ, though it certainly demands a new look at the traditional classical formulae. Schleiermacher in fact insists on the need to criticize such traditional statements, while agreeing with their intention of stating the divine and human in the one person of Christ.

Christ's redeeming work, for Schleiermacher, consists in the impartation of his God-consciousness to the believer. Through personal communion with Jesus, the inner life of the believer is re-created. Christ is truly the second, life-giving Adam. The nascent God-consciousness is enabled to flourish and to become dominant over the sensuous, self-centred emotions. Schleiermacher was not afraid to call his soteriology 'mystical', in order to stress the union between Christ and the believer. Redemption and reconciliation are founded in this union, not in any extra-personal transactions or ransom-payments or penal satisfactions for sin, as in certain traditional theories of atonement.

Schleiermacher, it was noted earlier, was remarkably interested in both a new dogmatic formulation of the person of Christ, and the historical Jesus. This dual interest was a strength, but it also put his christology under strain. More serious than the question of whether Schleiermacher 'psychologized' the 'divinity' of Christ, is the question whether the picture given of Jesus' God-consciousness in his christology can really be substantiated by the historical picture of Jesus he draws from the gospel narratives. Schleiermacher's Jesus is essentially that of the Fourth Gospel, and indeed on various grounds he prefers the Johannine to the synoptic gospels as sources for the life of Jesus. Many today would of course query the assumptions of such a preference. But also linked with that preference is the fact that Schleiermacher's historical Jesus is remarkably untroubled in his God-consciousness, and indeed in his mental and emotional states generally. The synoptic accounts of the agony in Gethsemane are to be seen as 'embellishments' under the influence of later martyr-spirituality. The Markan account of the cry of dereliction from the cross, 'My God, my God, why hast thou forsaken me?' is not to be taken without reference to the whole of Psalm 22, which overall is a song of triumphant praise to God of which that line is but the beginning. All along Schleiermacher plays down the aspects of suffering and anguish in Jesus' life and death, and he seems clearly threatened by the implications of those parts of the narratives which suggest that, at what is literally the crux of soteriology, Jesus' God-consciousness — if such it still was — was an ineffably dark experience of God's absence. To admit this element would clearly place a question-mark not only over the christology, but over Schleiermacher's doctrine of God as well. A God who is experienced as absent by the derelict Jesus is no longer one who is 'pure act'. Perhaps there *is* an element of passivity, of suffering, of withdrawal of himself by God in face of the world. Schleiermacher could scarcely contemplate that, and hardly any other theologian of the time would either. It was in fact Schleiermacher's philosophical counterpart at Berlin, Hegel, who sought to comprehend the experience of the 'death of God' within his intellectual system. But it was not until the more recent years of the twentieth century, in the thought of such as Bonhoeffer, Jüngel and Moltmann, and to some extent the 'Process Theologians' such as Hartshorne and Pittenger, that such far-reaching new conceptions of God have been seriously tackled in western theology.[50]

7. NATION, CHURCH AND STATE*

Schleiermacher, we have seen, was deeply stirred by Prussia's humiliation in 1806, and both in preaching and political activity shared in the struggle to promote a liberal reform of the Prussian state, to throw off the French yoke and, ultimately, to achieve greater unity among the German states. At least one major study has been produced of Schleiermacher's nationalism and the relation of this to his religious thought. If the thought of any theologian acquires significance in the light of his social and political context, in Schleiermacher's case some examination is required of how his theology and his patriotism related to each other. In his instance, this aspect becomes doubly significant in the view of the fateful development of German nationalism in the following century, and the question cannot be avoided whether Schleiermacher contributed to the historical roots of National Socialism. In any case, the issues of religious faith, national loyalty and the power of the state transcend Schleiermacher's own context and are with many of us today as well.

Schleiermacher's patriotism was far from being a crude glorification of the Fatherland, right or wrong. It was a highly moral crusade, and from the pulpit he tirelessly reiterated his belief that the nadir of 1806 was to be seen as a divine judgment — or at least a stern education — on the Prussians for the corruption which had overtaken their personal and public behaviour. Prussia had grown lax, dishonest, boastful without cause, the old virtues had been lost. The wrath of God had to strike ere there could be rebirth of the nation. When therefore the opportunity came to harry the doomed Napoleon retreating from Russia in 1813, Schleiermacher saw this as the heaven-sent signal for the Prussian revival. The sermon *A*

---

* For texts, see below pp. 235ff.

Nation's Duty in a War for Freedom was delivered as the troops marched from Berlin. It reveals both the extent and the sharp limits of the ethical element in Schleiermacher's Prussian loyalty. The present hour was the time of opportunity to repent of the deep corruption into which Prussia had fallen. A new unity, determination and readiness for sacrifice was uniting king and people (the whole tone is highly similar to the sermons preached in Britain on the outbreak of the First World War). A sense of moral release was sweeping the people. The issue had at last become clear: either total liberation or total defeat, either being infinitely preferable to the sickly condition of subservience.

It becomes clear, however, that for Schleiermacher the highest moral good is the existence, unique characteristics and independence of the Fatherland itself. A foreign element degrades a developed nation, 'for God has imparted to each its own nature, and has therefore marked out bounds and limits for the habitations of the different races of men on the face of the earth'.[51] Prussia must become truly Prussia, such is the divine purpose. It is at this point that the contemporary reader who has more than a slight acquaintance with the story of Nazism becomes uneasy, for such a theology of nationhood as being of the divine ordering was undoubtedly one of the entrenched Protestant beliefs which Nazi ideology was ready to exploit and incorporate into its own beliefs in blood, race and soil. Martin Redeker states of Schleiermacher's nationalism: 'This is not a nationalism which absolutizes the people and state.'[52] That is correct; that Schleiermacher was no state absolutist his own readiness to confront the authorities and even the sovereign show. But Redeker goes on to differentiate this from the twentieth century 'completely secularized and hence unrestrained nationalism and chauvinism'. This is somewhat innocent, for the 'unrestrained' nationalism which brought Adolf Hitler to power in 1933 was *not* 'completely secularized'. Certain brands of it were highly religious, more especially that promulgated by the so-called 'German Christians' who held that nation and race were indefeasible 'orders of creation' decreed by God and therefore to be maintained to the utmost degree by whatever means proved necessary. While it would be a travesty to view Schleiermacher as some kind of proto-Nazi, it must be admitted that the 'German Christians' who welcomed Hitler would have been only too glad to read in this most illustrious German Protestant of the preceding century that the nation which trusts in God 'is that nation . . . which means to defend at any price the distinctive aims and spirit which God has implanted in it, and is thus fighting for God's work'.[53]

The affinity between religious passion and nationalism is well-known to social and political historians.[54] Indeed it could be argued that in the modern age nationalism has itself become a kind of religion for many, providing a 'larger self' to which the individual can relate in devotion, following the collapse of the conventional theism. In the case of Germany, it has been pointed out, it was Pietism which particularly fed the warmth of devotion to the Fatherland. In Schleiermacher the connexion is supplied, theologically and philosophically, by his understanding of individuality. The uniqueness of the individual is paralleled by the larger 'individualities' of the social groups to which he or she belongs — home, church, society, nation. In each case, the God-given nature of the individual, person or group, is to be expressed. And just as individual piety is a matter of feeling, so the successively wider attachments will be marked by appropriate feelings of loyalty and devotion.

This is certainly the point where fundamentally critical issues arise for Schleiermacher's theology. Why, for instance, is 'nation' regarded as the widest boundary of human belonging? Is this simply a case of religious blessing being given to the structures of the world as they are, without examination of the acceptability of these structures in the light of the divine purpose? More fundamentally still, but leading on from this, in beginning with the emotions of the contemporary religious consciousness and working back to Jesus as the originator of that consciousness, does Schleiermacher simply accept the 'pious emotions' at their face value? It seems that the connexion between Jesus and the religious consciousness is established in such a way that there is no point of detachment by which Jesus himself can become a critical criterion for the authenticity of those emotions. We have already had cause to comment on certain aspects of Schleiermacher's 'Johannine' Jesus in the preceding section. The feelings of piety and, correspondingly, of patriotic devotion, appear to be regarded as intrinsically valid. This was certainly an ingredient in the development of German *Kulturprotestantismus,* an amalgam of Protestant bourgeois values with German identity and culture which by the end of the nineteenth century made it hard for many to distinguish being Christian from being German. That world collapsed in the 1914-18 War, in the aftermath of which Karl Barth led a new attempt at a specifically christocentric critique of all social and political values.

Schleiermacher had a clear theology of the Church in relation to secular power, and this is stated in *The Christian Faith* — interestingly, not in the ecclesiological but in the christological section. Here it is the Lutheran doctrine of the 'two kingdoms' which predominates. Christ's kingdom is essentially that of the Church. He does not yet possess the kingdom of power which belongs to the Father. Civil government has no jurisdiction in the Church, for it is part of the general divine government of the world, operating even where there is no Christian religion. Even where Christians are involved in positions of responsibility in secular government the fundamental separation between the two spheres remains. The Christian is one who is governed personally by Christ in an inner vital relationship. This simply means that 'everyone, whether magistrate or private citizen, has to seek in the directions given by Christ, *not indeed right directions for his conduct under civil government (for this is always a matter for the art of politics)*, but certainly the right temper of mind even in this relationship' (emphases mine).[55] Bismarck, the shaper of German destiny in the later nineteenth century who had sat in Schleiermacher's confirmation class in Berlin, in fact exemplified such a combination of piety and *Realpolitik*. Political direction is thus an autonomous area immune from Christian ethical scrutiny. Schleiermacher can label 'patriotism' and 'the common spirit of society' as 'fleshly motives' for the formation of a Church within any society — a remarkable description in view of his own patriotic fervour in the pulpit. The reason is that Schleiermacher, as has happened so often in Protestant history, was primarily concerned to ensure the freedom of the Church from state interference and control. Once that freedom was apparently safeguarded or at least claimed, interest in a theology of civil society as such was minimal. Not only could secular power become a law unto itself, but the 'fleshly motives' of national solidarity, left free to roam without theological examination, could too readily appeal to the Church for baptism in pious fervour. In the early nineteenth century, in a Germany pitifully divided and weak, constituting a vacuum of power in a Europe beset on the one hand by Napoleonic France and on the other by Tsarist Russia, that might seem a happy coincidence of interests serving the cause of national liberation, and indeed a move towards a sane international order in Europe. A century later it was to prove fatefully different.

8. CHRISTIANITY AND THE RELIGIONS*

The Enlightenment marked the end of an age of innocence for Christianity in its relations with other faiths. Of course the existence of Judaism,

* For texts, see below pp. 254ff.

Islam and Indian religions had long been known. But it was only relatively recently that such wide religious diversity among mankind began to be seen as having powerful implications for the questions of religious truth and authority. Deism represented one approach to the issue, by attempting to distil out of man's innate moral sense and powers of reason the essential, common truth to which all religions pointed and thus to arrive at a universal 'natural religion'. Problems of competing truth-claims would then be solved. Today the relationship between Christianity and 'other religions' is as open to debate as ever.

Schleiermacher was acutely aware of the questions posed by a multi-religious world for a Christianity claiming a specific knowledge of God through Christ. His own response was highly original for his time. He first trenchantly rejected the Enlightenment's 'natural religion'. Religion never effectively existed in such a generalized disembodied form as this 'set of truths'. Religion of any power always took the form of a positive, historical religion. Christianity was certainly one of these historical religions. Non-Christian religions were not to be categorized as wholly in error. For Schleiermacher, Christianity certainly did have a specific character, in the centrality of the experience of redemption brought by Jesus. But that did not make Christianity totally discontinuous with the inwardness of the other religions. It was the most highly developed religion — 'the *purest* form of Monotheism which has appeared in history', 'the *most perfect* of the most highly developed forms of religion' (emphases mine).[56] Such statements have been cited as evidence that Schleiermacher effectively sold out the decisive revelatory nature of Christianity to a general conception of 'religion' of which Christianity is simply a particular case — the most perfect maybe but even then only as a matter of degree.

Before coming to a final judgment on this issue the student should again carefully consider the context in which Schleiermacher was writing and the view he was primarily contending against, namely, the Enlightenment with its love of 'natural religion'. To Schleiermacher such a belief was a disembodied abstraction, wholly evacuated of what was truly religious, namely the *feeling* of dependence upon God. For Schleiermacher, while one could speak in general terms of 'religion' as feeling, such 'feeling' only occurred in distinct, specific, historically conditioned forms of existence, whether fetishistic, or polytheistic, or monotheistic, whether as ancient Greek religion or Judaism or Islam or Christianity. Again, Schleiermacher's notion of individuality surfaces here. Each religion must be examined in its own particular case and, by calling for a scientific study of the historical religions Schleiermacher can be justly recognized as a pioneer in the modern field of 'the study of religions'.

It is incidentally also interesting to note how Schleiermacher assesses the historical situation of the three great monotheisms — Judaism, Christianity and Islam.[57] Judaism he dismisses as 'being almost in process of extinction'. Its limitation of the love of its God to Israel 'betrays a lingering affinity with Fetishism' — and indeed its monotheism was not fully developed until after the exile. This last judgment is in accord with modern, standard historical criticism. The former sentiments may by some be thought to indicate an academic form of anti-Semitism (though Schleiermacher as a person showed no antipathy to Jews — his close confidante Henriette Herz was Jewish). Islam, on the other hand, is to be seen as, with Christianity, 'still contending for the mastery of the human race' — a testimony to just how long-lived after the mediaeval period was the European fear of Arab advance.

EPILOGUE: BARTH AND SCHLEIERMACHER

'Until better instructed, I can see no way from Schleiermacher or from his contemporary epigones, to the chroniclers, prophets, and wise ones of Israel, to those who narrate the story of the life, death, and resurrection of Jesus Christ, to the word of the apostles — no way to the God of Abraham, Isaac, and Jacob and the Father of Jesus Christ, no way to the great tradition of the Christian church. For the present I can see nothing here but a choice. And for me there can be no question as to how that choice is to be made.'[58]

This was Karl Barth's final word on Schleiermacher, the theologian whose works had inspired him during his student days, against whom he revolted during the First World War when he led the advance of the new theology of revelation, and with whom he conducted a continuing polemic. Schleiermacher, in Barth's eyes, was the 'common denominator' in that succession of Protestant liberal theologies which confused culture with Christian faith, and being found ethically bankrupt capitulated to the Kaiser's war policy in 1914. Moreover, in Barth's eyes it was Schleiermacher's shade which haunted the existential theologies of Bultmann and others. Worse still, Barth alleges, his presuppositions can be detected in the 'death of God' theology of the 1960s. 'That Schleiermacher made the christianly pious person into the criterion and content of his theology, while, after the "death of God" and the state-funeral dedicated to him, one now jubilantly wants to make the christianly impious person into its object and theme, these certainly are two different things. In the end and in principle, however, they probably amount to the same thing.'[59] The root fault, according to Barth, lay in Schleiermacher's self-confinement within the 'anthropological horizon'. His attention was given to the Christian, not the One in whom the Christian believes and worships. His attention was devoted to feelings of piety, not actually to God in his divine, utterly superior being. Only ambiguously is this theology rather than philosophy. Even when describing God as the source of the feeling of absolute dependence, Schleiermacher, according to Barth, is not unequivocal that faith is in relationship to 'an indispensable Other'.

The student will have to pursue his or her judgment on the issue between Schleiermacher and Barth after first-hand reading of both theologians, and some informed discussion of them. The issues are indeed fundamental and far-reaching, well beyond the historical interest that may be taken in the two theologians themselves. But one observation may be permitted here. This is, that any judgment made upon Schleiermacher must take into account the particular context in which he lived and thought, and what, to *him*, were the main parameters within which a doctrine of God had to be plotted. For Barth, faced with what seemed like the total collapse of the liberal and idealistic theology in 1914-18, it appeared that theology was faced with an antithesis, a fundamental choice between speaking of God in his own reality and glory as revealed in his Word, and speaking of man in his religious and moral potentialities. But that is not the antithesis which Schleiermacher was conscious of facing at the end of the Enlightenment, and it is hard to see how that antithesis could have occurred to him then. If there was an antithesis facing him, it was between treating the knowledge of God in abstract metaphysical or moral terms, and seeing it as a matter of immediate consciousness affecting human existence.

It must be said that Barth nevertheless had a warm regard for Schleiermacher the human being and pastor. He was genuinely glad to find Schleiermacher's bust amid the rubble at Bonn in 1946. He had lectured intensively on Schleiermacher at Göttingen in 1923-24, and he includes an important essay on him in his survey of nineteenth century Protestant theology.

Finally, after all the criticism he has tirelessly aimed at Schleiermacher's head, Barth typically leaves us with an intriguing, almost wistful, suggestion that all might not be completely lost with Schleiermacher.

What about, asks Barth, a theology 'predominantly and decisively of the Holy Spirit?' — 'A theology of which Schleiermacher was scarcely conscious, but which might actually have been the legitimate concern dominating even his theological activity.'[60] In other words, theology *must* take account of what is actually felt as the experience of God's activity in human awareness. This, Barth felt, would be the task of a new theological generation. If that is so, Schleiermacher's name will certainly not be forgotten.

SELECTED TEXTS

1

RELIGION AS FEELING AND
RELATIONSHIP *

On Religion. Speeches to Its Cultured Despisers *was Schleiermacher's first book and the work by which his name was made in his native Germany. The first edition appeared in 1799, when Schleiermacher was aged 31, and preacher at the Charité Hospital in Berlin. A second edition was produced in 1806 while Schleiermacher was teaching at the University of Halle. A third and final edition was published in 1822, when Schleiermacher was at the height of his reputation as professor in Berlin. The successive editions exhibit significant modifications to the text. After the first edition, Schleiermacher revised certain passages where, in his desire to posit 'feeling' as the means of apprehending God, in opposition to the Enlightenment tendency to rationalism and abstraction, he gave some of his critics the impression of pantheist leanings. Explanatory notes were also added to the later editions, where it is clear that from 1806 onwards the critical political situation in Prussia sharply increased Schleiermacher's historical sense.*

The texts used here are from the translation by John Oman (1893) of the third edition. There were five chapters — 'Speeches' — in all: Defence; The Nature of Religion; The Cultivation of Religion; Association in Religion, or Church and Priesthood; The Religions. Selections have been made from the first, second and fourth 'Speeches' to exhibit the heart of Schleiermacher's insistence on the inward, emotional nature of religion as feeling, his understanding of the individual in relation to others, to society and the universe, and his vital communal and historical sense which means that for him religion is always socially embodied. In view of later criticisms of Schleiermacher's 'subjectivity', Schleiermacher's intricate analysis of how the conscious self responds to realities external to it should be carefully noted.

---

* See also pp. 36ff. above.

FIRST SPEECH

DEFENCE

It may be an unexpected and even a marvellous undertaking, that any one should still venture to demand from the very class that have raised themselves above the vulgar, and are saturated with the wisdom of the centuries, attention for a subject so entirely neglected by them. And I confess that I am aware of nothing that promises any easy success, whether it be in winning for my efforts your approval, or in the more difficult and more desirable task of instilling into you my thought and inspiring you for my subject. From of old faith has not been every man's affair. At all times but few have discerned religion itself, while millions, in various ways, have been satisfied to juggle with its trappings. Now especially the life of cultivated people is far from anything that might have even a resemblance to religion. Just as little, I know, do you worship the Deity in sacred retirement, as you visit the forsaken temples. In your ornamented dwellings, the only sacred things to be met with are the sage maxims of our wise men, and the splendid compositions of our poets. Suavity and sociability, art and science have so fully taken possession of your minds, that no room remains for the eternal and holy Being that lies beyond the world. I know how well you have succeeded in making your earthly life so rich and varied, that you no longer stand in need of an eternity. Having made a universe for yourselves, you are above the need of thinking of the Universe that made you. You are agreed, I know, that nothing new, nothing convincing can any more be said on this matter, which on every side by sages and seers, and I might add by scoffers and priests, has been abundantly discussed. To priests, least of all, are you inclined to listen. They have long been outcasts for you, and are declared unworthy of your trust, because they like best to lodge in the battered ruins of their sanctuary and cannot, even there, live without disfiguring and destroying it still more. All this I know, and yet, divinely swayed by an irresistible necessity within me, I feel myself compelled to speak, and cannot take back my invitation that you and none else should listen to me.

Might I ask one question? On every subject, however small and unimportant, you would most willingly be taught by those who have devoted to it their lives and their powers. In your desire for knowledge you do not avoid the cottages of the peasant or the workshops of the humble artisans. How then does it come about that, in matters of religion alone, you hold every thing the more dubious when it comes from those who are experts, not only according to their own profession, but by recognition from the state, and from the people? Or can you perhaps, strangely enough, show that they are not more experienced, but maintain and cry up anything rather than religion? Scarcely, my good sirs! Not setting much store on a judgment so baseless I confess, as is right, that I also am a member of this order. I venture, though I run the risk, if you do not give me an attentive hearing, of being reckoned among the great crowd from which you admit so few exceptions.

This is at least a voluntary confession, for my speech would not readily have betrayed me. Still less have I any expectations of danger from the praise which my brethren will bestow on this undertaking, for my present aim lies almost entirely outside their sphere, and can have but small resemblance to what they would most willingly see and hear. With the cry of distress, in which most of them join, over the downfall of religion I have no sympathy, for I know no age that has given religion a better reception than the present. I have nothing to do with the conservative and barbarian lamentation whereby they seek to rear again the fallen walls and gothic pillars of their Jewish Zion.

Why then, as I am fully conscious that in all I have to say to you I entirely belie my profession, should I not acknowledge it like any other accident? Its prepossessions shall in no way hinder us. Neither in asking nor in answering shall the limits it holds sacred be valid between us. As a man I speak to you of the sacred secrets of mankind according to my views — of what was in me as with youthful enthusiasm I sought the unknown, of what since then I have thought and experienced, of the innermost springs of my being which shall for ever remain for me the highest, however I be moved by the changes of time and mankind. I do not speak from any reasoned resolve, nor from hope, nor from fear. Nor is it done from any caprice or accident. Rather it is the pure necessity of my nature; it is a divine call; it is that which determines my position in the world and makes me what I am. Wherefore, even if it were neither fitting nor prudent to speak of religion, there is something which compels me and represses with its heavenly power all those small considerations. . . .

To this very power I now submit, and of this very nature is my call. Permit me to speak of myself. You know that what is spoken at the instigation of piety cannot be pride, for piety is always full of humility. Piety was the mother's womb, in whose sacred darkness my young life was nourished and was prepared for a world still sealed for it. In it my spirit breathed ere it had yet found its own place in knowledge and experience. It helped me as I began to sift the faith of my fathers and to cleanse thought and feeling from the rubbish of antiquity. When the God and the immortality of my childhood vanished from my doubting eyes it remained to me. Without design of mine it guided me into active life. It showed me how, with my endowments and defects, I should keep myself holy in an undivided existence, and through it alone I have learnt friendship and love. In respect of other human excellences, before your judgment-seat, ye wise and understanding of the people, I know it is small proof of possession to be able to speak of their value. They can be known from description, from observation of others, or, as all virtues are known, from the ancient and general traditions of their nature. But religion is of such a sort and is so rare, that whoever utters anything of it, must necessarily have had it, for nowhere could he have heard it. Of all that I praise, all that I feel to be the true work of religion, you would find little even in the sacred books. To the man who has not himself experienced it, it would only be an annoyance and a folly.

Finally, if I am thus impelled to speak of religion and to deliver my testimony, to whom should I turn if not to the sons of Germany? Where else is an audience for my speech? It is not blind predilection for my native soil or for my fellows in government and language, that makes me speak thus, but the deep conviction that you alone are capable, as well as worthy, of having awakened in you the sense for holy and divine things. Those proud Islanders whom many unduly honour, know no watchword but *gain* and *enjoyment.* Their zeal for knowledge is only a sham to what is for you highest and dearest. To the roof of the temple I would lead you that you might survey the whole sanctuary and discover its innermost secrets.

Do you seriously expect me to believe that those who daily distress themselves most toilsomely about earthly things have pre-eminent fitness for becoming intimate with heavenly things, those who brood anxiously over the next moment and are fast bound to the nearest objects can extend their vision widest over the world, and that those, who, in the monotonous round of a dull industry have not yet found themselves will discover most clearly the living Deity! Surely you will not maintain that to your shame? You alone, therefore, I can invite, you who are called to leave the common standpoint of mankind, who do not shun the toilsome way into the depths of man's spirit to find his inmost emotions and see the living worth and connection of his outward works.

Since this became clear to me, I have long found myself in the hesitating mood of one who has lost a precious jewel, and does not dare to examine the last spot where it could be hidden. There was a time when you held it a mark of special courage to cast off partially the restraints of inherited dogma. You still were ready to discuss particular subjects, though it were only to efface one of those notions. Such a figure as religion moving gracefully, adorned in eloquence, still pleased you, if only that you wished to maintain in the gentler sex a certain feeling for sacred things. But that time is long past. Piety is now no more to be spoken of, and even the Graces, with most unwomanly hardness, destroy the tenderest blossoms of the human heart, and I can link the interest I require from you to nothing but your contempt. I will ask you, therefore, just to be well informed and thorough-going in this contempt.

Let us then, I pray you, examine whence exactly religion has its rise. Is it from some clear intuition, or from some vague thought? Is it from the different kinds and sects of religion found in history, or from some general idea which you have perhaps conceived arbitrarily? Some doubtless will profess the latter view. But here as in other things the ready judgment may be without ground, the matter being superficially considered and no trouble being taken to gain an accurate knowledge. Your general idea turns on fear of an eternal being, or, broadly, respect for his influence on the occurrences of this life called by you providence, on expectation of a future life after this one, called by you immortality. These two conceptions which you have rejected, are, you consider, in one way or another, the hinges of all religion. But say, my dear sirs, how you have found this; for there are two points of view from which everything taking place in man or proceeding from him may be regarded. Considered from the centre outwards, that is according to its inner quality, it is an expression of human nature, based in one of its necessary modes of acting or impulses or whatever else you like to call it, for I will not now quarrel with your technical language. On the contrary, regarded from the outside, according to the definite attitude and form it assumes in particular cases, it is a product of time and history. From what side have you considered religion that great spiritual phenomenon, that you have reached the idea that everything called by this name has a common content? You can hardly affirm that it is by regarding it from within. If so, my good sirs, you would have to admit that these thoughts are at least in some way based in human nature. And should you say that as now found they have sprung only from misinterpretations or false references of a necessary human aim, it would become you to seek in it the true and eternal, and to unite your efforts to ours to free human nature from the injustice which it always suffers when aught in it is misunderstood or misdirected.

By all that is sacred, and according to that avowal, something must be sacred to you, I adjure you, do not neglect this business, that mankind, whom with us you honour, do not most justly scorn you for forsaking them in a grave matter. If you find from what you hear that the business is as good as done, even if it ends otherwise than you expect, I venture to reckon on your thanks and approval.

But you will probably say that your idea of the content of religion is from the other view of this spiritual phenomenon. You start with the outside, with the opinions, dogmas and usages, in which every religion is presented. They always return to providence and immortality. For these externals you have sought an inward and original source in vain. Wherefore religion generally can be nothing but an empty pretence which, like a murky and oppressive atmosphere, has enshrouded part of the truth. Doubtless this is your genuine opinion. But if you really consider these two points the sum of religion in all the forms in which it has appeared in history, permit me to ask whether you have rightly observed all these phenomena and have rightly comprehended their common content? If your idea has had its rise in this way you must justify it by instances. If anyone says it is wrong and beside the mark, and if he point out something else in religion not hollow, but having a kernel of excellent quality and extraction, you must first hear and judge before you venture further to despise. Do not grudge, therefore, to listen to what I shall say to those who, from first to last, have more accurately and laboriously adhered to observation of particulars.

You are doubtless acquainted with the histories of human follies, and have reviewed the various structures of religious doctrine from the senseless fables of wanton peoples to the most refined Deism, from the rude superstition of human sacrifice to the ill-put-together fragments of metaphysics and ethics now called purified Christianity, and you have found them all without rhyme or reason. I am far from wishing to contradict you. Rather, if you really mean that the most cultured religious system is no better than the rudest, if you only perceive that the divine cannot lie in a series that ends on both sides in something ordinary and despicable, I will gladly spare you the trouble of estimating further all that lies between. Possibly they may all appear to you transitions and stages towards the final form. Out of the hand of its age each comes better polished and carved, till at length art has grown equal to that perfect plaything with which our century has presented history. But this consummation of doctrines and systems is often anything rather than consummation of religion. Nay, not infrequently, the progress of the one has not the smallest connection with the other. I cannot speak of it without indignation. All who have a regard for what issues from within the mind, and who are in earnest that every side of man be trained and exhibited, must bewail how the high and glorious is often turned from its destination and robbed of its freedom in order to be held in despicable bondage by the scholastic spirit of a barbarian and cold time. What are all these systems, considered in themselves, but the handiwork of the calculating understanding, wherein only by mutual limitation each part holds its place? What else can they be, these systems of theology, these theories of the origin and the end of the world, these analyses of the nature of an incomprehensible Being, wherein everything runs to cold argufying, and the highest can be treated in the tone of a common controversy? And this is certainly — let me appeal to your own feeling — not the character of religion.

If you have only given attention to these dogmas and opinions, therefore, you do not yet know religion itself, and what you despise is not it. Why have you not penetrated deeper to find the kernel of this shell? I am astonished at your voluntary ignorance, ye easy-going inquirers, and at the all too quiet satisfaction with which you linger by the first thing presented to you. Why do you not regard the religious life itself, and first those pious exaltations of the mind in which all other known activities are set aside or almost suppressed, and the whole soul is dissolved in the immediate feeling of the Infinite and Eternal? In such moments the disposition you pretend to despise reveals itself in primordial and visible form. He only who has studied and truly known man in these emotions can rediscover religion in those outward manifestations. He will assuredly perceive something more in them than you. Bound up in them all something of that spiritual matter lies, without which they could not have arisen. But in the hands of those who do not understand how to unbind it, let them break it up and examine it as they may, nothing but the cold dead mass remains.

This recommendation to seek rather in those scattered and seemingly undeveloped elements your object that you have not yet found in the developed and the complete to which you have hitherto been directed, cannot surprise you who have more or less busied yourselves with philosophy, and are acquainted with its fortunes. With philosophy, indeed, it should be quite otherwise. From its nature it must strive to fashion itself into the closest connection. That special kind of knowledge is only verified and its communication assured by its completeness, and yet even here you must commence with the scattered and incomplete. Recollect how very few of those who, in a way of their own, have penetrated into the secrets of nature and spirit, viewing and exhibiting their mutual relation and inner harmony in a light of their own, have put forth at once a system of their knowledge. In a finer, if more fragile form, they have communicated their discoveries.

On the contrary, if you regard the systems in all schools, how often are they mere habitations and nurseries of the dead letter. With few exceptions, the plastic spirit of high contemplation is too fleeting and too free for those rigid forms whereby those who would willingly grasp and retain what is strange, believe they are best helped. Suppose that any one held the architects of those great edifices of philosophy, without distinction, for true philosophers! Suppose he would learn from them the spirit of their research! Would you not advise him thus, 'See to it, friend, that you have not lighted upon those who merely follow, and collect, and rest satisfied with what another has furnished: with them you will never find the spirit of that art: to the discoverers you must go, on whom it surely rests.' To you who seek religion I must give the same advice. It is all the more necessary, as religion is as far removed, by its whole nature, from all that is systematic as philosophy is naturally disposed to it.

Consider only with whom those ingenious erections originate, the mutability of which you scorn, the bad proportions of which offend you, and the incongruity of which, with your contemptuous tendency, almost strikes you as absurd. Have they come from the heroes of religion? Name one among those who have brought down any kind of new revelation to us, who has thought it worth his while to occupy himself with such a labour of Sisyphus, beginning with Him who first conceived the idea of the kingdom of God, from which, if from anything in the sphere of religion, a system might have been produced to the new mystics or enthusiasts, as you are accustomed to call them, in whom, perhaps, an original beam of the inner light still shines. You will not blame me if I do not reckon among them the theologians of the letter, who believe the salvation of the world and the light of wisdom are to be found in a new vesture of formulae, or a new arrangement of ingenious proofs. In isolation only the mighty thunder of their speech, announcing that the Deity is revealing Himself through them, is accustomed to be heard when the celestial feelings are unburdened, when the sacred fires must burst forth from the overcharged spirit. Idea and word are simply the necessary and inseparable outcome of the heart, only to be understood by it and along with it. Doctrine is only united to doctrine occasionally to remove misunderstanding or expose unreality.

From many such combinations those systems were gradually compacted. Wherefore, you must not rest satisfied with the repeated oft-broken echo of that original sound. You must transport yourselves into the interior of a pious soul and seek to understand its inspiration. In the very act, you must understand the production of light and heat in a soul surrendered to the Universe. Otherwise you learn nothing of religion, and it goes with you as with one who should too late bring fuel to the fire which the steel has struck from the flint, who finds only a cold, insignificant speck of coarse metal with which he can kindle nothing any more.

I ask, therefore, that you turn from everything usually reckoned religion, and fix your regard on the inward emotions and dispositions, as all utterances and acts of inspired men direct. Despite your acquirements, your culture and your prejudices, I hope for good success. At all events, till you have looked from this standpoint without discovering anything real, or having any change of opinion, or enlarging your contemptuous conception, the product of superficial observation, and are still able to hold in ridicule this reaching of the heart towards the Eternal, I will not confess that I have lost. Then, however, I will finally believe that your contempt for religion is in accordance with your nature, and I shall have no more to say.

Yet you need not fear that I shall betake myself in the end to that common device of representing how necessary religion is for maintaining justice and order in the world. Nor shall I remind you of an all-seeing eye, nor of the unspeakable short-sightedness of human management, nor of the narrow bounds of human power to render help. Nor shall I say how religion is a faithful friend and useful stay of morality, how, by its sacred feelings and glorious prospects, it makes the struggle with self and the perfecting of goodness much easier for weak man. Those who profess to be the best friends and most zealous defenders do indeed speak in this way. Which of the two is more degraded in being thus thought of together, I shall not decide, whether justice and morality which are represented as needing support, or religion which is to support them, or even whether it be not you to whom such things are said.

Though otherwise this wise counsel might be given you, how could I dare to suppose that you play with your consciences a sort of fast and loose game, and could be impelled by something you have hitherto had no cause to respect and love to something else that without it you already honour, and to which you have already devoted yourselves? Or suppose that these Speeches were merely to suggest what you should do for the sake of the people! How could you, who are called to educate others and make them like yourselves, begin by deceiving them, offering them as holy and vitally necessary what is in the highest degree indifferent to yourselves, and which, in your opinion, they can again reject as soon as they have attained your level? I, at least, cannot invite you to a course of action in which I perceive the most ruinous hypocrisy towards the world and towards yourselves. To recommend religion by such means would only increase the contempt to which it is at present exposed. Granted that our civil organizations are still burdened with a very high degree of imperfection and have shown but small power to prevent or abolish injustice, it would still be a culpable abandonment of a weighty matter, a faint-hearted unbelief in the approach of better things, if religion that in itself is not otherwise desirable must be called in.

Answer me this one question. Could there be a legal constitution resting on piety? Would not the whole idea that you hold so sacred vanish as soon as you took such a point of departure? Deal with the matter directly, therefore, if it seems to be in such an evil plight. Improve the laws, recast the whole constitution, give the state an iron hand, give it a hundred eyes if it has not got them already. At least do not allow those it has to sleep veiled in delusion. If you leave a business like this to an intermediary, you have never managed it. Do not declare to the disgrace of mankind that your loftiest creation is but a parasitic plant that can only nourish itself from strange sap.

Speaking from your standpoint, law must not even require morality to assure for it the most unlimited jurisdiction in its own territory. It must stand quite alone. Statesmen must make it universal. Now quite apart from the question whether what only exists in so far as it proceeds from the heart can be thus arbitrarily combined, if this general jurisdiction is only possible when religion is combined with law, none but persons skilled to infuse the spirit of religion into the human soul should be statesmen. And in what dark barbarousness of evil times would that land us!

Just as little can morality be in need of religion. A weak, tempted heart must take refuge in the thought of a future world. But it is folly to make a distinction between this world and the next. Religious persons at least know only one. If the desire for happiness is foreign to morality, later happiness can be no more valid than earlier; if it should be quite independent of praise, dread of the Eternal cannot be more valid than dread of a wise man. If morality loses in splendour and stability by every addition, how much more must it lose from something that can never hide its foreign extraction.

All this, however, you have heard of sufficiently from those who defend the independence and might of the moral law. Yet let me add, that to wish to transport religion into another sphere that it may serve and labour is to manifest towards it also great contempt. It is not so ambitious of conquest as to seek to reign in a foreign kingdom. The power that is its due, being earned afresh at every moment, satisfies it. Everything is sacred to it, and above all everything holding with it the same rank in human nature. But it must render a special service; it must have an aim; it must show itself useful! What degradation! And its defenders should be eager for it!

At the last remove, morality and justice also must conduce to some further advantage. It were better that such utilitarians should be submerged in this eternal whirlpool of universal utility, in which everything good is allowed to go down, of which no man that would be anything for himself understands a single sensible word, than that they should venture to come forward as defenders of religion, for of all men they are least skilled to conduct its case. High renown it were for the heavenly to conduct so wretchedly the earthly concerns of man! Great honour for the free and unconcerned to make the conscience of man a little sharper and more alert! For such a purpose religion does not descend from heaven. What is loved and honoured only on account of some extraneous advantage may be needful, but it is not in itself necessary, and a sensible person simply values it according to the end for which it is desired. By this standard, religion would be valueless enough. I, at least, would offer little, for I must confess that I do not believe much in the unjust dealings it would hinder, nor the moral dealings it would produce. If that is all it could do to gain respect, I would have no more to do with its case. To recommend it merely as an accessory is too unimportant. An imaginery praise that vanishes on closer contemplation, cannot avail anything going about with higher pretensions. I maintain that in all better souls piety springs necessarily by itself; that a province of its own in the mind belongs to it, in which it has unlimited sway; that it is worthy to animate most profoundly the noblest and best and to be fully accepted and known by them. That is my contention, and it now behoves you to decide whether it is worth your while to hear me, before you still further strengthen yourselves in your contempt. *On Religion, Speeches . . .*, pp. 1-3, 8-21

*

SECOND SPEECH

THE NATURE OF RELIGION

. . . Religion is for you at one time a way of thinking, a faith, a peculiar way of contemplating the world, and of combining what meets us in the world: at another, it is a way of acting, a peculiar desire and love, a special kind of conduct and character. Without this distinction of a theoretical and practical you could hardly think at all, and though both sides belong to religion, you are usually accustomed to give heed chiefly to only one at a time. Wherefore, we shall look closely at religion from both sides.

We commence with religion as a kind of activity. Activity is twofold, having to do with life and with art. You would ascribe with the poet earnestness to life and cheerfulness to art; or, in some other way, you would contrast them. Separate them you certainly will. For life, duty is the watchword. The moral law shall order it, and virtue shall show itself the ruling power in it, that the individual may be in harmony with the universal order of the world, and may nowhere encroach in a manner to disturb and confuse. This life, you consider, may appear without any discernible trace of art. Rather is it to be attained by rigid rules that have nothing to do with the free and variable precepts of art. Nay, you look upon it almost as a rule that art should be somewhat in the background, and non-essential for those who are strictest in the ordering of life. On the other hand, imagination shall inspire the artist, and genius shall completely sway him. Now imagination and genius are for you quite different from virtue and morality, being capable of existing in the largest measure along with a much more meagre moral endowment. Nay you are inclined, because the prudent power often comes into danger by reason of the fiery power, to relax for the artist somewhat of the strict demands of life.

How now does it stand with piety, in so far as you regard it as a peculiar kind of activity? Has it to do with right living? Is it something good and praiseworthy, yet different from morality, for you will not hold them to be identical? But in that case morality does not exhaust the sphere which it should govern. Another power works alongside of it, and has both right and might to continue working. Or will you perhaps betake yourselves to the position that piety is a virtue, and religion a duty or section of duties? Is religion incorporated into morality and subordinated to it, as a part to the whole? Is it, as some suppose, special duties towards God, and therefore a part of all morality which is the performance of all duties? But, if I have rightly appreciated or accurately reproduced what you say, you do not think so. You rather seem to say that the pious person has something entirely peculiar, both in his doing and leaving undone, and that morality can be quite moral without therefore being pious.

And how are religion and art related? They can hardly be quite alien, because, from of old, what is greatest in art has had a religious character.

When, therefore, you speak of an artist as pious, do you still grant him that relaxation of the strict demands of virtue? Rather he is then subjected, like every other person. But then to make the cases parallel, you must secure that those who devote themselves to life do not remain quite without art. Perhaps this combination gives its peculiar form to religion. With your view, there seems no other possible issue.

Religion then, as a kind of activity, is a mixture of elements that oppose and neutralize each other. Pray is not this rather the utterance of your dislike than your conviction? Such an accidental shaking together, leaving both elements unaltered, does not, even though the most accurate equality be atained, make something specific. But suppose it is otherwise, suppose piety is something which truly fuses both, then it cannot be formed simply by bringing the two together, but must be an original unity. Take care, however, I warn you, that you do not make such an admission. Were it the case, morality and genius apart would be only fragments of the ruins of religion, or its corpse when it is dead. Religion were then higher than both, the true divine life itself. But, in return for this warning, if you accept it, and discover no other solution, be so good as tell me how your opinion about religion is to be distinguished from nothing? Till then nothing remains for me but to assume that you have not yet, by examination, satisfied yourselves about this side of religion. Perhaps we shall have better fortune with the other side — what is known as the way of thinking, or faith.

You will, I believe, grant that your knowledge, however many-sided it may appear, falls, as a whole, into two contrasted sciences. How you shall subdivide and name belongs to the controversies of your schools, with which at present I am not concerned. Do not, therefore, be too critical about my terminology, even though it comes from various quarters. Let us call the one division physics or metaphysics, applying both names indifferently, or indicating sections of the same thing. Let the other be ethics or the doctrine of duties or practical philosophy. At least we are agreed about the distinction meant. The former describes the nature of things, or if that seems too much, how man conceives and must conceive of things and of the world as the sum of things. The latter science, on the contrary, teaches what man should be for the world, and what he should do in it. Now, in so far as religion is a way of thinking of something and a knowledge about something, has it not the same object as these sciences? What does faith know about except the relation of man to God and to the world — God's purpose in making him, and the world's power to help or hinder him? Again it distinguishes in its own fashion a good action from a bad. Is then religion identical with natural science and ethics? You would not agree, you would never grant that our faith is as surely founded, or stands on the same level of certainty as your scientific knowledge! Your accusation against it is just that it does not know how to distinguish between the demonstrable and the probable. Similarly, you do not forget to remark diligently that very marvellous injunctions both to do and leave undone have issued from religion. You may be quite right; only do not forget that it has been the same with that which you call science. In both spheres you believe you have made improvements and are better than your fathers.

What then, are we to say that religion is? As before, that it is a mixture — mingled theoretical and practical knowledge? But this is even less permissible, particularly if, as appears, each of these two branches of knowledge has its own characteristic mode of procedure. Such a mixture of elements that would either counteract or separate, could only be made most arbitrarily. The utmost gain to be looked for would be to furnish us with another method for putting known results into shape for beginners, and for stimulating them to a further study. But if that be so, why do you strive against religion? You might, so long as beginners are to be found, leave it in peace and security. If we presumed to subject you, you might smile at our folly, but, knowing for certain that you have left it far behind, and that it is only prepared for us by you wiser people, you would be wrong in losing a serious word on the matter. But it is not so, I think. Unless I am quite mistaken, you have long been labouring to provide the mass of the people with just such an epitome of your knowledge. The name is of no consequence, whether it be 'religion' or 'enlightenment' or aught else. But there is something different which must first be expelled, or, at least, excluded. This something it is that you call belief, and it is the object of your hostility, and not an article you would desire to extend.

Wherefore, my friends, belief must be something different from a mixture of opinions about God and the world, and of precepts for one life or for two. Piety cannot be an instinct craving for a mess of metaphysical and ethical crumbs. If it were, you would scarcely oppose it. It would not occur to you to speak of religion as different from your knowledge, however much it might be distant. The strife of the cultured and learned with the pious would simply be the strife of depth and thoroughness with superficiality; it would be the strife of the master with pupils who are to emancipate themselves in due time.

Were you, after all, to take this view, I should like to plague you with all sorts of Socratic questions, till I compelled many of you to give a direct answer to the question, whether it is at all possible to be wise and pious at the same time. I should also wish to submit whether in other well-known matters you do not acknowledge the principle that things similar are to be placed together and particulars to be subordinated to generals? Is it that you may joke with the world about a serious subject, that in religion only the principle is not applied? But let us suppose you are serious. How does it come, then, that in religious faith, what, in science, you separate into two spheres, is united and so indissolubly bound together that one cannot be thought of without the other? The pious man does not believe that the right course of action can be determined, except in so far as, at the same time, there is knowledge of the relations of man to God; and again right action, he holds, is necessary for right knowledge. Suppose the binding principle lies in the theoretic side. Why then is a practical philosophy set over against a theoretic, and not rather regarded as a section? Or suppose the principle is in the practical side, the same would apply to a theoretic philosophy. Or both may be united, only in a yet higher, an original knowledge. That this highest, long-lost unity of knowledge should be religion you cannot believe, for you have found it most, and have opposed it most, in those who are furthest from science. I will not hold you to any such conclusion, for I would not take up a position that I cannot maintain. This, however, you may well grant, that, concerning this side of religion, you must take time to consider what is its proper significance.

Let us be honest with one another. As we recently agreed, you have no liking for religion. But, in carrying on an honourable war which is not quite without strain, you would not wish to fight against such a shadow as that with which we have so far been battling. It must be something special that could fashion itself so peculiarly in the human heart, something thinkable, the real nature of which can so be presented as to be spoken of and argued about, and I consider it very wrong that out of things so disparate as modes of knowing and modes of acting, you patch together an untenable something, and call it religion, and then are so needlessly ceremonious with it. But you would deny that you have not gone to work with straightforwardness. Seeing I have rejected systems, commentaries and apologies, you would demand that I unfold all the original sources of religion from the beautiful fictions of the Greeks to the sacred scriptures of the Christians. Should I not find everywhere the nature of the Gods, and the will of the Gods? Is not that man everywhere accounted holy and blessed who knows the former, and does the latter?

But that is just what I have already said. Religion never appears quite pure. Its outward form is ever determined by something else. Our task first is to exhibit its true nature, and not to assume off-hand, as you seem to do, that the outward form and the true nature are the same. Does the material world present you with any element in its original purity as a spontaneous product of nature? Must you, therefore, as you have done in the intellectual world, take very gross things for simple? It is the one ceaseless aim of all analysis to present something really simple. So also it is in spiritual things. You can only obtain what is original by producing it, as it were, by a second, an artificial creation in yourselves, and even then it is but for the moment of its production. Pray come to an understanding on the point, for you shall be ceaselessly reminded of it.

But let us go on to the sources and original writings of religion. To attach them to your sciences of resistance and of action, of nature and of spirit is an unavoidable necessity, because they are the sources of your terminology. Furthermore the best preparation for awakening consciousness for your own higher subject is to study what has already been more or less scientifically thought. The deepest and highest in a work is not always either first or last. Did you but know how to read between the lines! All sacred writings are like these modest books which were formerly in use in our modest Fatherland. Under a paltry heading they treated weighty matters, and, offering but few explanations, aimed at the most profound inquiry. Similarly, the sacred writings include metaphysical and moral conceptions. Except where they are more directly poetic, this seems the beginning and the end. But of you it is expected that, seeing through the appearance, you will recognize the real intent. It is as when nature gives precious metals alloyed with baser substances, and our skill knows how to discover them and restore them to their refulgent splendour. The sacred writings were not for perfect believers alone, but rather for children in belief, for novices, for those who are standing at the entrance and would be invited in, and how could they go to work except as I am now doing with you? They had to accept what was granted. In it they had to find the means for stimulating the new sense they would awake, by giving a severe concentration and lofty temper to the mind. Can you not recognize, even in the way these moral and metaphysical conceptions are treated, in the creative, poetic impulse, though it necessarily works in a poor and thankless speech, an endeavour to break through from a lower region to a higher? As you can easily see, a communication of this sort could be nothing other than poetical or rhetorical. Akin to the rhetorical is the dialect, and what method has from of old been more brilliantly or more successfully employed in revealing the higher nature, not only of knowledge, but of the deeper feelings? But if the vehicle alone satisfies, this end will not be reached. Wherefore, as it has become so common to seek metaphysics and ethics chiefly, in the sacred writings, and to appraise them accordingly, it seems time to approach the matter from the other end, and to begin with the clear cut distinction between our faith and your ethics and metaphysics, between our piety and what you call morality. This is what I would attain by this digression. I wished to throw some light on the conception that is dominant among you. That being done, I now return.

In order to make quite clear to you what is the original and characteristic possession of religion, it resigns, at once, all claims on anything that belongs either to science or morality. Whether it has been borrowed or bestowed it is now returned. What then does your science of being, your natural science, all your theoretical philosophy, in so far as it has to do with the actual world, have for its aim? To know things, I suppose, as they really are; to show the peculiar relations by which each is what it is; to determine for each its place in the whole, and to distinguish it rightly from all else; to present the whole real world in its mutually conditioned necessity; and to exhibit the oneness of all phenomena with their eternal laws. This is truly beautiful and excellent, and I am not disposed to depreciate. Rather, if this description of mine, so slightly sketched, does not suffice, I will grant the highest and most exhaustive you are able to give.

And yet, however high you go; though you pass from the laws to the Universal Lawgiver, in whom is the unity of all things; though you allege that nature cannot be comprehended without God, I would still maintain that religion has nothing to do with this knowledge, and that, quite apart from it, its nature can be known. Quantity of knowledge is not quantity of piety. Piety can gloriously display itself, both with originality and individuality, in those to whom this kind of knowledge is not original. They may only know it as everybody does, as isolated results known in connection with other things. The pious man must, in a sense, be a wise man, but he will readily admit, even though you somewhat proudly look down upon him, that, in so far as he is pious, he does not hold his knowledge in the same way as you.

Let me interpret in clear words what most pious persons only guess at and never know how to express. Were you to set God as the apex of your science as the foundation of all knowing as well as of all knowledge, they would accord praise and honour, but it would not be their way of having and knowing God. From their way, as they would readily grant, and as is easy enough to see, knowledge and science do not proceed.

It is true that religion is essentially contemplative. You would never call anyone pious who went about in impervious stupidity, whose sense is not open for the life of the world. But this contemplation is not turned, as your knowledge of nature is, to the existence of a finite thing, combined with and opposed to another finite thing. It has not even, like your knowledge of God — if for once I might use an old expression — to do with the nature of the first cause, in itself and in its relation to every other cause and operation. The contemplation of the pious is the immediate consciousness of the universal existence of all finite things, in and through the infinite, and of all temporal things in and through the eternal. Religion is to seek this and find it in all that lives and moves, in all growth and change, in all doing and suffering. It is to have life and to know life in immediate feeling, only as such an existence in the infinite and eternal. Where this is found religion is satisfied, where it hides itself there is for her unrest and anguish, extremity and death. Wherefore it is a life in the infinite nature of the whole, in the one and in the all, in God, having and possessing all things in God, and God in all. Yet religion is not knowledge and science, either of the world or of God. Without being knowledge, it recognizes knowledge and science. In itself it is an affection, a revelation of the infinite in the finite, God being seen in it and it in God.

Similarly, what is the object of your ethics, of your science of action? Does it not seek to distinguish precisely each part of human doing and producing, and at the same time to combine them into a whole, according to actual relations? But the pious man confesses that, as pious, he knows nothing about it. He does, indeed, contemplate human action, but it is not the kind of contemplation from which an ethical system takes its rise. Only one thing he seeks out and detects, action from God, God's activity among men. If your ethics are right, and his piety as well, he will not, it is true, acknowledge any action as excellent which is not embraced in your system. But to know and to construct this system is your business, ye learned, not his. If you will not believe, regard the case of women. You ascribe to them religion, not only as an adornment, but you demand of them the finest feeling for distinguishing the things that excel: do you equally expect them to know your ethics as a science?

It is the same, let me say at once, with action itself. The artist fashions what is given him to fashion, by virtue of his special talent. These talents are so different that the one he possesses another lacks; unless someone, against heaven's will, would possess all. But when anyone is praised to you as pious, you are not accustomed to ask which of these gifts dwell in him by virtue of his piety. The citizen — taking the word in the sense of the ancients, not in its present meagre significance — regulates, leads, and influences in virtue of his morality. But this is something different from piety. Piety has also a passive side. While morality always shows itself as manipulating, as self-controlling, piety appears as a surrender, a submission to be moved by the whole that stands over against man. Morality depends, therefore, entirely on the consciousness of freedom, within the sphere of which all that it produces falls. Piety, on the contrary, is not at all bound to this side of life. In the opposite sphere of necessity, where there is no properly individual action, it is quite as active. Wherefore the two are different. Piety does, indeed, linger with satisfaction on every action that is from God, and every activity that reveals the infinite in the finite, and yet it is not itself this activity. Only by keeping quite outside the range both of science and of practice can it maintain its proper sphere and character. Only when piety takes its place alongside of science and practice, as a necessary, an indispensable third, as their natural counterpart, not less in worth and splendour than either, will the common field be altogether occupied and human nature on this side complete.

But pray understand me fairly. I do not mean that one could exist without the other, that, for example, a man might have religion and be pious, and at the same time be immoral. That is impossible. But, in my opinion, it is just as impossible to be moral or scientific without being religious. But have I not said that religion can be had without science? Wherefore, I have myself begun the separation. But remember, I only said piety is not the measure of science. Just as one cannot be truly scientific without being pious, the pious man may not know at all, but he cannot know falsely. His proper nature is not of that subordinate kind, which, according to the old adage that like is only known to like, knows nothing except semblance of reality.

His nature is reality which knows reality, and where it encounters nothing it does not suppose it sees something. And what a precious jewel of science, in my view, is ignorance for those who are captive to semblance. If you have not learned it from my Speeches or discovered it for yourselves, go and learn it from your Socrates. Grant me consistency at least. With ignorance your knowledge will ever be mixed, but the true and proper opposite of knowledge is presumption of knowledge. By piety this presumption is most certainly removed, for with it piety cannot exist.

Such a separation of knowledge and piety, and of action and piety, do not accuse me of making. You are only ascribing to me, without my deserving it, your own view and the very confusion, as common as it is unavoidable, which it has been my chief endeavour to show you in the mirror of my Speech. Just because you do not acknowledge religion as the third, knowledge and action are so much apart that you can discover no unity, but believe that right knowing can be had without right acting, and *vice versa*. I hold that is it only in contemplation that there is division. There, where it is necessary, you despise it, and instead transfer it to life, as if in life itself objects could be found independent one of the other. Consequently you have no living insight into any of these activities. Each is for you a part, a fragment. Because you do not deal with life in a living way, your conception bears the stamp of perishableness, and is altogether meagre. True science is complete vision; true practice is culture and art self-produced; true religion is sense and taste for the infinite. To wish to have true science or true practice without religion, or to imagine it is possessed, is obstinate, arrogant delusion, and culpable error. It issues from the unholy sense that would rather have a show of possession by cowardly purloining than have secure possession by demanding and waiting. What can man accomplish that is worth speaking of, either in life or in art, that does not arise in his own self from the influence of this sense for the infinite? Without it, how can anyone wish to comprehend the world scientifically, or if, in some distinct talent, the knowledge is thrust upon him, how should he wish to exercise it? What is all science, if not the existence of things in you, in your reason? What is all art and culture if not your existence in the things to which you give measure, form and order? And how can both come to life in you except in so far as there lives immediately in you the eternal unity of reason and nature, the universal existence of all finite things in the infinite?

Wherefore, you will find every truly learned man devout and pious. Where you see science without religion, be sure it is transferred, learned up from another. It is sickly, if indeed it is not that empty appearance which serves necessity and is no knowledge at all. And what else do you take this deduction and weaving together of ideas to be, which neither live nor correspond to any living thing? Or in ethics, what else is this wretched uniformity that thinks it can grasp the highest human life in a single dead formula? The former arises because there is no fundamental feeling of that living nature which everywhere presents variety and individuality, and the latter because the sense fails to give infinity to the finite by determining its nature and boundaries only from the infinite. Hence the dominion of the mere notion; hence the mechanical erections of your systems instead of an organic structure; hence the vain juggling with analytical formulae, in which, whether categorical or hypothetical, life will not be fettered. Science is not your calling, if you despise religion and fear to surrender yourself to reverence and aspiration for the primordial. Either science must become as low as your life, or it must be separated and stand alone, a division that precludes success. If man is not one with the eternal in the unity of intuition and feeling which is immediate, he remains, in the unity of consciousness which is derived, for ever apart.

What, then, shall become of the highest utterance of the speculation of our days, complete rounded idealism, if it do not again sink itself in this unity, if the humility of religion do not suggest to its pride another realism than that which it so boldly and with such perfect right, subordinates to itself? It annihilates the universe, while it seems to aim at constructing it. It would degrade it to a mere allegory, to a mere phantom of the one-sided limitation of its own empty consciousness. Offer with me reverently a tribute to the manes of the holy, rejected Spinoza. The high world-spirit pervaded him; the infinite was his beginning and his end; the universe was his only and his everlasting love. In holy innocence and in deep humility he beheld himself mirrored in the eternal world, and perceived how he also was its most worthy mirror. He was full of religion, full of the Holy Spirit. Wherefore, he stands there alone and unequalled; master in his art, yet without disciples and without citizenship, sublime above the profane tribe.

Why should I need to show that the same applies to art? Because, from the same causes, you have here also a thousand phantoms, delusions, and mistakes. In place of all else I would point to another example which should be as well known to you all. I would point in silence — for pain that is new and deep has no words. It is that superb youth, who has too early fallen asleep, with whom everything his spirit touched became art. His whole contemplation of the world was forthwith a great poem. Though he had scarce more than struck the first chords, you must associate him with the most opulent poets, with those select spirits who are as profound as they are clear and vivacious. See in him the power of the enthusiasm and the caution of a pious spirit, and acknowledge that when the philosophers shall become religious and seek God like Spinoza, and the artists be pious and love Christ like Novalis, the great resurrection shall be celebrated for both worlds.

But, in order that you may understand what I mean by this unity and difference of religion, science and art, we shall endeavour to descend into the inmost sanctuary of life. There, perhaps, we may find ourselves agreed. There alone you discover the original relation of intuition and feeling from which alone this identity and difference is to be understood. But I must direct you to your own selves. You must apprehend a living movement. You must know how to listen to yourselves before your own consciousness. At least you must be able to reconstruct from your consciousness your own state. What you are to notice is the rise of your consciousness and not to reflect upon something already there. Your thought can only embrace what is sundered. Wherefore as soon as you have made any given definite activity of your soul an object of communication or of contemplation, you have already begun to separate. It is impossible, therefore, to adduce any definite example, for, as soon as anything is an example, what I wish to indicate is already past. Only the faintest trace of the original unity could then be shown. Such as it is, however, I will not despise it, as a preliminary.

Consider how you delineate an object. Is there not both a stimulation and a determination by the object, at one and the same time, which for one particular moment forms your existence? The more definite your image, the more, in this way, you become the object, and the more you lose yourselves. But just because you can trace the growing preponderance of one side over the other, both must have been one and equal in the first, the original moment that has escaped you. Or sunk in yourselves, you find all that you formerly regarded as a disconnected manifold compacted now indivisibly into the one peculiar content of your being. Yet when you give heed, can you not see as it disappears, the image of an object, from whose influence, from whose magical contact this definite consciousness has proceeded? The more your own state sways you the paler and more unrecognizable your image becomes. The greater your emotion, the more you are absorbed in it, the more your whole nature is concerned to retain for the memory an imperishable trace of what is necessarily fleeting, to carry over to what you may engage in, its colour and impress, and so unite two moments into a duration, the less you observe the object that caused it. But just because it grows pale and vanishes, it must before have been nearer and clearer. Originally it must have been one and the same with your feeling. But, as was said, these are mere traces. Unless you will go back on the first beginning of this consciousness, you can scarcely understand them.

And suppose you cannot? Then say, weighing it quite generally and originally, what is every act of your life in itself and without distinction from other acts. What is it merely as act, as movement? Is it not the coming into being of something for itself, and at the same time in the whole? It is an endeavour to return into the whole, and to exist for oneself at the same time. These are the links from which the whole chain is made. Your whole life is such an existence for self in the whole. How now are you in the whole? By your senses. And how are you for yourselves? By the unity of your self-consciousness, which is given chiefly in the possibility of comparing the varying degrees of sensation. How both can only rise together, if both together fashion every act of life, is easy to see. You become sense and the whole becomes object. Sense and object mingle and unite, then each returns to its place, and the object rent from sense is a perception, and you rent from the object are for yourselves, a feeling. It is this earlier moment I mean, which you always experience yet never experience. The phenomenon of your life is just the result of its constant departure and return. It is scarcely in time at all, so swiftly it passes; it can scarcely be described, so little does it properly exist. Would that I could hold it fast and refer to it your commonest as well as your highest activities.

Did I venture to compare it, seeing I cannot describe it, I would say it is fleeting and transparent as the vapour which the dew breathes on blossom and fruit, it is bashful and tender as a maiden's kiss, it is holy and fruitful as a bridal embrace. Nor is it merely like, it is all this. It is the first contact of the universal life with an individual. It fills no time and fashions nothing palpable. It is the holy wedlock of the universe with the incarnated reason for a creative, productive embrace. It is immediate, raised above all error and misunderstanding. You lie directly on the bosom of the infinite world. In that moment, you are its soul. Through one part of your nature you feel, as your own, all its powers and its endless life. In that moment it is your body, you pervade, as your own, its muscles and members and your thinking and forecasting set its inmost nerves in motion. In this way every living, original movement in your life is first received. Among the rest it is the source of every religious emotion. But it is not, as I said, even a moment. The incoming of existence to us, by this immediate union, at once stops as soon as it reaches consciousness. Either the intuition displays itself more vividly and clearly, like the figure of the vanishing mistress to the eyes of her lover; or feeling issues from your heart and overspreads your whole being, as the blush of shame and love over the face of the maiden. At length your consciousness is finally determined as one or other, as intuition or feeling. Then, even though you have not quite surrendered to this division and lost consciousness of your life as a unity, there remains nothing but the knowledge that they were originally one, that they issued simultaneously from the fundamental relation of your nature. Wherefore, it is in this sense true what an ancient sage has taught you, that all knowledge is recollection. It is recollection of what is outside of all time, and is therefore justly to be placed at the head of all temporal things.

And, as it is with intuition and feeling on the one hand, so it is with knowledge which includes both and with activity on the other. Through the constant play and mutual influence of these opposites, your life expands and has its place in time. Both knowledge and activity are a desire to be identified with the universe through an object. If the power of the objects preponderates, if, as intuition or feeling, it enters and seeks to draw you into the circle of their existence, it is always a knowledge. If the preponderating power is on your side, so that you give the impress and reflect yourselves in the objects, it is activity in the narrower sense, external working. Yet it is only as you are stimulated and determined that you can communicate yourselves to things. In founding or establishing anything in the world you are only giving back what that original act of fellowship has wrought in you, and similarly everything the world fashions in you must be by the same act. One must mutually stimulate the other. Only in an interchange of knowing and activity can your life consist. A peaceful existence, wherein one side did not stimulate the other, would not be your life. It would be that from which it first developed, and into which it will again disappear.

There then you have the three things about which my Speech has so far turned — perception, feeling and activity, and you now understand what I mean when I say they are not identical and yet are inseparable. Take what belongs to each class and consider it by itself. You will find that those moments in which you exercise power over things and impress yourselves upon them, form what you call your practical, or, in the narrower sense, your moral life; again the contemplative moments, be they few or many, in which things produce themselves in you as intuition, you will doubtless call your scientific life. Now can either series alone form a human life? Would it not be death? If each activity were not stimulated and renewed by the other, would it not be self-consumed? Yet they are not identical. If you would understand your life and speak comprehensibly of it, they must be distinguished. As it stands with these two in respect of one another, it must stand with the third in respect of both. How then are you to name this third, which is the series of feeling? What life will it form? The religious as I think, and as you will not be able to deny, when you have considered it more closely. . . .

Not by examples which are rare, but by passing through these and similar feelings you discover in yourselves the outlines of the fairest and the basest, the noblest and the most despicable. You not only find at times all the manifold degrees of human powers within you, but when self-love is quite submerged in sympathy, all the countless mixture of human tendencies that you have ever seen in the characters of others appears simply arrested impulses of your own life. There are moments when, despite all distinction of sex, culture, or environment, you think, feel, and act as if you were really this or that person. In your own order, you have actually passed through all those different forms. You are a compendium of humanity. In a certain sense your single nature embraces all human nature. Your ego, being multiplied and more clearly outlined, is in all its smallest and swiftest changes immortalized in the manifestations of human nature. As soon as this is seen, you can love yourselves with a pure and blameless love. Humility, that never forsakes you, has its counterpart in the feeling that the whole of humanity lives and works in you. Even contrition is sweetened to joyful self-sufficiency. This is the completion of religion on this side. It works its way back to the heart, and there finds the infinite. The man in whom this is accomplished, is no more in need of a mediator for any sort of intuition of humanity. Rather he is himself a mediator for many.

But there is not merely the swinging of feeling between the world and the individual, in the present moment. Except as something going on, we cannot comprehend what affects us, and we cannot comprehend ourselves, except as thus progressively affected. Wherefore, as feeling persons, we are ever driven back into the past. The spirit furnishes the chief nourishment for our piety, and history immediately and especially is for religion the richest source. History is not of value for religion, because it hastens or controls in any way the progress of humanity in its development, but because it is the greatest and most general revelation of the deepest and holiest. In this sense, however, religion begins and ends with history. Prophecy and history are for religion the same and indistinguishable, and all true history has at first had a religious purpose, and has taken its departure from religious ideas.

What is finest and tenderest in history, moreover, cannot be communicated scientifically, but can only be comprehended in the feeling of a religious disposition. The religious mind recognizes the transmigration of spirits and souls, which to others is but graceful fiction, as, in more than one sense, a wonderful arrangement of the universe for comparing the different periods of humanity according to a sure standard. After a long period, during which nature could produce nothing similar, some distinguished individual almost entirely the same returns. But only the seers recognize him, and it is they who should judge by his works the signs of different times. A movement of humanity returns exactly like something of which some distant foretime has left you an image, and you are to recognize from the various causes which have now produced it, the course of development and the formula of its law. The genius of some human endowment awakes as from slumber. Here and there rising and falling, it has already finished its course. Now it appears in a new life in another place and under different circumstances. Its quicker increase, its deeper working, its fairer stronger form, indicate how much the climate of humanity has improved, and how much fitter the soil has grown to nourish nobler plants. Peoples and generations of mortals appear as all alike necessary for the completeness of history, though, like individuals, of different worth. Some are estimable and spirited, and work strongly without ceasing, permeating space and defying time. Others are common and insignificant, fitted only to show some peculiar shade of some single form of life. For one moment only they are really living and noticeable. One thought they exhibit, one conception they produce, and then they hasten towards destruction that the power that produced them may be given to something else. As vegetable nature, from the destruction of whole species, and from the ruins of whole generations of plants, produces and nourishes a new race, so spiritual nature rears from the ruins of a glorious and beautiful world of men, a new world that draws its first vital strength from elements decomposed and wondrously transformed. Being deeply impressed with this sense of a universal connection, your glance perhaps passes so often directly from least to greatest and greatest to least, going backwards and forwards, till through dizziness it can neither distinguish great nor small, cause nor effect, preservation nor destruction. This state continues, and then that well-known figure of an eternal fate appears. Its features bear the impress of this state, being a marvellous mixture of obstinate self-will and deep wisdom, of rude unfeeling force and heartfelt love, of which first one seizes you and then another, now inviting you to impotent defiance and now to childlike submission.

Penetrate further and compare this partial striving of the individual, the fruit of opposing views, with the quiet uniform course of the whole. You will see how the high world-spirit smilingly marches past all that furiously opposes him. You will see how dread Nemesis, never wearied, follows his steps, meting out punishment to the haughty who resist the gods. Even the stoutest and choicest who have with steadfastness, worthy perhaps of praise and wonder, refused to bow before the gentle breath of the great Spirit, it mows down with iron hand. Would you comprehend the proper character of all changes and of all human progress, a feeling resting on history must show you more surely than aught else, that living gods rule who hate nothing so much as death, and that nothing is to be persecuted and destroyed like this first and last foe of the spirit. The rude, the barbarian, the formless are to be absorbed and recast. Nothing is to be a dead mass that moves only by impact and resists only by unconscious collision; all is to be individual, connected, complex, exalted life. Blind instinct, unthinking custom, dull obedience, everything lazy and passive, all those sad symptoms of the death slumber of freedom and humanity are to be abolished. To this the work of the minutes and the centuries is directed, it is the great ever advancing work of redemptive love.

Some prominent emotions of religion connected with nature and humanity, I have now sketched in vague outline. I have brought you to the limits of your horizon. Here is the end and summit of religion for all to whom humanity is the whole world. But consider that in your feeling there is something that despises these bounds, something in virtue of which you cannot stay where you are. Beyond this point only infinity is to be looked into. I will not speak of the presentiments which define themselves and become thoughts which might by subtilty be established, that humanity, being capable of motion and cultivation, being not only differently manifested in the individual, but here and there really being different, cannot possibly be the highest, the sole manifestation of the unity of spirit and matter. As the individual is only one form of humanity, so humanity may be only one form of this unity. Beside it many other similar forms may exist, bounding it and standing over against it. But in our own feeling we all find something similar. The dependence of our earth, and therefore of the highest unity it has produced, upon other worlds, has been impressed upon us both by nature and by education. Hence this ever active but seldom understood presentiment of some other marriage of spirit and matter, visible and finite, but above humanity, higher and closer and productive of more beautiful forms. But any sketch that could be drawn would be too definite. Any echo of the feeling could only be fleeting and vague. Hence it is exposed to misconception and is so often taken for folly and superstition.

This is sufficient reference to a thing so immeasurably far from you. More would be incomprehensible. Had you only the religion that you could have! Were you but conscious of what you already have! Were you to consider the few religious opinions and feelings that I have so slightly sketched, you would be very far from finding them all strange to you. Something of the same kind you must have had in your thoughts before. But I do not know whether to lack religion quite, or not to understand it, is the greater misfortune. In the latter case also it fails of its purpose, and you impose upon yourselves in addition.

Two things I would specially blame in you. Some things you select and stamp as exclusively religious, other things you withdraw from religion as exclusively moral. Both you apparently do on the same ground. Religion with you is the retribution which alights on all who resist the spirit of the whole, it is the hatred everywhere active against haughtiness and audacity, the steady advance of all human things to one goal. You are conscious of the feeling that points to this unfailing progress. After it has been purified from all abuses, you would willingly see it sustained and extended. But you will then have it that this is exclusively religion, and you would exclude other feelings that take their rise from the same operation of the mind in exactly the same way.

How have you come to this torn off fragment? I will tell you. You do not regard it as religion but as an echo of moral action, and you simply wish to foist the name upon it, in order to give religion the last blow. What we have agreed to acknowledge as religion does not arise exclusively in the moral sphere, not at least in the narrow sense in which you understand the word. Feeling knows nothing of such a limited predilection. If I direct you specially to the sphere of the spirit and to history, it does not follow that the moral world is religion's universe. In your narrow sense of it the moral world would produce very few religious emotions. The pious man can detect the operation of the world-spirit in all that belongs to human activity, in play and earnest, in smallest things and in greatest. Everywhere he perceives enough to move him by the presence of this spirit and without this influence nothing is his own. Therein he finds a divine Nemesis that those who, being predominantly ethical or rather legal, would, by selecting from religion only the elements suited to this purpose, make of it an insignificant appendage to morals, do yet, purify religion as they may, irrecoverably corrupt their moral doctrine itself and sow in it the seed of new errors. When anyone succumbs in moral action, it sounds well to say it is the will of the eternal, and that what does not succeed through us, will sometime, by others, come to pass. But if this high assurance belonged to moral action, moral action would be dependent on the degree of receptivity for this assurance in each person at any moment. Morality cannot include immediately aught of feeling without at once having its original power and purity disturbed.

With all those feelings, love, humility, joy, and the others that I pictured as the undulation of the mind between the two points of which the world is one, and your ego the other, you deal in another way. The ancients knew what was right. They called them all piety. For them those feelings were an essential part of religion, the noblest part. You also recognize them, but you try to persuade yourselves that they are an essential section of your moral action. You would justify these sentiments on moral principles, and assign them their place in your moral system. But in vain, for, if you remain true to yourselves, they will there neither be desired nor endured. If action proceed directly from the emotions of love or affection, it will be insecure and thoughtless. Moral action should not proceed from such a momentary influence of an outward object. Wherefore your doctrine of morals, when it is strict and pure, acknowledges no reverence except for its own law. Everything done from pity or gratitude it condemns as impure, almost as selfish. It makes light of, almost despises, humility. If you talk of contrition it speaks of lost time being needlessly increased. Your own feeling must assure you that the immediate object of all these sentiments is not action. They are spontaneous functions of your deepest and highest life, coming by themselves and ending by themselves. Why do you make such an ado, and beg for grace for them, where they have no right to be? Be content to consider them religion, and then you will not need to demand anything for them except their own sure rights, and you will not deceive yourselves with the baseless claims which you are disposed to make in their name. Return them to religion: the treasure belongs to it alone. As the possessor of it, religion is for morality and all else that is an object of human doing, not the handmaid, but an indispensable friend and sufficient advocate with humanity. This is the rank of religion, as the sum of all higher feelings.

That it alone removes man from one-sidedness and narrowness I have already indicated. Now I am in a position to be more definite. In all activity and working, be it moral or artistic, man must strive for mastery. But when man becomes quite absorbed, all mastery limits and chills, and makes one-sided and hard. The mind is directed chiefly to one point, and this one point cannot satisfy it. Can man, by advancing from one narrow work to another, really use his whole power? Will not the larger part be unused, and turn, in consequence, against himself and devour him? How many of you go to ruin because you are too great for yourselves? A superfluity of power and impulse that never issues in any work, because there is no work adequate, drives you aimlessly about, and is your destruction. To resist this evil would you have those who are too great for one object of human endeavour, unite them all — art, science, life, and any others you may know of? This would simply be your old desire to have humanity complete everywhere, your ever recurring love of uniformity. But is it possible? Those objects, as soon as they are attended to separately, all alike strive to rouse and dominate the mind. Each tendency is directed to a work that should be completed, it has an ideal to be copied, a totality to be embraced. This rivalry of several objects of endeavour can only end by one expelling the others. Nay, even within this one sphere, the more eminent a mastery a man would attain, the more he must restrict himself. But if this pre-eminence entirely occupy him, and if he lives only to attain it, how shall he duly participate in the world, and how shall his life become a whole? Hence most virtuosos are one-sided and defective, or at least, outside of their own sphere, they sink into an inferior kind of life.

The only remedy is for each man, while he is definitely active in some one department, to allow himself, without definite activity, to be affected by the infinite. In every species of religious feeling he will then become conscious of all that lies beyond the department which he directly cultivates. The infinite is near to everyone, for whatever be the object you have chosen for your deliberate technical working, it does not demand much thought to advance from it to find the universe. In it you discover the rest as precept, or inspiration or revelation. The only way of acquiring what lies outside the direction of the mind we have selected, is to enjoy and comprehend it thus as a whole, not by will as art, but by instinct for the universe as religion.   *On Religion, Speeches . . .*, pp. 27-45, 79-86

*

FOURTH SPEECH

ASSOCIATION IN RELIGION

How many of the perverse efforts and the sad destinies of mankind you ascribe to religion, I do not need to recount. In a thousand utterances of the most esteemed among you it is clear as day. And I will not pause to refute those charges in detail and derive them from other causes. Rather let us subject the whole idea of the church to a new consideration, reconstructing it from the centre outwards, unconcerned about how much is fact and experience.

If there is religion at all, it must be social, for that is the nature of man, and it is quite peculiarly the nature of religion. You must confess that when an individual has produced and wrought out something in his own mind, it is morbid and in the highest degree unnatural to wish to reserve it to himself. He should express it in the indispensable fellowship and mutual dependence of action. And there is also a spiritual nature which he has in common with the rest of his species which demands that he express and communicate all that is in him. The more violently he is moved and the more deeply he is impressed, the stronger that social impulse works. And this is true even if we regard it only as the endeavour to find the feeling in others, and so to be sure that nothing has been encountered that is not human.

You see that this is not the case of endeavouring to make others like ourselves, nor of believing that what is in one man is indispensable for all. It is only the endeavour to become conscious of and to exhibit the true relation of our own life to the common nature of man.

But indisputably the proper subjects for this impulse to communicate are the conscious states and feelings in which originally man feels himself passive. He is urged on to learn whether it may not be an alien and unworthy power that has produced them. Those are the things which mankind from childhood are chiefly engaged in communicating. His ideas, about the origin of which he can have no doubts, he would rather leave in quiet. Still more easily he resolves to reserve his judgments. But of all that enters by the senses and stirs the feelings he will have witnesses and participators. How could he keep to himself the most comprehensive and general influences of the world when they appear to him the greatest and most irresistible? How should he wish to reserve what most strongly drives him out of himself and makes him conscious that he cannot know himself from himself alone? If a religious view become clear to him, or a pious feeling stir his soul, it is rather his first endeavour to direct others to the same subject and if possible transmit the impulse.

The same nature that makes it necessary for the pious person to speak, provides him also with an audience. No element of life, so much as religion, has implanted along with it so vivid a feeling of man's utter incapacity ever to exhaust it for himself alone. No sooner has he any sense for it than he feels its infinity and his own limits. He is conscious that he grasps but a small part of it, and what he cannot himself reach he will, at least, so far as he is able, know and enjoy from the representations of those who have obtained it. This urges him to give his religion full expression, and, seeking his own perfection, to listen to every note that he can recognize as religious. Thus mutual communication organizes itself, and speech and hearing are to all alike indispensable.

But the communication of religion is not like the communication of ideas and perceptions to be sought in books. In this medium, too much of the pure impression of the original production is lost. Like dark stuffs that absorb the greater part of the rays of light, so everything of the pious emotion that the inadequate signs do not embrace and give out again, is swallowed up. In the written communication of piety, everything needs to be twice or thrice repeated, the original medium requiring to be again exhibited, and still its effect on men in general in their great unity can only be badly copied by multiplied reflection. Only when it is chased from the society of the living, religion must hide its varied life in the dead letter.

Nor can this intercourse with the heart of man be carried on in common conversation. Many who have a regard for religion have upbraided our times, because our manners are such that in conversation in society and in friendly intercourse, we talk of all weighty subjects except of God and divine things. In our defence I would say, this is neither contempt nor indifference, but a very correct instinct. Where mirth and laughing dwell, and even earnestness must pliantly associate with joke and witticism, there can be no room for what must ever be attended by holy reserve and awe. Religious views, pious feelings, and earnest reflections, are not to be tossed from one to another in such small morsels as the materials of a light conversation. On sacred subjects it would be rather sacrilegious than fitting to be ready with an answer to every question and a response to every address. Religion, therefore, withdraws itself from too wide circles to the more familiar conversation of friendship or the dialogue of love, where glance and action are clearer than words, and where a solemn silence also is understood.

By way of the light and rapid exchange of retorts common in society divine things cannot be treated, but there must be a higher style and another kind of society entirely consecrated to religion. On the highest subject with which language has to deal, it is fitting that the fulness and splendour of human speech be expended. It is not as if there were any ornament that religion could not do without, but it would be impious and frivolous of its heralds, if they would not consecrate everything to it, if they would not collect all they possess that is glorious, that religion may, if possible, be presented in all power and dignity. Without poetic skill, therefore, religion can only be expressed and communicated rhetorically, in all power and skill of speech, and in its swiftness and inconstancy the service of every art that could aid, is willingly accepted. Hence a person whose heart is full of religion, only opens his mouth before an assembly where speech so richly equipped might have manifold working.

Would that I could depict to you the rich, the superabundant life in this city of God, when the citizens assemble, each full of native force seeking liberty of utterance and full at the same time of holy desire to apprehend and appropriate what others offer. When one stands out before the others he is neither justified by office nor by compact; nor is it pride or ignorance that inspires him with assurance. It is the free impulse of his spirit, the feeling of heart-felt unanimity and completest equality, the common abolition of all first and last, of all earthly order. He comes forward to present to the sympathetic contemplation of others his own heart as stirred by God, and, by leading them into the region of religion where he is at home, he would infect them with his own feeling. He utters divine things and in solemn silence the congregation follow his inspired speech. If he unveils a hidden wonder, or links with prophetic assurance the future to the present, or by new examples confirms old truths, or if his fiery imagination enchants him in visions into another part of the world and into another order of things, the trained sense of the congregation accompanies him throughout. On returning from his wanderings through the Kingdom of God into himself, his heart and the hearts of all are but the common seat of the same feeling. Let this harmony of view announce itself, however softly, then there are sacred mysteries discovered and solemnized that are not mere insignificant emblems, but, rightly considered, are natural indications of a certain kind of consciousness and certain feelings. It is like a loftier choir that in its own noble tone answers the voice that calls.

And this is not a mere simile, but, as such a speech is music without song or melody, there may be a music among the saints that is speech without words, giving most definite and comprehensible expression to the heart.

The muse of harmony, the intimate relation of which to religion has been long known, though acknowledged by few, has from of old laid on the altars of religion the most gorgeous and perfect works of her most devoted scholars. In sacred hymns and choruses to which the words of the poet are but loosely and airily appended, there are breathed out things that definite speech cannot grasp. The melodies of thought and feeling interchange and give mutual support, till all is satiated and full of the sacred and the infinite.

Of such a nature is the influence of religious men upon each other. Thus their natural and eternal union is produced. It is a heavenly bond, the most perfect production of the spiritual nature of man, not to be attained till man, in the highest sense, knows himself. Do not blame them if they value it more highly than the civil union which you place so far above all else, but which nevertheless will not ripen to manly beauty. Compared with that other union, it appears far more forced than free, far more transient than eternal. *On Religion, Speeches . . .*, pp. 148-152

*

Schleiermacher's crowning theological achievement was The Christian Faith, *published 1821-1822, intended both as the presentation of his lectures in systematic theology over the years, and as a new dogmatics for the Prussian Protestant Church, which under the policies of King Friedrich Wilhelm III had seen a measure of union achieved between the Lutheran and Reformed traditions. No less than in the early* Speeches, *however, the basis of all Schleiermacher's theology lies in the religious consciousness, and this is expounded early on in* The Christian Faith, *not polemically as in the* Speeches, *but relatively simply and concisely. Indeed, the 'pious emotions' are now defined precisely as 'the feeling of absolute dependence' — perhaps better expressed as 'the feeling of being utterly dependent'. Again, Schleiermacher sets the religious feeling firmly within the self's total experience of living in the finite, historical and natural world; and again, religion is ineluctably communal.*

> *The common element in all howsoever diverse expressions of piety, by which these are conjointly distinguished from all other feelings, or, in other words, the self-identical essence of piety, is this: the consciousness of being absolutely dependent, or, which is the same thing, of being in relation with God.*

1. In any actual state of consciousness, no matter whether it merely accompanies a thought or action or occupies a moment for itself, we are never simply conscious of our selves in their unchanging identity, but are always at the same time conscious of a changing determination of them. The ego in itself can be represented objectively; but every consciousness of self is at the same time the consciousness of a variable state of being. But in this distinction of the latter from the former, it is implied that the variable does not proceed purely from the self-identical, for in that case it could not be distinguished from it. Thus in every self-consciousness there are two elements which we might call respectively a self-caused element (*ein Sichselbstsetzen*) and a non-self-caused element (*ein Sichselbstnichtsogesetzthaben*); or a being and a having-by-some-means-come-to-be (*ein Sein und ein Irgendwiegewordensein*). The latter of these presupposes for

99

every self-consciousness another factor besides the ego, a factor which is the source of the particular determination, and without which the self-consciousness would not be precisely what it is. But this other is not objectively presented in the immediate self-consciousness with which alone we are here concerned. For though, of course, the double constitution of self-consciousness causes us always to look objectively for an other to which we can trace the origin of our particular state, yet this search is a separate act with which we are not at present concerned. In self-consciousness there are only two elements: the one expresses the existence of the subject for itself, the other its co-existence with an other.

Now to these two elements, as they exist together in the temporal self-consciousness, correspond in the subject its *receptivity* and its (spontaneous) *activity*. If we could think away the co-existence with an other, but otherwise think ourselves as we are, then a self-consciousness which predominantly expressed an affective condition of receptivity would be impossible, and any self-consciousness could then express only activity — an activity, however, which, not being directed to any object, would be merely an urge outwards, an indefinite 'agility' without form or colour. But as we never do exist except along with an other, so even in every outward-tending self-consciousness the element of receptivity, in some way or other affected, is the primary one; and even the self-consciousness which accompanies an action (acts of knowing included), while it predominantly expresses spontaneous movement and activity, is always related (though the relation is often a quite indefinite one) to a prior moment of affective receptivity, through which the original 'agility' received its direction. To these propositions assent can be unconditionally demanded; and no one will deny them who is capable of a little introspection and can find interest in the real subject of our present inquiries.

2. The common element in all those determinations of self-consciousness which predominantly express a receptivity affected from some outside quarter is the *feeling of dependence*. On the other hand, the common element in all those determinations which predominantly express spontaneous movement and activity is the *feeling of freedom*. The former is the case not only because it is by an influence from some other quarter that we have come to such a state, but particularly because we *could* not so become except by means of an other. The latter is the case because in these instances an other is determined by us, and without our spontaneous activity could not be so determined. These two definitions may, indeed, seem to be still incomplete, inasmuch as there is also a mobility of

the subject which is not connected with an other at all, but which seems to be subject to the same antithesis as that just explained. But when we become such-and-such from within outwards, for ourselves, without any other being involved, that is the simple situation of the temporal development of a being which remains essentially self-identical, and it is only very improperly that this can be referred to the concept 'freedom'. And when we cannot ourselves, from within outwards, become such-and-such, this only indicates the limits which belong to the nature of the subject itself as regards spontaneous activity, and this could only very improperly be called 'dependence'.

Further, this antithesis must on no account be confused with the antithesis between gloomy or depressing and elevating or joyful feelings, of which we shall speak later. For a feeling of dependence may be elevating, if the 'having-become-such-and-such' which it expresses is complete; and similarly a feeling of freedom may be dejecting, if the moment of predominating receptivity to which the action can be traced was of a dejecting nature, or again if the manner and method of the activity prove to be a disadvantageous combination.

Let us now think of the feeling of dependence and the feeling of freedom as *one*, in the sense that not only the subject but the corresponding other is the same for both. Then the total self-consciousness made up of both together is one of *reciprocity* between the subject and the corresponding other. Now let us suppose the totality of all moments of feeling, of both kinds, as one whole: then the corresponding other is also to be supposed as a totality or as one, and then that term 'reciprocity' is the right one for our self-consciousness in general, inasmuch as it expresses our connection with everything which either appeals to our receptivity or is subjected to our activity. And this is true not only when we particularize this other and ascribe to each of its elements a different degree of relation to the twofold consciousness within us, but also when we think of the total 'outside' as one, and moreover (since it contains other receptivities and activities to which we have a relation) as one together with ourselves, that is, as a *world*. Accordingly our self-consciousness, as a consciousness of our existence in the world or of our co-existence with the world, is a series in which the feeling of freedom and the feeling of dependence are divided. But neither an absolute feeling of dependence, *i.e.* without any feeling of freedom in relation to the co-determinant, nor an absolute feeling of freedom, *i.e.* without any feeling of dependence in relation to the co-determinant, is to be found in this whole realm. If we consider our relations to nature, or those which exist in human society, there we shall find a large number of objects in regard to which freedom and dependence maintain very much of an equipoise: these constitute the field of equal reciprocity. There are other objects which exercise a far greater influence upon our receptivity than our activity exercises upon them, and also *vice versa*, so that one of the two may diminish until it is imperceptible. But neither of the two members will ever completely disappear. The feeling of dependence predominates in the relation of children to their parents, or of citizens to their fatherland; and yet individuals can, without losing their relationship, exercise upon their fatherland not only a directive influence, but even a counter-influence. And the dependence of children on their parents, which very soon comes to be felt as a gradually diminishing and fading quantity, is never from the start free from the admixture of an element of spontaneous activity towards the parents: just as even in the most absolute autocracy the ruler is not without some slight feeling of dependence. It is the same in the case of nature: towards all the forces of nature — even, we may say, towards the heavenly bodies — we ourselves do, in the same sense in which they influence us, exercise a counter-influence, however minute. So that our whole self-consciousness in relation to the world or its individual parts remains enclosed within these limits.

3. There can, accordingly, be for us no such thing as a feeling of absolute freedom. He who asserts that he has such a feeling is either deceiving himself or separating things which essentially belong together. For if the feeling of freedom expresses a forthgoing activity, this activity must have an object which has been somehow given to us, and this could not have taken place without an influence of the object upon our receptivity. Therefore in every such case there is involved a feeling of dependence which goes along with the feeling of freedom, and thus limits it. The contrary could only be possible if the object altogether came into existence through our activity, which is never the case absolutely, but only relatively. But if, on the other hand, the feeling of freedom expresses only an inward movement of activity, not only is every such individual movement bound up with the state of our stimulated receptivity at the moment, but, further, the totality of our free inward movements, considered as a unity, cannot be represented as a feeling of absolute freedom, because our whole existence does not present itself to our consciousness as having proceeded from our own spontaneous activity. Therefore in any temporal existence a feeling of absolute freedom can have no place. As regards the feeling of absolute dependence which, on the other hand, our proposition does postulate: for just the same reason, this feeling cannot

in any wise arise from the influence of an object which has in some way to be *given* to us; for upon such an object there would always be a counter-influence, and even a voluntary renunciation of this would always involve a feeling of freedom. Hence a feeling of absolute dependence, strictly speaking, cannot exist in a single moment as such, because such a moment is always determined, as regards its total content, by what is *given*, and thus by objects towards which we have a feeling of freedom. But the self-consciousness which accompanies all our activity, and therefore, since that is never zero, accompanies our whole existence, and negatives absolute freedom, is itself precisely a consciousness of absolute dependence; for it is the consciousness that the whole of our spontaneous activity comes from a source outside of us in just the same sense in which anything towards which we should have a feeling of absolute freedom must have proceeded entirely from ourselves. But without any feeling of freedom a feeling of absolute dependence would not be possible.

4. As regards the identification of absolute dependence with 'relation to God' in our proposition: this is to be understood in the sense that the *whence* of our receptive and active existence, as implied in this self-consciousness, is to be designated by the word 'God', and that this is for us the really original signification of that word. In this connection we have first of all to remind ourselves that, as we have seen in the foregoing discussion, this 'whence' is not the world, in the sense of the totality of temporal existence, and still less is it any single part of the world. For we have a feeling of freedom (though, indeed, a limited one) in relation to the world, since we are complementary parts of it, and also since we are continually exercising an influence on its individual parts; and, moreover, there is the possibility of our exercising influence on all its parts; and while this does permit a limited feeling of dependence, it excludes the absolute feeling. In the next place, we have to note that our proposition is intended to oppose the view that this feeling of dependence is itself conditioned by some previous knowledge about God. And this may indeed be the more necessary since many people claim to be in the sure possession of a concept of God, altogether a matter of conception and original, *i.e.* independent of any feeling; and in the strength of this higher self-consciousness, which indeed may come pretty near to being a feeling of absolute freedom, they put far from them, as something almost infra-human, that very feeling which for us is the basic type of all piety. Now our proposition is in no wise intended to dispute the existence of such an original knowledge, but simply to set it aside as something with which, in a system of Christian doctrine, we could never have any concern, because plainly

enough it has itself nothing to do directly with piety. If, however, word and idea are always originally one, and the term 'God' therefore presupposes an idea, then we shall simply say that this idea, which is nothing more than the expression of the feeling of absolute dependence, is the most direct reflection upon it and the most original idea with which we are here concerned, and is quite independent of that original knowledge (properly so called), and conditioned only by our feeling of absolute dependence. So that in the first instance God signifies for us simply that which is the co-determinant in this feeling and to which we trace our being in such a state; and any further content of the idea must be evolved out of this fundamental import assigned to it. Now this is just what is principally meant by the formula which says that to feel oneself absolutely dependent and to be conscious of being in relation with God are one and the same thing; and the reason is that absolute dependence is the fundamental relation which must include all others in itself. This last expression includes the God-consciousness in the self-consciousness in such a way that, quite in accordance with the above analysis, the two cannot be separated from each other. The feeling of absolute dependence becomes a clear self-consciousness only as this idea comes simultaneously into being. In this sense it can indeed be said that God is given to us in feeling in an original way; and if we speak of an original revelation of God to man or in man, the meaning will always be just this, that, along with the absolute dependence which characterizes not only man but all temporal existence, there is given to man also the immediate self-consciousness of it, which becomes a consciousness of God. In whatever measure this actually takes place during the course of a personality through time, in just that measure do we ascribe piety to the individual. On the other hand, any possibility of God being in any way *given* is entirely excluded, because anything that is outwardly given must be given as an object exposed to our counter-influence, however slight this may be. The transference of the idea of God to any perceptible object, unless one is all the time conscious that it is a piece of purely arbitrary symbolism, is always a corruption, whether it be a temporary transference, *i.e.* a theophany, or a constitutive transference, in which God is represented as permanently a particular perceptible existence.

The religious self-consciousness, like every essential element in human nature, leads necessarily in its development to fellowship or communion; a communion which, on the one hand, is variable and fluid, and, on the other hand, has definite limits, i.e. *is a Church.*

1. If the feeling of absolute dependence, expressing itself as consciousness of God, is the highest grade of immediate self-consciousness, it is also an essential element of human nature. This cannot be controverted on the ground that there is for every individual man a time when that consciousness does not yet exist. For this is the period when life is incomplete, as may be seen both from the fact that the animal confusion of consciousness has not yet been overcome, and from the fact that other vital functions too are only developing themselves gradually. Nor can it be objected that there are always communities of men in which this feeling has not yet been awakened; for these likewise only exhibit on a large scale that undeveloped state of human nature which betrays itself also in other functions of their lives. Similarly it cannot be argued that the feeling is accidental (non-essential), because even in a highly developed religious environment individuals may be found who do not share it. For these people cannot but testify that the whole matter is not so alien to them but that they have at particular moments been gripped by such a feeling, though they may call it by some name that is not very honouring to themselves. . . .

2. The truth that every essential element of human nature becomes the basis of a fellowship or communion, can only be fully explicated in the context of a scientific theory of morals. Here we can only allude to the essential points of this process, and then ask everybody to accept it as a fact. Fellowship, then, is demanded by the *consciousness of kind* which dwells in every man, and which finds its satisfaction only when he steps forth beyond the limits of his own personality and takes up the facts of other personalities into his own. It is accomplished through the fact that everything inward becomes, at a certain point of its strength or maturity, an outward too, and, as such, perceptible to others. Thus feeling, as a self-contained determination of the mind (which on the other side passes into thought and action, but with that we are not here concerned), will, even *qua* feeling, and purely in virtue of the consciousness of kind, not exist exclusively for itself, but becomes an outward, originally and without any definite aim or pertinence, by means of facial expression, gesture, tones, and (indirectly) words; and so becomes to other people a revelation of the inward. This bare expression of feeling, which is entirely

105

caused by the inward agitation, and which can be very definitely distinguished from any further and more separate action into which it passes, does indeed at first arouse in other people only an idea of the person's state of mind. But, by reason of the consciousness of kind, this passes into living imitation; and the more able the percipient is (either for general reasons, or because of the greater liveliness of the expression, or because of closer affinity) to pass into the same state, the more easily will that state be produced by imitation. Everybody must in his own experience be conscious of this process from both sides, the expressing and the perceiving, and must thus confess that he always finds himself, with the concurrence of his conscience, involved in a multifarious communion of feeling, as a condition quite in conformity with his nature, and therefore that he would have co-operated in the founding of such a communion if it had not been there already.

As regards the feeling of absolute dependence in particular, everyone will know that it was first awakened in him in the same way, by the communicative and stimulative power of expression or utterance.

3. Our assertion that this communion is at first variable and fluid follows from what we have just been saying. For as individuals in general resemble each other in variable degrees, both as regards the strength of their religious emotions and as regards the particular region of sensible self-consciousness with which their God-consciousness most easily unites, each person's religious emotions have more affinity with those of one of his fellows than with those of another, and thus communion of religious feeling comes to him more easily with the former than with the latter. If the difference is great, he feels himself attracted by the one and repelled by the others; yet not repelled directly or absolutely, so that he could not enter into any communion of feeling with them at all; but only in the sense that he is more powerfully attracted to others; and thus he could have communion even with these, in default of the others, or in circumstances which specially drew them together. For there can hardly exist a man in whom another would recognize no religious affection whatever as being in any degree similar to his own, or whom another would know to be quite incapable of either moving or being moved by him. It remains true, however, that the more uninterrupted the communion is to be, *i.e.* the more closely the kindred emotions are to follow each other, and the more easily the emotions are to communicate themselves, so much the smaller must be the number of people who can participate. We may conceive as great an interval as we like between the two extremes, that of the closest and that of the feeblest communion; so that

the man who experiences the fewest and feeblest religious emotions can have the closest kind of communion only with those who are equally little susceptible to these emotions, and is not in a position to imitate the utterances of those who derive religious emotion from moments where he himself never finds it. A similar relation holds between the man whose piety is purer, in the sense that in every moment of it he clearly distinguishes the religious content of his self-consciousness from the sensible to which it is related, and the man whose piety is less pure, *i.e.* more confused with the sensible. However, we may conceive the interval between these extremes as being, for each person, filled up with as many intermediate stages as we like; and this is just what constitutes the fluidity of the communion.

4. This is how the interchange of religious consciousness appears when we think of the relation of individual men to each other. But if we look at the actual condition of men, we also find well-established relationships in this fluid, and therefore (strictly speaking) undefined communion or fellowship. In the first place, as soon as human development has advanced to the point of a domestic life, even if not a completely regulated one, every family will establish within itself such a communion of the religious self-consciousness — a communion which, however, has quite definite limits as regards the outside world. For the members of the family are bound together in a peculiar manner by definite congruity and kinship and, moreover, their religious emotions are associated with the same occasions, so that strangers can only have an accidental and transitory, and therefore a very unequal, share in them.

But we also find families not isolated but standing collectively in distinctly defined combinations, with common language and customs, and with some knowledge or inkling of a closer common origin. And then religious communion becomes marked off among them, partly in the form of predominating similarity in the individual families, and partly by one family, which is particularly open to religious emotions, coming to predominate as the paramountly active one, while the others, being as it were scarcely out of their nonage, display only receptivity (a state of affairs which exists wherever there is a hereditary priesthood). Every such relatively closed religious communion, which forms an ever self-renewing circulation of the religious self-consciousness within certain definite limits, and a propagation of the religious emotions arranged and organized within the same limits, so that there can be some kind of definite understanding as to which individuals belong to it and which do not — this we designate a *Church*.   *The Christian Faith*, pp. 12-18, 26-29

2

THE DISTINCTIVENESS OF CHRISTIANITY: REDEMPTION THROUGH JESUS CHRIST*

Schleiermacher, as has been seen earlier, achieved a remarkable Christ-centredness in his theology, which has subsequently become axiomatic for much more modern Christian thought. His presentation of the distinctiveness of Christianity is most concisely set out in the early chapters of his dogmatics, The Christian Faith. *Everything in Christianity is related to the experienced redemption wrought by the historical Jesus of Nazareth. This means that Schleiermacher relativizes much which had traditionally been thought of as essential belief, in the light of the one truly essential belief: that in Jesus a perfect God-consciousness existed, and that this same Jesus enables the religious consciousness to triumph in us. All else — miracles, prophetic fulfilment, biblical inspiration etc. — find their meaning only if the living communion with the Redeemer, and the effect he brings, is apprehended first and in its own strength. This emphasis upon the personal encounter with Jesus and his spiritual influence, placing 'supernatural', metaphysical or doctrinal formulae in a secondary position, was to be one of the hallmarks of liberal Protestant thought for several generations.*

PRESENTATION OF CHRISTIANITY IN ITS PECULIAR ESSENCE: PROPOSITIONS BORROWED FROM APOLOGETICS

Christianity is a monotheistic faith, belonging to the teleological type of religion, and is essentially distinguished from other such faiths by the fact that in it everything is related to the redemption accomplished by Jesus of Nazareth.

1. The only pertinent way of discovering the peculiar essence of any particular faith and reducing it as far as possible to a formula is by showing the element which remains constant throughout the most diverse religious affections within this same communion, while it is absent from analogous affections within other communions. Now since we have little reason to expect that this peculiarity is equally strongly marked in all the different varieties of emotions, there is all the greater possibility of our

---

* See also pp. 40ff. above.

missing the mark in this attempt, and so coming in the end to the opinion that there is no hard-and-fast inward difference at all, but only the outward difference as determined by time and place. However, we may with some certainty conclude from what has been said above, that we shall be least likely to miss the peculiarity if we keep principally to what is most closely connected with the basal fact, and this is the procedure which underlies the formula of our proposition. But Christianity presents special difficulties, even in this fact alone, that it takes a greater variety of forms than other faiths and is split up into a multiplicity of smaller communions or churches; and thus there arises a twofold task, first, to find the peculiar essence, common to all these communions, of Christianity as such, and secondly, to find the peculiar essence of the particular communion whose right is to be authenticated or whose system of doctrine is to be established. But still further difficulty lies in the fact that even in each particular ecclesiastical communion almost every doctrine appears with the most multifarious variations at different times and places; and this implies as its basis, not indeed, perhaps, an equally great diversity in the religious affections themselves, but always at least a great diversity in the manner of understanding and appraising them. Indeed, the worst of all is that, owing to this variation, the bounds of the Christian realm become a matter of dispute even among Christians themselves, one asserting of this form of teaching, and another of that form, that though it was indeed engendered within Christianity it is nevertheless really un-Christian in content. Now, if he who wishes to solve our problem belongs himself to one of these parties, and assumes at the outset that only what is found within the realm of that one view ought to be taken into account in ascertaining what is distinctive of Christianity, he is at the outset taking controversies as settled, for the settlement of which he professes to be only discovering the conditions. For only when the peculiar essence of Christianity has been ascertained can it be decided how far this or that is compatible or incompatible with it. But if the investigator succeeds in freeing himself from all partiality, and therefore takes into account everything, however opposed, so long as it professes to be Christian, then on the other hand he is in danger of reaching a result far scantier and more colourless in its content, and consequently less suitable to the aims of our present task. That is the present state of affairs, and it cannot be concealed. Now since each man, the more religious he is, usually brings his individual religion the more into this investigation, there is a large majority of the people who form their idea of the peculiar essence of Christianity according to the interests of their party. But for the interests of apologetics as well as of dogmatics it seems advisable rather to be content with a scanty result at the beginning and to hope for its completion in the course of further procedure, than to begin with a narrow and exclusive formula, which is of necessity confronted by one or more opposing formulae, with which there must be a conflict sooner or later. And it is in this sense that the formula of our proposition is set up.

2. It is indisputable that all Christians trace back to Christ the communion to which they belong. But here we are also presupposing that the term *Redemption* is one to which they all confess: not only that they all *use* the word, with perhaps different meanings, but that there is some common element of meaning which they all have in mind, even if they differ when they come to a more exact description of it. The term itself is in this realm merely figurative, and signifies in general a passage from an evil condition, which is represented as a state of captivity or constraint,* into a better condition — this is the passive side of it. But it also signifies the help given in that process by some other person, and this is the active side of it. Further, the usage of the word does not essentially imply that the worse condition must have been preceded by a better condition, so that the better one which followed would really be only a restoration: that point may at the outset be left quite open. But now apply the word to the realm of religion, and suppose we are dealing with the teleological type of religion. Then the evil condition can only consist in an obstruction or arrest of the vitality of the higher self-consciousness, so that there comes to be little or no union of it with the various determinations of the sensible self-consciousness, and thus little or no religious life. We may give to this condition, in its most extreme form, the name of *Godlessness*, or, better, *God-forgetfulness*. But we must not think this means a state in which it is quite impossible for the God-consciousness to be kindled. For if that were so, then, in the first place, the lack of a thing which lay outside of one's nature could not be felt to be an evil condition; and in the second place, a re-creating in the strict sense would then be needed in order to make this lack, and that is not included in the idea of redemption. The possibility, then, of kindling the God-consciousness remains in reserve even where the evil condition of that consciousness is painted in the darkest colours.† Hence we can only designate it as an absence of facility for introducing the God-consciousness into the course of our actual lives and retaining it there. This certainly makes it seem as if these two condi-

* [This does not apply as precisely to the English word *redemption* as to the German word *Erlösung*, which primarily means release or deliverance. — TRANSL.]

† Rom. 1:18ff.

110

tions, that which exists before redemption and that which is to be brought about by redemption, could only be distinguished in an indefinite way, as a more and a less; and so, if the idea of redemption is to be clearly established, there arises the problem of reducing this indefinite distinction to a relative opposition. Such an opposition lies in the following formulae. Given an activity of the sensible self-consciousness, to occupy a moment of time and to connect it with another: its 'exponent' or 'index' will be greater than that of the higher self-consciousness for uniting itself therewith; and given an activity of the higher self-consciousness, to occupy a moment of time through union with a determination of the sensible, its 'exponent' or 'index' will be less than that of the activity of the sensible for completing the moment for itself alone. Under these conditions no satisfaction of the impulse towards the God-consciousness will be possible; and so, if such a satisfaction is to be attained, a redemption is necessary, since this condition is nothing but a kind of imprisonment or constraint of the feeling of absolute dependence. These formulae, however, do not imply that in all moments which are so determined the God-consciousness or the feeling of absolute dependence is at zero, but only that in some respect it does not dominate the moment; and in proportion as that is the case the above designations of Godlessness and God-forgetfulness may fitly be applied to it.

3. The recognition of such a condition undeniably finds a place in all religious communions. For the aim of all penances and purifications is to put an end to the consciousness of this condition or to the condition itself. But our proposition establishes two points which in this connection distinguish Christianity from all other religious communions. In the first place, in Christianity the incapacity and the redemption, and their connection with each other, do not constitute simply one particular religious element among others, but all other religious emotions are related to this, and this accompanies all others, as the principal thing which makes them distinctively Christian. And secondly, redemption is posited as a thing which has been universally and completely accomplished by Jesus of Nazareth. And these two points, again, must not be separated from each other, but are essentially interconnected. Thus it could not by any means be said that Christian piety is attributable to every man who in all his religious moments is conscious of being in process of redemption, even if he stood in no relation to the person of Jesus or even knew nothing of him — a case which, of course, will never arise. And no more could it be said that a man's religion is Christian if he traces it to Jesus, even supposing that therein he is not at all conscious of being in process of redemption — a

case which also, of course, will never arise. The reference to redemption is in every Christian consciousness simply because the originator of the Christian communion is the Redeemer; and Jesus is founder of a religious communion simply in the sense that its members become conscious of redemption through him. Our previous exposition ensures that this will not be understood to mean that the whole religious consciousness of a Christian can have no other content than simply Jesus and redemption, but only that all religious moments, so far as they are free expressions of the feeling of absolute dependence, are set down as having come into existence through that redemption, and, so far as the feeling appears still unliberated, are set down as being in need of that redemption. It likewise goes without saying that, while this element is always present, different religious moments may and will possess it in varying degrees of strength or weakness, without thereby losing their Christian character. But it *would*, of course, follow from what has been said, that if we conceive of religious moments in which all reference to redemption is absent, and the image of the Redeemer is not introduced at all, these moments must be judged to belong no more intimately to Christianity than to any other monotheistic faith.

4. The more detailed elaboration of our proposition, as to how the redemption is effected by Christ and comes to consciousness within the Christian communion, falls to the share of the dogmatic system itself. Here, however, we have still to discuss, with reference to the general remarks we made above, the relation of Christianity to the other principal monotheistic communions. These also are traced back each to an individual founder. Now if the difference of founder were the only difference, this would be a merely external difference, and the same thing would be true if these others likewise set up their founder as a redeemer and thus related everything to redemption. For that would mean that in all these religions the religious moments were of like content, only that the personality of the founder was different. But such is not the case: rather must we say that only through Jesus, and thus only in Christianity, has redemption become the central point of religion. For inasmuch as these other religions have instituted particular penances and purifications for particular things, and these are only particular parts of their doctrine and organization, the effecting of redemption does not appear as their main business. It appears rather as a derivative element. Their main business is the founding of the communion upon definite doctrine and in definite form. If, however, there are within the communion considerable differences in the free development of the God-consciousness, then some

people, in whom it is most cramped, are more in need of redemption, and others, in whom it works more freely, are more capable of redemption; and thus through the influence of the latter there arises in the former an approximation to redemption; but only up to the point at which the difference between the two is more or less balanced, simply owing to the fact that there exists a communion or fellowship. In Christianity, on the other hand, the redeeming influence of the Founder is the primary element, and the communion exists only on this presupposition, and as a communication and propagation of that redeeming activity. Hence within Christianity these two tendencies always rise and fall together: the tendency to give pre-eminence to the redeeming work of Christ, and the tendency to ascribe great value to the distinctive and peculiar elements in Christian piety. And the same is true of the two opposite tendencies: the tendency to regard Christianity simply as a means of advancing and propagating religion in general (its own distinctive nature being merely accidental and secondary), and the tendency to regard Christ principally as a teacher and the organizer of a communion, while putting the redeeming activity in the background.

Accordingly, in Christianity the relation of the Founder to the members of the communion is quite different from what it is in the other religions. For those other founders are represented as having been, as it were, arbitrarily elevated from the mass of similar or not very different men, and as receiving just as much for themselves as for other people whatever they do receive in the way of divine doctrine and precept. Thus even an adherent of those faiths will hardly deny that God could just as well have given the law through another as through Moses, and the revelation could just as well have been given through another as through Mohammed. But Christ is distinguished from all others as Redeemer alone and for all, and is in no wise regarded as having been at any time in need of redemption himself; and is therefore separated from the beginning from all other men, and endowed with redeeming power from his birth.

Not that we mean here to exclude at the outset from the Christian communion all those who differ from this presentation of the matter (which is itself capable of manifold shades of variation) in holding that Christ was only later endowed with redeeming power, provided only that this power is recognized as something different from the mere communication of doctrine and rule of life. But if Christ is regarded entirely on the analogy of the founders of other religions, then the distinctive peculiarity of Christianity can only be asserted for the content of the doctrine and rule of life, and the three monotheistic faiths remain separate only in so far as each holds unflinchingly to what it has received. But now suppose them all together capable of advancing still to perfection, and suppose they were able to find for themselves, sooner or later, the better doctrines and precepts of Christianity: then the inward difference would entirely disappear. Suppose that finally the Christian Church is likewise to move on beyond what has been received from Christ: then nothing else remains for Christ but to be regarded as an outstanding point in the development, and this in such a sense that there is a redemption *from* him as well as a redemption through him. And since the perfecting principle can only be reason, and this is everywhere the same, all distinction between the progress of Christianity and that of other monotheistic faiths would gradually disappear, and all alike would only have a validity limited to a definite period, so far as their distinctive character was concerned.

In this way the difference becomes clear between two widely divergent conceptions of Christianity. But at the same time the lines leading from the one to the other become visible. If the latter of the two conceptions were ever to present itself as a complete doctrine, such a communion would perhaps of its own accord sever its connection with the other Christian communions. But otherwise it could still be recognized as a Christian communion, unless it actually declared itself to be now freed from the necessity of adherence to Christ. Still less should participation in the Christian communion be denied to *individuals* who approximate to that view, so long as they desire to maintain in themselves a living consciousness of God along with, and by means of, that communion.

5. This development of the argument will, it is hoped, serve to confirm what we have established for the purpose of determining the distinctive element of Christianity. For we have tried, as it were by way of experiment, to single out from among the common elements of Christian piety that element by which Christianity is most definitely distinguished externally; and in this attempt we were guided by the necessity of regarding the inner peculiarity and the outward delimitation in their interconnection. Perhaps in a universal philosophy of religion, to which, if it were properly recognized, apologetics could then appeal, the inner character of Christianity in itself could be exhibited in such a way that its particular place in the religious world would thereby be definitely fixed. This would also mean that all the principal moments of the religious consciousness would be systematized, and from their interconnection it would be seen which of them were fitted to have all the others related to them and to be themselves a constant concomitant of all the others. If, then, it should be

seen that the element which we call 'redemption' becomes such a moment as soon as a liberating fact enters a region where the God-consciousness was in a state of constraint, Christianity would in that case be vindicated as a distinct form of faith and its nature in a sense construed. But even this could not properly be called a proof of Christianity, since even the philosophy of religion could not establish any necessity, either to recognize a particular fact as redemptive, or to give the central place actually in one's own consciousness to any particular moment, even though that moment should be capable of occupying such a place. Still less can this present account claim to be such a proof; for here, in accordance with the line we have taken, and since we can only start from a historical consideration, we cannot even pretend to do as much as might be done in a complete philosophy of religion. Moreover, it is obvious that an adherent of some other faith might perhaps be completely convinced by the above account that what we have set forth is really the peculiar essence of Christianity, without being thereby so convinced that Christianity is actually the truth, as to feel compelled to accept it. Everything we say in this place is relative to dogmatics, and dogmatics is only for Christians; and so this account is only for those who live within the pale of Christianity, and is intended only to give guidance, in the interests of dogmatics, for determining whether the expressions of any religious consciousness are Christian or not, and whether the Christian quality is strongly and clearly expressed in them, or rather doubtfully. We entirely renounce all attempt to prove the truth or necessity of Christianity; and we presuppose, on the contrary, that every Christian, before he enters at all upon inquiries of this kind, has already the inward certainty that his religion cannot take any other form than this. *The Christian Faith*, pp. 52-60

*

There is no other way of obtaining participation in the Christian communion than through faith in Jesus as the Redeemer.

1. To participate in the Christian communion means to seek in Christ's institution an approximation to the above-described state of absolute facility and constancy of religious emotions. No one can wish to belong to the Christian Church on any other ground. But since each can only enter through a free resolve of his own, this must be preceded by the certainty that the influence of Christ puts an end to the state of being in need of redemption, and produces that other state; and this certainty is just faith in Christ. That is to say, this term always signifies, in our present province, the certainty which accompanies a state of the higher self-con-

sciousness, and which is therefore different from, but not for that reason less than, the certainty which accompanies the objective consciousness. In the same sense we spoke above of faith in God, which was nothing but the certainty concerning the feeling of absolute dependence, as such, *i.e.* as conditioned by a being placed outside of us, and as expressing our relation to that being. The faith of which we are now speaking, however, is a purely factual certainty, but a certainty of a fact which is entirely inward. That is to say, it cannot exist in an individual until, through an impression which he has received from Christ, there is found in him a beginning — perhaps quite infinitesimal, but yet a real premonition — of the process which will put an end to the state of needing redemption. But the term 'faith in Christ' here (as the term 'faith in God' formerly) relates the state of redemption, as effect, to Christ as cause. That is how John describes it. And so from the beginning only those people have attached themselves to Christ in his new community whose religious self-consciousness had taken the form of a need of redemption, and who now became assured in themselves of Christ's redeeming power.* So that the more strongly those two phases appeared in any individual, the more able was he, by representation of the fact (which includes description of Christ and his work) to elicit this inward experience in others. Those in whom this took place became believers, and the rest did not.† This, moreover, is what has ever since constituted the essence of all direct Christian preaching. Such preaching must always take the form of testimony; testimony as to one's own experience, which shall arouse in others the desire to have the same experience. But the impression which all later believers received in this way from the influence of Christ, *i.e.* from the common Spirit communicated by him and from the whole communion of Christians, supported by the historical representation of his life and character, was just the same impression which his contemporaries received from him directly. Hence those who remained unbelieving were not blamed because they had not let themselves be persuaded by reasons, but simply because of their lack of self-knowledge, which must always be the explanation when the Redeemer is truly and correctly presented and people show themselves unable to recognize him as such. But even Christ himself represented this lack of self-knowledge, *i.e.* of the consciousness of needing redemption, as the limit to his activity. And so the ground of unbelief is the same in all ages, as is also the ground of belief or faith.

---

* John 1:45.46, 6:68.69, Matt. 16:15-18.
† Acts 2:37-41.

2. The attempt has often been made to demonstrate the necessity of redemption, but always in vain. We need not, however, appeal to these cases, for it is clear in itself that the thing is impossible. Any man who is capable of being satisfied with himself as he is will always manage to find a way out of the argument. And no more can it be demonstrated, once the consciousness of this need has been awakened, that Christ is the only One who can work redemption. In his own time there were many who did believe that redemption was near, and yet did not accept him. And even when we have a more correct idea of the end to be sought, it is not easy to see how it could be proved that any particular individual is in a position to achieve the desired effect. For in this matter we are concerned with amount of spiritual power, which we have no means of calculating; and even if we had, we should also require some fixed datum against which the calculation could be set. It cannot even be proved in a general way that such a redemption is bound to come, even if we presuppose a general knowledge not only of what men are like but also of what God is like. There would still be plenty of room for different sophistical arguments to draw opposite conclusions from the same data, according as God's purpose for man was conceived in one way or in another.

Agreed, then, that we must adhere to the kind of certainty which we have just described, and that faith is nothing other than the incipient experience of the satisfaction of that spiritual need by Christ: there can still be very diverse ways of experiencing the need and the succour, and yet they will all be faith. Moreover, the consciousness of need may be present for a long time in advance, or it may, as is often the case, be fully awakened only by the contrast which the perfection of Christ forms with our own condition, so that the two things come into existence simultaneously, the supreme consciousness of need and the beginning of its satisfaction.

3. It is true that in the Scriptures themselves proofs are often mentioned, which the witnesses of the Gospel employed.* Yet it is never asserted that faith sprang from the proof, but from the preaching. Those proofs were only applied among the Jews, with reference to their current ideas of the coming Messiah, in order to repulse the opposition presented by these ideas to the witness of the Gospel, or to anticipate any such opposition. This was an indispensable line of defence for witnesses of Christ who were Jews and who were dealing with Jews. If they wished to assert that they themselves had never expected any other kind of redemp-

---

* Acts 6:9.10, 9:20-22, also 18:27.28.

tion than this, or that their expectations had been transformed by the appearing and the influence of Christ, they must either break with the whole Jewish religion, which they had no warrant for doing, or show that the prophetic representations were applicable to this Jesus as Redeemer. If we took the other view of the matter, it would mean that the faith of the Gentile Christians was not the same as that of the Jewish Christians; and then it would not have been possible for these two to become really one, but the Gentiles would have had to become Jews first, in order then to be brought to Christ by the authority of the prophets.

Postscript. — Our proposition says nothing of any intermediate link between faith and participation in the Christian communion, and is accordingly to be taken as directly combining the two, so that faith of itself carries with it that participation; and not only as depending on the spontaneous activity of the man who has become a believer, but also as depending on the spontaneous activity of the communion (Church), as the source from which the testimony proceeded for the awakening of faith. At the same time, in shutting up the whole process between these two points, the witness or testimony and its effect, our proposition is intended to make an end of everything which, in the form of demonstration, is usually brought to the aid of the proper witness or even substituted for it. This refers principally to the attempts to bring about a recognition of Christ by means of the miracles which he performs, or the prophecies which predicted him, or the special character of the testimonies originally borne to him, regarded as the work of divine inspiration. In all this there seems to be more or less illusion on the following point: that the efficacy of these things somehow always presupposes faith, and therefore cannot produce it.

First consider *miracle*, taking the word in its narrower sense, so that prophecy and inspiration are not included, but simply phenomena in the realm of physical nature which are supposed not to have been caused in a natural manner. Whether we confine ourselves to those performed by Jesus himself, or include those which took place in connection with him, these miracles cannot bring about a recognition of him at all. In the first place, we know of these miracles only from those same holy Scriptures (for the miracles related in less pure sources are never adduced along with them) which relate similar miracles of people who did not adhere to Christianity at all, but are rather to be reckoned among its enemies; and Scripture gives us no marks for distinguishing evidential miracles from non-evidential. But further, Scripture itself bears witness that faith has been produced without miracles, and also that miracles have failed to produce it; from which it may be concluded that even when it has existed along with miracles it was not produced by miracles but in its own original way. Hence if the purpose of miracles had been to produce faith, we should have to conclude that God's breaking into the order of nature proved ineffectual. Accordingly, many find the purpose of miracles simply in the fact that they turn the attention to Christ. But this, again, is at least so far contradicted by Christ's oft-repeated command not to make the miracles more widely known, that we should have to limit their efficacy to the immediate eye-witnesses, and thus this efficacy would no longer exist today. But, finally, the following question cannot be avoided. In any other context than that of such faith and its realm, we may encounter any number of facts which we cannot explain naturally, and yet we never think of miracle, but simply regard the explanation as deferred until we have a more exact knowledge both of the fact in question and of the laws of nature. But when such a fact occurs in connection with some faith-realm which has to be established, we think at once of miracle; only, each man claims miracle as real for the realm of his own faith alone, and sets down the others as false. On what is this distinction based? The question can hardly be answered except as follows. In general we do, perhaps, assume so exclusive a connection between miracles and the information of a new faith-realm, that we only admit miracle for this kind of case; but the state of each individual's faith determines his judgment of the alleged miracle, and so the miracle does not produce the faith. As regards that universal connection, however, the state of the case seems to be as follows. Where a new point in the development of the spiritual life, and indeed primarily of the self-consciousness, is assumed to exist, new phenomena in physical nature, mediated by the spiritual power which is manifested, are also expected, because both the contemplative and the outwardly active spiritual states all proceed from the self-consciousness, and are determined by its movements. Thus, once Christ is recognized as Redeemer, and consequently as the beginning of the supreme development of human nature in the realm of the self-consciousness, it is a natural assumption that, just because at the point where such an existence communicates itself most strongly, spiritual states appear which cannot be explained from what went before, he who exercises such a peculiar influence upon human nature around him will be able, in virtue of the universal connection of things, to manifest also a peculiar power of working upon the physical side of human nature and upon external nature. That is to say, it is natural to expect miracles from him who is the supreme divine revelation; and yet they can be called miracles only in a relative sense, since our ideas of the susceptibility of physical nature to the influence of the spirit and of the causality of the will acting upon physical nature are as far from being finally settled and as capable of being perpetually widened by new experiences as are our ideas of the forces of physical nature themselves. Now, since, in connection with the divine revelation in Christ, phenomena presented themselves which could be brought under this concept of miracle, it was natural that they should actually come to be regarded from this point of view, and adduced as confirmation of the fact that this was a new point of development. But this confirmation will be effectual only where there is already present a beginning of faith; failing that, the miracle would either be declared false or be reserved, as regards the understanding of it, for some natural explanation which the future would reveal. Still less could it be proved from the miracles which accompanied it that Christianity is the supreme revelation, since similar phenomena are on the same grounds to be expected in the lower faiths too, and miracles themselves cannot, as such, be divided into higher and lower. Indeed, the possibility cannot be excluded that similar phenomena might occur even apart from all connection with the realm of religion, whether as accompanying other kinds of development or as signalizing deeper movements in physical nature itself. Similarly, on the other hand, it seems to be a matter of course that such supernatural phenomena, which accompany revelation, disappear again in proportion as the new development, freed from its point of origin in the external realm, is organized, and so becomes mature.

The same thing may be said with regard to *Prophecies,* in case anyone should wish to assign to them a more powerful rôle than that which we have granted above. Let us confine ourselves to the prophecies of the Jewish prophets regarding Christ, for in more recent times the heathen prophecies have been universally set aside, and we are not here immediately concerned with the prophecies of Christ and his apostles. Suppose, then, that we wished to make more use of those prophetic utterances among Jews. It is quite conceivable that a Jew should become a Christian because he came to see that those prophecies were to be referred to Jesus, and that nevertheless he should possess neither the real faith nor the true participation in the Christian communion, understanding it all, perhaps, in a quite different way, because he did not feel any need of redemption. But suppose these prophecies were to be universally set before unbelievers, in order to produce in them the will to enter into communion with Christ. It might be made out at the start that these prophecies are all to be regarded as belonging together, that they all have in view an individual, and indeed one and the same individual (for otherwise the fulfilment of them all in one and the same person would really be a non-fulfilment), and further that they have all come to fulfilment in Christ, each in the sense in which it was meant, not those figuratively meant being fulfilled in a literal sense and those literally meant in a figurative sense (for that also would not be a real fulfilment). But, after all, it always comes to this in the end: that Jesus must be taken to be the Redeemer, because the Redeemer was predicted with descriptive details which are found in him. But this argument presupposes that people already have faith in the prophets who predicted, as such; and it is impossible to imagine how an unbeliever outside of Judaism should come to have such a faith, except on the supposition that the inspiration of the prophets is proved to him, and with this we shall deal below. Without such a faith the collocation of prophecies and their fulfilments would be a mere signpost, giving an impulse to seek fellowship with Christ only to those people who were already feeling the need of redemption; and this only in so far as the need expressed in the prophecies is analogous to their own, and at the same time the thing prophesied has a manifest connection with that need;* that is to say, in so far as each man could himself have prophesied the same thing out of his own need. The impulse, however, could only issue in his seeking to have the experience for himself,† and only when this attempt succeeded would there be faith. And certainly this impulse can now, when facts speak so loud, be given much more powerfully and surely in other ways than by means of the prophecies. This becomes especially clear when we reflect how the case really stands with regard to the above-mentioned presuppositions; namely, that it can never be proved that those prophets foresaw Christ as he really was, and still less the messianic kingdom as it really developed in Christianity. Thus it must be admitted that a proof from prophecy of Christ as the Redeemer is impossible; and in particular, the zealous attempt to seek out for this purpose prophecies or prototypes which relate to accidental circumstances in the story of Christ must appear simply as a mistake. A clear distinction must, therefore, be made between the apologetical use which the apostles made of the prophecies in their intercourse with the Jews, and a general use which might be made of them as evidences. When, however, faith in the Redeemer is already present, then we can dwell with great pleasure on all

* In this sense perhaps the prophecy quoted in Matt. 12:19.20 is the most pregnant prophecy.
†John 1:41.46.

expressions of the longing for redemption awakened by earlier and inadequate revelations. And this is the real significance (and it has, of course, a confirmative and corroborative value) of messianic prophecies, wherever they appear and in however obscure presentiments they are shrouded: they disclose to us a striving of human nature towards Christianity, and at the same time give it as the confession of the best and most inspired of earlier religious communions, that they are to be regarded only as preparatory and transitory institutions. As for the prophecies made by Christianity itself, it is, of course, natural that at the beginning of the development of a new thing the outlook is directed very much towards the future, *i.e.* towards its completion, and so one can understand the questions of the disciples, to which answers — on the basis of which they afterwards made further prophecies — could not altogether be denied. But Christ's prophecies cannot serve as a proof of his unique office and his exclusive vocation as Redeemer, for the simple reason that others also have admittedly prophesied. Again, it was equally natural that the more the new dispensation became established as an historical phenomenon, the more the interest in the future decreased and prophecy disappeared.

Now from all this it follows that, if faith in the revelation of God in Christ and in redemption through him has not already arisen in the direct way through experience as the demonstration of the Spirit and of power, neither miracles nor prophecies can produce it, and indeed that this faith would be just as immovable even if Christianity had neither prophecies nor miracles to show. For the lack of these could never refute that demonstration, or prove a mere delusion the experience of need satisfied in the fellowship of Christ. From the lack of these, indeed, nothing could be concluded except that those natural assumptions do not always prove true, and that the beginning of the most perfect form of religious self-consciousness appeared more suddenly, and confined its working more closely to its own immediate realm.

We come finally to *inspiration*. In Christianity this conception has a wholly subordinate significance. It cannot be related at all to Christ, since the divine revelation through him, however it is conceived, is always conceived as identical with his whole being, and not as appearing fragmentarily in sporadic moments. And as for what the apostles received from the Spirit, Christ traces that entirely to his own instruction, and those who through their testimony became believers did not believe because the testimony sprang from inspiration, for of that they knew nothing. The conception therefore relates only in the first place to the prophets of the Old Covenant, and in the second place to the composition of the New Testament Scriptures; and so we have to deal with it here only in so far as concerns the attempt to compel faith demonstratively by means of holy Scripture, when this is first assumed to be inspired. But as regards the Old Testament, prophecy cannot be understood alone without law and history; and this whole, taken all together, is so consistently theocratic that (while we can indeed distinguish in it two 'poles', one of which exercises attraction, the other repulsion, towards the New Testament), if, apart from the New Testament, we succeeded in making anyone believe in the prophetic inspiration (which, however, could hardly be accomplished except upon their own testimony that the word of God came to them), yet from this there could not be developed a faith in Christ as the end of the Law. We shall rather express the whole truth if we say that we believe in the prophetic inspiration simply because of the use which Christ and his apostles make of the utterances of the prophets. As regards the New Testament, the faith had been disseminated for two hundred years before that Testament was unanimously established as having peculiar validity. And, moreover, it was not a matter of Christian faith being in the meantime always mediated by faith in the Old Testament, for among the great mass of the heathen, who went over to Christianity without having been previously Judaized, this was by no means the case. But even now, and even supposing that the inspiration of the New Testament Scriptures can be proved from these Scriptures themselves, this would nevertheless presuppose a very perfect understanding of these Scriptures. And thus, since this is possible only for a few, we should still require some other way in which faith might arise, so that there would be two kinds of faith. And further, it is still impossible to see how an objective conviction of this kind could exercise such an influence on the self-consciousness, that, from the mere knowledge that those people were inspired who asserted that men need redemption and that Christ is their Redeemer, this assertion would immediately come to contain for all an inward truth. All that this conviction in itself can do is merely to give an impulse towards the awakening of a fuller self-consciousness and towards the winning of a total impression of Christ; and only from this will faith then proceed.   *The Christian Faith*, pp. 68-76

3

THEOLOGY AS REFLECTION
AND COMMUNICATION*

In On Religion. Speeches to Its Cultured Despisers, *Schleiermacher was at pains to distinguish as sharply as possible the essential nature of religion as* feeling *for the Infinite, from all ideas, conceptualizations and doctrines about it. Only by this distinction between vital religious emotion and the 'miserable love of system' could the rationalist mockery of orthodox doctrine be countered. Here Schleiermacher is certainly at his closest to the Romantic spirit of the age, but it must be remembered that the* Speeches *as a whole stress the need for specific, concrete communal expressions of religion, that is, a form of church. Romantics like Goethe found such elements in the* Speeches *unacceptable. Schleiermacher, for his part, had a profound understanding of individuality, but was not an individualist. The individual finds true individuality only in belonging to a community. The second of the* Speeches, *however, certainly shows Schleiermacher at the point where, on first reading, he might well seem to be so concerned to separate 'feeling' from 'knowledge' that he leaves little place for any form of that knowledge which is theology.*

SECOND SPEECH

THE NATURE OF RELIGION

. . . There is no sensation that is not pious, except it indicate some diseased and impaired state of the life, the influence of which will not be confined to religion. Wherefore, it follows that ideas and principles are all foreign to religion. This truth we here come upon for the second time. If ideas and principles are to be anything, they must belong to knowledge which is a different department of life from religion.

Now that we have some ground beneath us, we are in a better position to inquire about the source of this confusion. May there not be some reason for this constant connection of principles and ideas with religion? In the same way is there not a cause for the connection of action with religion? Without such an inquiry it would be vain to proceed farther. The

---

* See also pp. 43ff. above.

misunderstanding would be confirmed, for you would change what I say into ideas and begin seeking for principles in them. Whether you will follow my exposition, who can tell? What now is to hinder that each of the functions of life just indicated should not be an object for the others? Or does it not rather manifestly belong to their inner unity and equality that they should in this manner strive to pass over into one another? So at least it seems to me. Thus, as a feeling person, you can become an object to yourself and you can contemplate your own feeling. Nay, you can, as a feeling person, become an object for yourself to operate upon and more and more to impress your deepest nature upon. Would you now call the general description of the nature of your feelings that is the product of this contemplation a principle, and the description of each feeling, an idea, you are certainly free to do so. And if you call them religious principles and ideas, you are not in error. But do not forget that this is scientific treatment of religion, knowledge about it, and not religion itself.

Nor can the description be equal to the thing described. The feeling may dwell in many sound and strong, as for example in almost all women, without ever having been specially a matter of contemplation. Nor may you say religion is lacking, but only knowledge about religion. Furthermore, do not forget what we have already established, that this contemplation presupposes the original activity. It depends entirely upon it. If the ideas and principles are not from reflection on a man's own feeling, they must be learned by rote and utterly void. Make sure of this, that no man is pious, however perfectly he understands these principles and conceptions, however much he believes he possesses them in clearest consciousness, who cannot show that they have originated in himself and, being the outcome of his own feeling, are peculiar to himself. Do not present him to me as pious, for he is not. His soul is barren in religious matters, and his ideas are merely supposititious children which he has adopted, in the secret feeling of his own weakness. As for those who parade religion and make a boast of it, I always characterize them as unholy and removed from all divine life. One has conceptions of the ordering of the world and formulae to express them, the other has prescriptions whereby to order himself and inner experiences to authenticate them. The one weaves his formulae into a system of faith, and the other spins out of his prescriptions a scheme of salvation. It being observed that neither has any proper standing ground without feeling, strife ensues as to how many conceptions and declarations, how many precepts and exercises, how many emotions and sensations must be accepted in order to conglomerate a sound religion that shall be neither specially cold nor enthusiastic, dry nor shallow. O fools, and slow of heart! They do not know that all this is mere analysis of the religious sense, which they must have made for themselves, if it is to have any meaning.

But if they are not conscious of having anything to analyse, whence have they those ideas and rules? They have memory and imitation, but that they have religion do not believe. They have no ideas of their own from which formulae might be known, so they must learn them by rote, and the feelings which they would have accompanying them are copies, and like all copies, are apt to become caricatures. And out of this dead, corrupt, second-hand stuff, a religion is to be concocted! The members and juices of an organized body can be dissected; but take these elements now and mix them and treat them in every possible way; and will you be able to make heart's blood of them? Once dead, can it ever again move in a living body? Such restoration of the products of living nature out of its component parts, once divided, passes all human skill, and, just as little, would you succeed with religion, however completely the various kindred elements be given from without. From within, in their original, characteristic form, the emotions of piety must issue. They must be indubitably your own feelings, and not mere stale descriptions of the feelings of others, which could at best issue in a wretched imitation.

Now the religious ideas which form those systems can and ought to be nothing else than such a description, for religion cannot and will not originate in the pure impulse to know. What we feel and are conscious of in religious emotions is not the nature of things, but their operation upon us. What you may know or believe about the nature of things is far beneath the sphere of religion. The universe is ceaselessly active and at every moment is revealing itself to us. Every form it has produced, everything to which, from the fulness of its life, it has given a separate existence, every occurrence scattered from its fertile bosom is an operation of the universe upon us. Now religion is to take up into our lives and to submit to be swayed by them, each of these influences and their consequent emotions, not by themselves but as a part of the whole, not as limited and in opposition to other things, but as an exhibition of the infinite in our life. Anything beyond this, any effort to penetrate into the nature and substance of things is no longer religion, but seeks to be a science of some sort.

On the other hand, to take what are meant as descriptions of our feelings for a science of the object, in some way the revealed product of religion, or to regard it as science and religion at the same time, necessarily leads to mysticism and vain mythology. For example, it was religion when the ancients, abolishing the limitations of time and space, regarded every special form of life throughout the whole world as the work and as the kingdom of a being who in this sphere was omnipresent and omnipotent, because one peculiar way in which the universe operates was present as a definite feeling, and they described it after this fashion. It was religion when they assigned a peculiar name and built a temple to the god to whom they ascribed any helpful occurrence whereby in an obvious, if accidental, way, the laws of the world were revealed, because they had comprehended something as a deed of the universe, and after their own fashion set forth its connection and peculiar character. It was religion when they rose above the rude iron age, full of flaws and inequalities, and sought again the golden age on Olympus in the joyous life of the gods, because beyond all change and all apparent evil that results only from the strife of finite forms, they felt the ever-stirring, living and serene activity of the world and the world-spirit. But when they drew up marvellous and complex genealogies of the gods, or when a later faith produced a long series of emanations and procreations, it was not religion. Even though these things may have their source in a religious presentation of the relation of the human and the divine, of the imperfect and the perfect, they were, in themselves, vain mythology, and, in respect of science, ruinous mysticism. The sum total of religion is to feel that, in its highest unity, all that moves us in feeling is one; to feel that aught single and particular is only possible by means of this unity; to feel, that is to say, that our being and living is a being and living in and through God. But it is not necessary that the deity should be presented as also one distinct object. To many this view is necessary, and to all it is welcome, yet it is always hazardous and fruitful in difficulties. It is not easy to avoid the appearance of making him susceptible of suffering like other objects. It is only one way of characterizing God, and, from the difficulties of it, common speech will probably never rid itself. But to treat this objective conception of God just as if it were a perception, as if apart from his operation upon us through the world the existence of God before the world, and outside of the world, though for the world, were either by or in religion exhibited as science is, so far as religion is concerned, vain mythology. What is only a help for presentation is treated as a reality. It is a misunderstanding very easily made, but it is quite outside the peculiar territory of religion.

From all this you will at once perceive how the question, whether religion is a system or not, is to be treated. It admits of an entire negative, and also of a direct affirmative, in a way that perhaps you scarce expected. Religion is certainly a system, if you mean that it is formed according to an inward and necessary connection. That the religious sense of one person is moved in one way, and that of another in another is not pure accident, as if the emotions formed no whole, as if any emotions might be caused in the same individual by the same object. Whatever occurs anywhere, whether among many or few as a peculiar and distinct kind of feeling is in itself complete, and by its nature necessary. What you find as religious emotions among Turks or Indians, cannot equally appear among Christians. The essential oneness of religiousness spreads itself out in a great variety of provinces, and again, in each province it contracts itself, and the narrower and smaller the province there is necessarily more excluded as incompatible and more included as characteristic. Christianity, for example, is a whole in itself, but so is any of the divisions that may at any time have appeared in it, down to Protestantism and Catholicism in modern times. Finally, the piety of each individual, whereby he is rooted in the greater unity, is a whole by itself. It is a rounded whole, based on his peculiarity, on what you call his character, of which it forms one side. Religion thus fashions itself with endless variety, down even to the single personality.

Each form again is a whole and capable of an endless number of characteristic manifestations. You would not have individuals issue from the whole in a finite way, each being at a definite distance from the other, so that one might be determined, construed and numbered from the others, and its characteristics be accurately determined in a conception? Were I to compare religion in this respect with anything it would be with music, which indeed is otherwise closely connected with it. Music is one great whole; it is a special, a self-contained revelation of the world. Yet the music of each people is a whole by itself, which again is divided into different characteristic forms, till we come to the genius and style of the individual. Each actual instance of this inner revelation in the individual contains all these unities. Yet while nothing is possible for a musician, except in and through the unity of the music of his people, and the unity of music generally, he presents it in the charm of sound with all the pleasure and joyousness of boundless caprice, according as his life stirs in him, and the world influences him. In the same way, despite the necessary elements in its structure, religion is, in its individual manifestations whereby it displays itself immediately in life, from nothing farther removed than from all semblance of compulsion or limitation. In life, the necessary element is taken up, taken up into freedom. Each emotion appears as the free self-determination of this very disposition, and mirrors one passing moment of the world.

It would be impious to demand here something held in constraint, something limited and determined from without. If anything of this kind lies in your conception of system then you must set it quite aside. A system of perceptions and feelings you may yourselves see to be somewhat marvellous. Suppose now you feel something. Is there not at the same time an accompanying feeling or thought — make your own choice — that you would have to feel in accordance with this feeling, and not otherwise were but this or that object, which does not now move you, to be present? But for this immediate association your feeling would be at an end, and a cold calculating and refining would take its place. Wherefore it is plainly an error to assert that it belongs to religion, to be conscious of the connection of its separate manifestations, not only to have it within, and to develop it from within, but to see it described and to comprehend it from without, and it is presumption to consider that, without it, piety is poverty-stricken. The truly pious are not disturbed in the simplicity of their way, for they give little heed to all the so-called religious systems that have been erected in consequence of this view.

Poor enough they are too, far inferior to the theories about music, defective though they be. Among those systematizers there is less than anywhere, a devout watching and listening to discover in their own hearts what they are to describe. They would rather reckon with symbols, and complete a designation which is about as accidental as the designation of the stars. It is purely arbitrary and never sufficient, for something new that should be included is always being discovered, and a system, anything permanent and secure, anything corresponding to nature, and not the result of caprice and tradition, is not to be found in it. The designation, let the forms of religion be ever so inward and self-dependent, must be from without. Thousands might be moved religiously in the same way, and yet each, led, not so much by disposition, as by external circumstances, might designate his feeling by different symbols. Furthermore, those systematizers are less anxious to present the details of religion than to subordinate them one to the other, and to deduce them from a higher. Nothing is of less importance to religion, for it knows nothing of deducing and connecting. There is no single fact in it that can be called original and chief. Its facts are one and all immediate. Without dependence on any other, each exists for itself. True, a special type of religion is constituted by one definite kind and manner of feeling, but it is mere perversion to call it a principle, and to treat it as if the rest could be deduced from it.

This distinct form of a religion is found, in the same way, in every single element of religion. Each expression of feeling bears on it immediately this peculiar impress. It cannot show itself without it, nor be comprehended without it. Everything is to be found immediately, and not proved from something else. Generals, which include particulars, combination and connection belong to another sphere, if they rest on reality, or they are merely a work of phantasy and caprice. Every man may have his own regulation and his own rubrics. What is essential can neither gain nor lose thereby. Consequently, the man who truly knows the nature of his religion, will give a very subordinate place to all apparent connection of details, and will not sacrifice the smallest for the sake of it.

By taking the opposite course, the marvellous thought has arisen of a universality of one religion, of one single form which is true, and in respect of which all others are false. Were it not that misunderstanding must be guarded against, I would say that it is only by such deducing and connecting that such a comparison as true and false, which is not peculiarly appropriate to religion, has ever been reached. It only applies where we have to do with ideas. Elsewhere the negative laws of your logic are not in place. All is immediately true in religion, for except immediately how could anything arise? But that only is immediate which has not yet passed through the stage of idea, but has grown up purely in the feeling. All that is religious is good, for it is only religious as it expresses a common higher life. But the whole circumference of religion is infinite, and is not to be comprehended under one form, but only under the sum total of all forms. It is infinite, not merely because any single religious organization has a limited horizon, and, not being able to embrace all, cannot believe that there is nothing beyond; but more particularly, because everyone is a person by himself, and is only to be moved in his own way, so that for everyone the elements of religion have most characteristic differences. Religion is infinite, not only because something new is ever being produced in time, by the endless relations both active and passive between different minds and the same limited matter; not only because the capacity for religion is never perfected, but is ever being developed anew, is ever being more beautifully reproduced, is ever entering deeper into the nature of man; but religion is infinite on all sides. As the knowledge of its eternal truth and infallibility accompanies knowledge, the consciousness of this infinity accompanies religion. It is the very feeling of religion, and must therefore accompany everyone that really has religion. He must be conscious that his religion is only part of the whole; that about the same circumstances there may be views and sentiments quite different from his, yet just as pious; and that there may be perceptions and feelings belonging to other modifications of religion, for which the sense may entirely fail him.

You see how immediately this beautiful modesty, this friendly, attractive forbearance springs from the nature of religion. How unjustly, therefore, do you reproach religion with loving persecution, with being malignant, with overturning society, and making blood flow like water. Blame those who corrupt religion, who flood it with an army of formulae and definitions, and seek to cast it into the fetters of a so-called system. What is it in religion about which men have quarrelled and made parties and kindled wars? About definitions, the practical sometimes, the theoretical always, both of which belong elsewhere. Philosophy, indeed, seeks to bring those who would know to a common knowledge. Yet even philosophy leaves room for variety, and the more readily the better it understands itself. But religion does not, even once, desire to bring those who believe and feel to one belief and one feeling. Its endeavour is to open in those who are not yet capable of religious emotions, the sense for the unity of the original source of life. But just because each seer is a new priest, a new mediator, a new organ, he flees with repugnance the bald uniformity which would again destroy this divine abundance.

This miserable love of system rejects what is strange, often without any patient examination of its claims, because, were it to receive its place, the closed ranks would be destroyed, and the beautiful coherence disturbed. There is the seat of the art and love of strife. War must be carried on, and persecution, for by thus relating detail to finite detail, one may destroy the other, while, in its immediate, relation to the infinite, all stand together in their original genuine connection, all is one and all is true. These systematizers, therefore, have caused it all. Modern Rome, godless but consequent, hurls anathemas and ejects heretics. Ancient Rome, truly pious, and, in a high style religious, was hospitable to every god. The adherents of the dead letter which religion casts out, have filled the world with clamour and turmoil.

Seers of the infinite have ever been quiet souls. They abide alone with themselves and the infinite, or if they do look around them, grudge to no one who understands the mighty word his own peculiar way. By means of this wide vision, this feeling of the infinite, they are able to look beyond their own sphere. There is in religion such a capacity for unlimited many-sidedness in judgment and in contemplation as is nowhere else to be found. I will not except even morality and philosophy, not at least so much of them as remains after religion is taken away. Let me appeal to your own experience. Does not every other object whereto man's thinking and striving are directed, draw around him a narrow circle, inside of which all that is highest for him is enclosed, and outside of which all appears common and unworthy? The man who only thinks methodically, and acts from principle and design, and will accomplish this or that in the world, unavoidably circumscribes himself, and makes everything that does not forward him an object of antipathy. Only when the free impulse of seeing, and of living is directed towards the infinite and goes into the infinite, is the mind set in unbounded liberty. Religion alone rescues it from the heavy fetters of opinion and desire. For it, all that is is necessary, all that can be is an indispensable image of the infinite. In this respect, it is all worthy of preservation and contemplation, however much, in other respects, and in itself, it is to be rejected. To a pious mind religion makes everything holy, even unholiness and commonness, whether he comprehends it or does not comprehend it, whether it is embraced in his system of thought, or lies outside, whether it agrees with his peculiar mode of acting or disagrees. Religion is the natural and sworn foe of all narrowmindedness, and of all onesidedness.

These charges, therefore, do not touch religion. They rest upon the confusion between religion and that knowledge which belongs to theology. It is a knowledge, whatever be its value, and is to be always distinguished from religion. . . .   *On Religion, Speeches . . .*, pp. 46-56

*

What is operation of grace? Nothing else manifestly than the common expression for revelation and inspiration, for interchange between the entrance of the world into man, through intuition and feeling, and the outgoing of man into the world, through action and culture. It includes both, in their originality and in their divine character, so that the whole life of the pious simply forms a series of operations of divine grace.

You see that all these ideas, in so far as religion requires, or can adopt ideas, are the first and the most essential. They indicate in the most characteristic manner a man's consciousness of his religion, because they indicate just what necessarily and universally must be in it. The man who does not see miracles of his own from the standpoint from which he contemplates the world, the man in whose heart no revelation of his own arises, when his soul longs to draw in the beauty of the world, and to be permeated by its spirit; the man who does not, in supreme moments, feel, with the most lively assurance, that a divine spirit urges him, and that he speaks and acts from holy inspiration, has no religion. The religious man must, at least, be conscious of his feelings as the immediate product of the universe; for less would mean nothing. He must recognize something individual in them, something that cannot be imitated, something that guarantees the purity of their origin from his own heart. To be assured of this possession is the true belief.

Belief, on the contrary, usually so called, which is to accept what another has said or done, or to wish to think and feel as another has thought and felt, is a hard and base service. So far is it from being the highest in religion, as is asserted, that it must be rejected by all who would force their way into the sanctuary of religion. To wish to have and hold a faith that is an echo, proves that a man is incapable of religion; to demand it of others, shows that there is no understanding of religion. You wish always to stand on your own feet and go your own way, and this worthy intent should not scare you from religion. Religion is no slavery, no captivity, least of all for your reason. You must belong to yourselves. Indeed, this is an indispensable condition of having any part in religion.

Every man, a few choice souls excepted, does, to be sure, require a guide to lead and stimulate, to wake his religious sense from its first slumber, and to give it its first direction. But this you accord to all powers and functions of the human soul, and why not to this one? For your satisfaction, be it said, that here, if anywhere, this tutelage is only a passing state. Hereafter, shall each man see with his own eyes, and shall produce some contribution to the treasures of religion; otherwise, he deserves no place in its kingdom, and receives none. You are right in despising the wretched echoes who derive their religion entirely from another, or depend on a dead writing, swearing by it and proving out of it.

Every sacred writing is in itself a glorious production, a speaking monument from the heroic time of religion, but, through servile reverence, it would become merely a mausoleum, a monument that a great spirit once was there, but is now no more. Did this spirit still live and work, he would look with love, and with a feeling of equality upon his work which yet could only be a weaker impress of himself. Not every person has religion who believes in a sacred writing, but only the man who has a lively and immediate understanding of it, and who, therefore, so far as he himself is concerned, could most easily do without it.

On Religion, Speeches . . ., pp. 90-1

*

The writer who in his younger days had produced the Speeches *exalting religion as feeling over theology as knowledge, nevertheless produced the highly systematic* The Christian Faith *in his mature years. As a work of dog-*

*matics this does indeed have a 'system' intended as an explication of the Prot-
estant faith. The mature Schleiermacher is no less emphatic on the primary
status of 'feeling' or 'consciousness' in religion. But now, as well as making
the distinction between religion and theology, he is also able to state suc-
cinctly the positive relationship between them. Early on in* The Christian
Faith, *therefore, the necessity of dogmatics for piety is stated. The rationale
is part anthropological — feelings are to be expressed and communicated,
and speech is the means of communication — and part christological. Christian piety is communicated from person to person, resulting in speech which
requires reflection since ultimately it is the speech of a community, and its
historical origin is in the 'self-proclamation' of Jesus himself. Only through
his speaking, and the speaking of the historical church, is the Christian pious
consciousness transmitted and fostered. Theology is the consideration of
this speech.*

THE RELATION OF DOGMATICS TO
CHRISTIAN PIETY

*Christian doctrines are accounts of the Christian religious affections set forth
in speech.*

1. All religious emotions, to whatever type and level of religion they
belong, have this in common with all other modifications of the affective
self-consciousness, that as soon as they have reached a certain stage and a
certain definiteness they manifest themselves outwardly by mimicry in
the most direct and spontaneous way, by means of facial features and
movements of voice and gesture, which we regard as their expression.
Thus we definitely distinguish the expression of devoutness from that of
a sensuous gladness or sadness, by the analogy of each man's knowledge
of himself. Indeed, we can even conceive that, for the purpose of maintaining the religious affections and securing their repetition and propagation (especially if they were common to a number of people), the elements of that natural expression of them might be put together into
sacred signs and symbolical acts, without the thought having perceptibly
come in between at all. But we can scarcely conceive such a low development of the human spirit, such a defective culture, and such a meagre use
of speech, that each person would not, according to the level of reflection
on which he stands, become in his various mental states likewise an
object to himself, in order to comprehend them in idea and retain them in
the form of thought. Now this endeavour has always directed itself particularly to the religious emotions; and this, considered in its own inward

meaning, is what our proposition means by an account of the religious affections. But while thought cannot proceed even inwardly without the use of speech, nevertheless there are, so long as it remains merely inward, fugitive elements in this procedure, which do indeed in some measure indicate the object, but not in such a way that either the formation or the synthesis of concepts (in however wide a sense we take the word 'concept') is sufficiently definite for communication. It is only when this procedure has reached such a point of cultivation as to be able to represent itself outwardly in definite speech, that it produces a real doctrine (*Glaubenssatz*), by means of which the utterances of the religious consciousness come into circulation more surely and with a wider range than is possible through the direct expression. But no matter whether the expression is natural or figurative, whether it indicates its object directly or only by comparison and delimitation, it is still a doctrine.

2. Now Christianity everywhere presupposes that consciousness has reached this stage of development. The whole work of the Redeemer himself was conditioned by the communicability of his self-consciousness by means of speech, and similarly Christianity has always and everywhere spread itself solely by preaching. Every proposition which can be an element of the Christian preaching (κήρυγμα) is also a doctrine, because it bears witness to the determination of the religious self-consciousness as inward certainty. And every Christian doctrine is also a part of the Christian preaching, because every such doctrine expresses as a certainty the approximation to the state of blessedness which is to be effected through the means ordained by Christ. But this preaching very soon split up into three different types of speech, which provide as many different forms of doctrine: the poetic, the rhetorical (which is directed partly outwards, as combative and commendatory, and partly inwards, as rather disciplinary and challenging), and finally the descriptively didactic. But the relation of communication through speech to communication through symbolic action varies very much according to time and place, the former having always retreated into the background in the Eastern Church (for when the letter of doctrine has become fixed and unalterable, it is in its effect much nearer to symbolic action than to free speech), and having become ever prominent in the Western Church. And in the realm of speech it is just the same with these three modes of communication. The relation in which they stand to each other, the general degree of richness, and the amount of living intercourse in which they unfold themselves, as they nourish themselves on one another and pass over into one another — these things testify not so much to the degree or

level of piety as rather to the character of the communion or fellowship and its ripeness for reflection and contemplation. Thus this communication is, on the one hand, something different from the piety itself, though the latter cannot, any more than anything else which is human, be conceived entirely separated from all communication. But, on the other hand, the doctrines in all their forms have their ultimate ground so exclusively in the emotions of the religious self-consciousness, that where these do not exist the doctrines cannot arise.

Dogmatic propositions are doctrines of the descriptively didactic type, in which the highest possible degree of definiteness is aimed at.

1. The poetic expression is always based originally upon a moment of exaltation which has come purely from within, a moment of enthusiasm or inspiration; the rhetorical upon a moment whose exaltation has come from without, a moment of stimulated interest which issues in a particular definite result. The former is purely descriptive (*darstellend*), and sets up in general outlines images and forms which each hearer completes for himself in his own peculiar way. The rhetorical is purely stimulative, and has, in its nature, to do for the most part with such elements of speech as, admitting of degrees of signification, can be taken in a wider or narrower sense, content if at the decisive moment they can accomplish the highest, even though they should exhaust themselves thereby and subsequently appear to lose somewhat of their force. Thus both of these forms possess a different perfection from the logical or dialectical perfection described in our proposition. But, nevertheless, we can think of both as being primary and original in every religious communion, and thus in the Christian Church, in so far as we ascribe to everyone in it a share in the vocation of preaching. For when anyone finds himself in a state of unusually exalted religious self-consciousness, he will feel himself called to poetic description, as that which proceeds from this state most directly. And, on the other hand, when anyone finds himself particularly challenged by insistent or favourable outward circumstances to attempt an act of preaching, the rhetorical form of expression will be the most natural to him for obtaining from the given circumstances the greatest possible advantage. But let us conceive of the comprehension and appropriation of what is given in a direct way in these two forms, as being now also wedded to language and thereby made communicable: then this cannot again take the poetic form, nor yet the rhetorical; but, being independent of that which was the important element in those two forms, and express-

ing as it does a consciousness which remains self-identical, it becomes, less as preaching than as confession (ὁμολογία), precisely that third form — the didactic — which, with its descriptive instruction, remains distinct from the two others, and is made up of the two put together, as a derivative and secondary form.

2. But let us confine ourselves to Christianity, and think of its distinctive beginning, namely, the self-proclamation of Christ, who, as subject of the divine revelation, could not contain in himself any distinction of stronger and weaker emotion, but could only partake in such a diversity through his common life with others. Then we shall not be able to take either the poetic or the rhetorical form of expression as the predominating, or even as the really primary and original, form of his self-proclamation. These have only a subordinate place in parabolic and prophetic discourses. The essential thing in his self-proclamation was that he had to bear witness regarding his ever unvarying self-consciousness out of the depths of its repose, and consequently not in poetic but in strictly reflective form; and thus had to set himself forth, while at the same time communicating his alone true objective consciousness of the condition and constitution of men in general, thus instructing by description or representation, the instruction being sometimes subordinate to the description, and sometimes *vice versa*. But this descriptively didactic mode of expression used by Christ is not included in our proposition, and such utterances of the Redeemer will hardly be set up anywhere as dogmatic propositions; they will only, as it were, provide the text for them. For in such essential parts of the self-proclamation of Christ the definiteness was absolute, and it is only the perfection of the apprehension and appropriation which reproduces these, that can be characterized by the endeavour after the greatest possible definiteness. Subordinate to these, however, there do appear genuinely dogmatic propositions in the discourse of Christ, namely, at those points at which he had to start from the partly erroneous and partly confused ideas current among his contemporaries.

3. As regards the poetic and rhetorical forms of expression, it follows directly from what we have said, that they may fall into apparent contradiction both with themselves and with each other, even when the self-consciousness which is indicated by different forms of expression is in itself one and the same. And a solution will only be possible, in the first place, when it is possible in interpreting propositions that are apparently contradictory to take one's bearings from the original utterances of Christ (a thing which can in very few cases be done directly), and, in the

second place, when the descriptively didactic expression, which has grown out of those three original forms put together, is entirely or largely free from those apparent contradictions. This, however, will not be possible of achievement so long as the descriptively didactic expression itself keeps vacillating between the emotional and the didactic, in its presentation to the catechumens or the community, and approaches sometimes more to the rhetorical and sometimes more to the figurative. It will only be possible in proportion as the aim indicated in our proposition underlies the further development of the expression and its more definite separation from the rhetorical and the poetic, both of which processes are essentially bound up with the need of settling the conflict. Now, of course, this demand, that the figurative expression be either exchanged for a literal one or transformed into such by being explained, and that definite limits be imposed on the corresponding element in the rhetorical expressions, is unmistakably the interest which science has in the formation of language; and it is mainly with the formation of religious language that we are here concerned. Hence dogmatic propositions develop to any considerable extent and gain recognition only in such religious communions as have reached a degree of culture in which science is organized as something distinct both from art and from business, and only in proportion as friends of science are found and have influence within the communion itself, so that the dialectical function is brought to bear on the utterances of the religious self-consciousness, and guides the expression of them. Such a union with organized knowledge has had a place in Christianity ever since the earliest ages of the Church, and therefore in no other religious communion has the form of the dogmatic proposition evolved in such strict separation from the other forms, or developed in such fulness.

Postscript. — This account of the origin of dogmatic propositions, as having arisen solely out of logically ordered reflection upon the immediate utterances of the religious self-consciousness, finds its confirmation in the whole of history. The earliest specimens of preaching preserved for us in the New Testament Scriptures already contain such propositions; and on closer consideration we can see in all of them, in the first place, their derivation from the original self-proclamation of Christ, and, in the second place, their affinity to figurative and rhetorical elements which, for permanent circulation, had to approximate more to the strictness of a formula. Similarly in later periods it is clear that the figurative language, which is always poetic in its nature, had the most decided influence upon the dogmatic language, and always preceded its development, and also that the majority of the dogmatic definitions were called forth by contradictions to which the rhetorical expressions had led.

But when the transformation of the original expressions into dogmatic propositions is ascribed to the logical or dialectical interest, this is to be understood as applying only to the form. A proposition which had originally proceeded from the speculative activity, however akin it might be to our propositions in content, would not be a dogmatic proposition. The purely scientific activity, whose task is the contemplation of existence, must, if it is to come to anything, either begin or end with the supreme being; and so there may be forms of philosophy containing propositions of speculative import about the supreme being which, in spite of the fact that they arose out of the purely scientific interest, are, when taken individually, difficult to distinguish from the corresponding propositions which arose purely out of reflection upon the religious emotions, but have been worked out dialectically. But when they are considered in their connections, these two indubitably show differences of the most definite kind. For dogmatic propositions never make their original appearance except in trains of thought which have received their impulse from religious moods of mind; whereas, not only do speculative propositions about the supreme being appear for the most part in purely logical or natural-scientific trains of thought, but even when they come in as ethical presuppositions or corollaries, they show an unmistakable leaning towards one or other of those two directions. Moreover, in the dogmatic developments of the earliest centuries, if we discount the quite unecclesiastical Gnostic schools, the influence of speculation upon the content of dogmatic propositions may be placed at zero. At a later time, certainly, when the classical organization of knowledge had fallen into ruins, and the conglomerate-philosophy of the Middle Ages took shape within the Christian Church, and at the same time came to exercise its influence upon the formation of dogmatic language, a confusion of the speculative with the dogmatic, and consequently a mingling of the two, was almost inevitable. But this was for both an imperfect condition, from which philosophy freed itself by means of the avowal, growing ever gradually louder, that at that time it had stood under the tutelage of ecclesiastical faith, and therefore under an alien law. Having, however, since then made so many fresh starts in its own proper development, it was able to escape from the wearisome task of inquiring exactly as to what kind of speculative propositions were at that time taken to be dogmatic, and *vice versa*. For the Christian Church, however, which is not in a position ever and anon to begin the development of its doctrine over again from the start, this separation is of the greatest importance, in order to secure that speculative matter (by which neither the poetic and rhetorical nor the popular expression can consent to be guided) may not continue to be offered to it as dogmatic. The Evangelical (Protestant) Church in particular is unanimous in feeling that the distinctive form of its dogmatic propositions does not depend on any form or school of philosophy, and has not proceeded at all from a speculative interest, but simply from the interest of satisfying the immediate self-consciousness solely through the means ordained by Christ, in their genuine and uncorrupted form. Thus it can consistently adopt as dogmatic propositions of its own no propositions except such as can show this derivation. Our dogmatic theology will not, however, stand on its proper ground and soil with the same assurance with which philosophy has so long stood upon its own, until the separation of the two types of proposition is so complete that, *e.g.*, so extraordinary a question as whether the same proposition can be true in philosophy and false in Christian theology, and *vice versa*, will no longer be asked, for the simple reason that a proposition cannot appear in the one context precisely as it appears in the other: however similar it sounds, a difference must always be assumed. But we are still very far from this goal, so long as people take pains to base or deduce dogmatic propositions in the speculative manner, or even set themselves to work up the products of speculative activity and the results of the study of religious affections into a single whole.   *The Christian Faith*, pp. 76-83

*

All propositions which the system of Christian doctrine has to establish can be regarded either as descriptions of human states, or as conceptions of divine attributes and modes of action, or as utterances regarding the constitution of the world; and all three forms have always subsisted alongside of each other.

1. Since the feeling of absolute dependence, even in the realm of redemption, only puts in an appearance, *i.e.* becomes a real self-consciousness in time, in so far as it is aroused by another determination of the self-consciousness and unites itself therewith, every formula for that feeling is a formula for a definite state of mind; and consequently all propositions of dogmatics must be capable of being set up as such formulae. But any such sensible determination of the self-consciousness points back to a determinant outside of the self-consciousness. Now since, in virtue of the general coherence always postulated in every human consciousness, this determinant always appears as a part thereof, any modification which has so arisen of the feeling of absolute dependence may be known if we can

get a description of that element of existence on which the state in question is based. Thus conceived, the dogmatic propositions become utterances regarding the constitution of the world, but only for the feeling of absolute dependence and with reference to it. Finally, not only is the feeling of absolute dependence in itself a co-existence of God in the self-consciousness, but the totality of being from which, according to the position of the subject, all determinations of the self-consciousness proceed, is comprehended under that feeling of dependence; and therefore all modifications of the higher self-consciousness may also be represented by our describing God as the basis of this togetherness of being in its various distributions.

2. If we compare these three possible forms with each other, it is clear that descriptions of human states of mind with this content can only be taken from the realm of inner experience, and that therefore in this form nothing alien can creep into the system of Christian doctrine; whereas, of course, utterances regarding the constitution of the world may belong to natural science, and conceptions of divine modes of action may be purely metaphysical; in which case both are engendered on the soil of science, and so belong to the objective consciousness and its conditions, and are independent of the inner experience and the facts of the higher self-consciousness. Thus these two forms (the first of which includes, of course, all propositions of a generally anthropological content) do not in themselves afford any guarantee that all propositions so conceived are genuinely dogmatic. Hence we must declare the description of human states of mind to be the fundamental dogmatic form; while propositions of the second and third forms are permissible only in so far as they can be developed out of propositions of the first form; for only on this condition can they be really authenticated as expressions of religious emotions.

3. If, then, all propositions which belong to the system of Christian doctrine can indisputably be expressed in the fundamental form, and propositions which assert attributes of God and qualities of the world must be reduced to propositions of that first form before we can be safe from the creeping in of alien and purely scientific propositions, then it would seem that Christian dogmatics has only to carry through consistently that fundamental form in order to complete the analysis of Christian piety, while the other two forms might be entirely set aside as superfluous. But if anyone were to attempt at the present time to treat Christian dogmatics in this way, his work would be left isolated without any historical support; and not only would it lack a really ecclesiastical character, but, however perfectly it rendered the content of Christian doctrine, it could not fulfil

the real purpose of all dogmatics. For since dogmatic language only came to be formed gradually out of the language which was current in the public communication of religion, the rhetorical and hymnic elements in this latter must have been especially favourable to the formation of conceptions of divine attributes, and indeed these became necessary in order that those expressions should be kept within due proportions. Similarly there arose, partly out of these, and partly out of the need for fixing the relation between the Kingdom of God and the world, utterances regarding the constitution of the world. Then, as the habit increased of treating metaphysics in combination with dogmatics, these two kinds of proposition became more numerous through the addition of similar ones of alien content, whereas the fundamental form naturally came to be left behind, and scarcely found any place except in presentations of a less scientific character. Hence a work which at the present time tried to confine itself entirely to the proper fundamental form would have no link with the past, and just for that reason would be of little practical use, either for purging the doctrinal system of alien elements, or for maintaining the clarity and verity of the rhetorical and poetic communications.

Thus the division outlined above will have to be fully worked out according to all these three forms of reflection upon the religious affections; but always and everywhere on this same basis, namely, the direct description of the religious affections themselves.

1. As the elements of dogmatics have taken shape in a fragmentary manner, and the science itself has therefore been fitted together externally out of these elements rather than generated organically, it is easy to understand how, generally speaking, propositions of all three kinds have been placed together without distinction, while none of the forms has been worked out with completeness and perspicuity. But such a state of affairs by no means satisfies the demands which may justly be made of dogmatic science; and in place of that we must of necessity (since, as we have seen, we cannot confine ourselves to the fundamental form alone) introduce that completeness of treatment which our proposition indicates. Nothing else can satisfy the present need. Now the general description of the Christian religion given above underlies this whole presentation so fundamentally that even our division of the subject-matter rests upon it. And so each individual section will have to be prefaced by a similar general description, to which in turn the further articulation of that section will have reference; and with this the ecclesiastical doctrines belonging

to the same province will be brought into connection: first, those which come nearest to the direct exposition of the religious affections, and then those which express the same thing in the form of divine attributes and qualities of the world.

2. From this it follows that the doctrine of God, as set forth in the totality of the divine attributes, can only be completed simultaneously with the whole system: whereas it is usually treated continuously and without a break, and before any other points of doctrine. But this divergence from the usual order can hardly be viewed as a disadvantage. For, not to mention the fact that divine attributes and modes of action which bear exclusively on the development of human soul-states (and this can be said of all the so-called moral attributes of God) cannot be understood without previous knowledge of these states, it is in general undeniable that the usual arrangement is peculiarly apt to conceal the relation of those doctrines both to the feeling of absolute dependence in general and to the fundamental facts of the Christian religion, and to give the impression of a quite independent speculative theory. Whereas our method not only makes that connection most luminous, but also places in closer juxtaposition things which can only be understood alongside of and by means of each other.

Postscript. — Further comparison of the schematism here set forth with those more common in our older and newer textbooks and systems would exceed the limits of an Introduction which is not obliged to be polemical. The method here adopted can only be justified by the finished argument itself.   *The Christian Faith,* pp. 125-128

*

The Brief Outline of the Study of Theology *was produced by Schleiermacher in 1810, coincident with the opening of the new University of Berlin. Schleiermacher had taken a leading part in the preparations and planning for this centre of learning and research, and was appointed to the chair of theology. The* Brief Outline *sets out Schleiermacher's comprehensive view of how all the theological disciplines relate to each other forming an academic subject with its own integrity, and yet, as an overall aim, shaped to serve the Church in its ministry. After an Introduction, the* Brief Outline *sets out Schleiermacher's three-fold structure of theology as Philosophical, Historical, and Practical Theology. The last-named is the culmination of theology, and it must be remembered that throughout his professorship Schleiermacher was also an active pastor and preacher in Berlin. Theology is always to be rooted in the human situation, and even dogmatics is not allowed to be an isolated ethereal subject on its own. It is subsumed under* Historical *Theology, being the theology of the Church in its* present *historical situation.*

INTRODUCTION

1. Theology, in the sense in which the word is constantly taken here, is a positive science, the parts of which are connected into a whole, only by their common relation to a determinate mode of faith, that is, a determinate form of the God-consciousness; those of Christian theology, therefore, by their relation to Christianity.

A positive science, namely, is, in general, a body of scientific elements which have a connectedness of their own — not as if, by a necessity arising out of the very idea of science, they formed a constituent part of the scientific organization — but only in so far as they are requisite in order to the solution of a practical problem. If, on the other hand, a rational theology has, in past times, been exhibited as an essential part of the scientific organization: it is true that this also has reference to the God of our God-consciousness; yet, being a speculative science, it is altogether a different thing from the theology with which we have to do.

2. A theology will be formed in connection with every determinate mode of faith, in the measure in which the latter is communicated rather by the aid of mental representations than of symbolical actions, and in the measure in which, at the same time, it obtains historical importance and independence; which theology, again, may be different for every different mode of faith, because it is connected with the individual character of the latter, as it respects both form and contents.

Only in the measure stated; because, in a community of small extent, the necessity for a theology, properly so called, does not arise; and because, in the case of a preponderance of symbolical actions, the ritual technology [*Technik*] which contains the interpretation of the latter, hardly deserves the name of a science.

3. Theology is not the business of all who belong to a particular Church, nor in so far as they belong to it; but only when and in so far as they have a share in the guidance of the Church: so that the contrast between such persons and the mass [of church members], and the prominent appearance of theology, are matters each of which implies the existence of the other.

The expression 'guidance of the Church' is here to be taken in the broadest sense, without reference to any one particular form.

4. The more the Church advances in its development, and the more numerous the regions of language and of culture over which it extends itself, the more many-partedly does theology also become organized; for which reason, Christian theology is that which has attained to the highest state of cultivation.

For, the more these two things come to pass, the more numerous are the differences, both in men's conceptions and in their modes of life, which theology has to connect together, and the more various the historical material which it has to investigate.

5. Christian theology, accordingly, is the collective embodiment of those branches of scientific knowledge and those rules of art, without the possession and application of which a harmonious guidance of the Christian Church, that is a Christian church-government, is not possible.

This, namely, is the relation laid down in 1; for the Christian faith, in and for itself, does not need such an apparatus in order to its efficacious activity, either in the individual soul, or in the circumstances connected with the social life of the family.

6. The said branches of knowledge, when they are acquired and possessed without reference to the government of the Church, cease to have a theological character, and become assignable to those sciences to which, according to the nature of their contents, they respectively belong.

These sciences are, then, according to the nature of the case, philology and history, psychology and morals; together with certain disciplinae which are off-shoots from the latter — the doctrine of art in general, and the philosophy of religion.

7. By virtue of this relation, the variety of knowledge referred to is, to the will to be efficient in the guidance of the Church, as the body to the soul.

Without this will, the unity of theology is lost; and its parts become disintegrated into the different elements of which it is composed.

8. But, as these heterogeneous branches of knowledge are connected into such a whole, only by the presence of an interest in Christianity, so also this interest in Christianity can manifest itself in an appropriate activity, only by being coupled with the possession of the said branches of knowledge.

According to 2, a guidance of the Church can proceed only from a highly developed historical consciousness; but it can become truly useful, moreover, only by means of a clear knowledge respecting the relations of [men's] religious states towards all that are of a different kind.

9. If we conceive of an interest in religion and a scientific spirit, existing

in a state of union, in the highest degree and in the greatest possible equilibrium, and with a view to both theory and practice — we have the idea of a *prince of the Church*.

This appellation for the theological ideal is, it must be admitted, appropriate only when the disparity between the members of the Church is great, and when, at the same time, the exercise of influence over an extensive region of the Church is possible. But it seems more suitable than the term 'father of the Church', which has already received the stamp of currency for a particular circle; and, for the rest, it does not in the least involve any allusion to an official relation.

10. If we conceive of this equilibrium as done away: then, he who has, in his own person, cultivated chiefly the knowledge that relates to Christianity, is a theologian in the more restricted sense of the term; and he, on the other hand, who cultivates especially the activity which has to do with the government of the Church, is a *minister* [Kleriker].

This natural sundering of the two characters shows itself outwardly with different degrees of prominence at different times; and the more it prevails, the more indispensable is a lively interaction between the two classes, in order that the Church may maintain its ground. For the rest, the term *theologian* will, in the remaining portion of this work, be taken for the most part in the broader sense, as comprehending both tendencies.

11. Every dealing with any branches of theological knowledge as such, whatever its nature, is always to be reckoned within the department of Church-guidance; and whatever process of thought — whether it be more of a constructive, or more of a regulative character — may be pursued concerning that activity which has to do with the *guidance of the Church* — the said thinking always belongs to the department of the theologian in the stricter sense of the term.

Even the scientific activity of the theologian must have for its object the promotion of the Church's welfare — and partakes, therefore, of a clerical character; and all technical prescriptions with regard even to the properly clerical forms of activity, have their place within the circle of the theological sciences.

12. If, according to what has been said, all true theologians also take part in the guidance of the Church, and all who are active in the government of the Church also have their life in theology; it follows that, notwithstanding the one-sided tendency of each class, both these characteristics — an interest in the well-being of the Church, and a scientific spirit — must be united in every individual.

For as in the opposite case, the scholar would no longer be a theologian, but would merely be occupied in working up certain elements of theology in the spirit of that particular science from which they might happen to be derived; so also the activity of the minister would be, not a guidance technically correct, or even directed by prudent thoughtfulness, but simply a confused exercise of influence.

13. Every one who finds himself called to the exercise of the guiding activity in the Church, determines for himself the mode of his working, according to the measure in which one or the other of these two elements preponderates in him.

Without such an inward calling, no one is in truth either a theologian or a minister; but neither of these modes of working is in any way dependent upon the circumstance, that the government of the Church constitutes the basis of a particular civil status.

14. No one can be perfectly possessed of the various branches of theological knowledge in their full extent; partly because every discipline in particular is susceptible of an infinite development in detail, and partly because the diversity of *disciplinae* requires a variety of talents, which can hardly be all possessed in an equal degree by any one individual.

This capability of development, even to the extent of an infinity of detail, applies as well to all that is historical, and all that is connected with the historical, as to all technical rules in relation to the variety of cases that may possibly arise.

15. If, however, every one should determine on this account to confine himself wholly to some one part of theology; the whole would have existence neither in any one nor in all together.

Not in the latter — because, with such a kind of distribution, no cooperation could take place between the individual occupants of different departments; nay, strictly speaking, there could not be even a communication amongst them.

16. A mastery, therefore, of all the theological *disciplinae* in their essential features, is the condition under which alone even but one of them can be dealt with in the manner and the spirit which are proper to theology.

For only thus — when every individual, along with his own particular discipline, possesses also a general comprehension of the whole — is it possible for communication to take place between all and sundry; and only thus is it possible for each, by means of the discipline to which he specially devotes himself, to exercise an efficient influence upon the whole.

17. Whether a man labours with a view to the perfecting of a particular

discipline, and what discipline he selects for this purpose, are matters which are determined chiefly by the peculiar character of the talent possessed by the individual, but also, in part, by his views with regard to the prevailing need of the Church at the time.

The prosperous advancement of theology in general, depends in great measure upon the satisfaction of this condition — that there shall be found, at any and every given period, distinguished talents for that, the onward cultivation of which is most needed. Those persons, however, can always be efficient in the greatest variety of ways, who have mastered the largest number of disciplinae in a certain degree of proportionateness, without aiming at special proficiency in any one of them; whereas, on the contrary, those who devote themselves exclusively to a single department, are capable of accomplishing most as scholars.

18. The following, therefore, are matters which are indispensable to every theologian. In the first place, a correct view of the mutual connection existing between the different parts of theology, and of the particular value of each in relation to the common object. In the next place, a knowledge of the internal organization of every discipline in particular, and of those leading topics included in it, which are the most essential with regard to the entire connection. Further, an acquaintance with those helps by means of which he may at any time procure immediately whatever information he may require. Finally, practice and certainty in the application of those precautions which are necessary, in order to his making the best and most correct use of the results presented by the labours of others.

The first two particulars are frequently united, under the title *Theological Encyclopaedia;* and the third, too (namely, *Theological Bibliography*), is possibly drawn into the same connection. The fourth is a section of the art of criticism which has not been worked out as a separate discipline, and concerning which but few rules can be given in the way of teaching; so that its attainment depends almost exclusively upon the possession of a certain natural capacity, and upon practice.

19. Every one who wishes to make himself master of a particular discipline in its whole extent, must make it his object to sift and to supplement what others have already accomplished therein.

Without an effort of this kind he would, whatever the completeness of his knowledge, be but a mere depositary of tradition; a mental activity which is, of all, the most subordinate and the least important.

20. The encyclopaedian outline which is intended to be given here,

relates merely to the first of the general requisites above mentioned (18); only that it deals, at the same time, with the individual disciplinae in the same manner as with the whole.

Such an outline is usually called a formal encyclopaedia; in contradistinction to which, those which are denominated material are intended rather to present a brief sketch of the leading contents of the individual disciplinae, but are less exact in setting forth their organization. Inasmuch as encyclopaedia is, in its very nature, the first introduction to the study of theology, it certainly has connected with it, also, the technology of the order according to which one ought to proceed in the said study — or what is usually called methodology. But this, in so far as it does not present itself spontaneously, upon an exhibition of the inward connection [of the various theological disciplinae], depends, in the present condition of our academical institutions, as well as of our literature, too much upon accidental circumstances, to make it worth while that we should constitute this a particular section, even, of the discipline with which we are occupied.

21. There is no such thing as a knowledge with regard to Christianity, so long as men — instead of endeavouring, on the one hand, to understand the essential nature of Christianity in its contrast to other modes of faith and other churches — and on the other, to understand the essential nature of religion and of religious communities in connection with the other activities of the human mind — content themselves with a merely empirical mode of apprehension.

The fact that the essential nature of Christianity is connected with a certain history, merely determines more particularly the mode of the understanding insisted upon; it is a circumstance which cannot prejudice the problem itself.

22. Unless religious communities are to be looked upon as practical mistakes, it must be possible to show that the existence of such associations is a necessary element in order to the development of the human mind.

The first part of the alternative has recently been exemplified in the 'Reflections on the Essential Nature of Protestantism'. What constitutes atheism, properly so called, is just a looking at religion itself in the very same way.

23. The farther development of the notion of religious communities must also yield an indication, in what manner and in what degree one may be different from another; and likewise, how that which is individually characteristic in the fellowships of faith which are historically given, is related to these differences [which are conceived of as possible]. And the

place for this is in the philosophy of religion.

The latter name, employed in this (certainly not yet altogether usual) sense, designates a discipline which, in relation to the idea of the Church, stands in the same position with regard to ethics, as a certain other discipline which has to do with the idea of the state, and a third, which has to do with the idea of art.

24. All that is necessary in order to a proper exhibition (upon the basis just pointed out), of the essential nature of Christianity, by virtue of which it is a peculiar mode of faith — as also of the form of the Christian community — and, at the same time, of the manner in which each of these, again, is subdivided and differenced — all this, taken together, forms the division of Christian Theology which we call *philosophical theology*.

The appellation is justified, on the one hand, by the connection of the problem involved with the science of ethics, and on the other, by the nature of the contents of that problem; which has to do for the most part with notional definitions. Such a discipline, however, has not hitherto been exhibited or recognized as a unity, because the necessity for it, in the form in which it is here conceived of, does not arise until we come to deal with the problem of organizing the theological sciences. Still, the matter of the discipline in question has already been worked up with a tolerable degree of completeness, in consequence of certain practical necessities which have grown out of various circumstances of the age.

25. The purpose of Christian church-guidance is both extensively and intensively conservative and progressive; and the knowledge relating to this activity forms a technology which we, grouping together all its different branches, designate by the name, *practical theology*.

In the cultivation of this discipline, too, up to the present time, there has been a very unequal distribution of the labour applied. The details, namely, of official duty, have been discussed with great copiousness; but, on the other hand, that which relates to the work of guidance and arrangement upon the whole, has received but scanty attention — indeed, the connection proper to a disciplinary treatment of the subject has been observed only with regard to individual portions of it.

26. But church-guidance requires also that there shall be a knowledge of the whole that is to be guided, as viewed in its existing condition; which condition, (since the whole referred to is of a historical character) is capable of being understood only when it is viewed as a product of the past; and this apprehension [of the past and the present as antecedent and consequent, and of the latter as explained by the former], in its

entire extent, constitutes *historical theology,* in the wider sense of the term.

The present cannot be rightly dealt with as the germ of a future which is to correspond more nearly to the [true] notion [of the thing referred to — *i.e.* Christianity organized in the form of a Christian community], unless it is perceived how this present has itself been developed out of the past.

27. If historical theology exhibits every point of time [in the history of Christianity] in its true relation to the idea of Christianity; it is at once not merely the foundation of practical, but also the verification of philosophical theology.

It will be both, of course, in so much the greater degree, the more manifold the developments which are already presented to our view. For this reason, church-guidance was, at first, a matter rather of correct instinct [than of careful study], and philosophical theology manifested itself in attempts of but little power.

28. Historical theology, accordingly, forms the proper body of theological study; and is connected with science, strictly so called, by means of philosophical, and with the active Christian life by means of practical theology.

Historical theology also includes within itself, historically, the practical division of the science; since the correct understanding of any particular period must needs show also what were the leading views in accordance with which the Church was governed during that period. And by reason of the connection which was pointed out in 27, philosophical theology must also, in like manner, be mirrored in historical theology.

29. If philosophical theology, as a discipline, were brought to a proper degree of perfection, it might form the commencement of the entire course of theological study. As it is, on the contrary, the individual portions of it are to be acquired only in a fragmentary manner, in connection with the study of historical theology; but even this can take place only when the study of ethics — which we have to regard as being at the same time the science of the principles of history — has gone before.

Without a constant reference to ethical principles, even the study of historical theology can be nothing but an unconnected preliminary exercise, and must needs degenerate into unintelligent tradition. This enables us, to a great extent, to explain the state of confusion in which the theological disciplinae are so often presented, and the total want of certainty which is manifested in their application to the guidance of the Church.

30. Not only is it impossible for the technology which is yet wanting for the purposes of church-guidance, to present itself, except as a result of the perfecting of historical by means of philosophical theology; but even the customary imparting of rules respecting the details of official duty, can work only in the manner of a mechanical prescription unless it is preceded by the study of historical theology.

The consequences of occupying one's self prematurely with this technology, are a practical superficiality, and an indifference to scientific progress.

31. Within this trilogy — philosophical, historical, and practical theology — the entire course of theological study is included: and the most natural order for the present outline is, indisputably, to begin with philosophical theology, and conclude with practical.

Brief Outline of the Study of Theology, pp. 91-103

*

DOGMATIC THEOLOGY

196. A *dogmatic* treatment of the system of doctrine, apart from personal conviction, is not possible; on the other hand, it is not necessary that all those elaborations of it which have reference to the same period of the same church-community should agree amongst themselves.

One might be disposed to deduce both the propositions which are here contradicted, from this fact, that the dogmatic treatment has to do merely with the doctrine current at the given time. But the man to whom this doctrine is not a matter of conviction — though he may, indeed, furnish a report concerning it, and concerning the manner, too, in which its inward connection is conceived of — cannot establish this connection by means of the exhibition which he gives of it. Yet it is the latter circumstance alone which gives to the mode of treatment a dogmatic character; the former is merely a historical exhibition, such as may be given in like manner of all systems by one and the same man, if possessed of the requisite knowledge. — On the other hand, there is, in the Evangelical Church, no necessity for entire agreement, for this reason, that even at one and the same time, different views have currency side by side. Everything namely, is to be looked upon as having currency, which is officially asserted and officially heard, without calling forth an official contradiction. The limits of this difference, therefore, certainly, are sometimes broader and sometimes narrower, according to time and circumstances.

197. We should not give the name of a system of dogmatics, either to the laying down and supporting by proof of a body of propositions which were prevailingly characterized by a deviation from the views generally current, and which expressed merely the conviction of the individual; or, on the other hand, to such a system as, in a period marked by the prevalence of diverse theories, would only consent to admit that, in regard to which no controversy existed.

No one will deny the former part of this assertion. But the controversial question, too, proceeding thence — as to whether text-books can be admitted to have a dogmatic character, when they merely give a historical report concerning the current system of doctrine, and, on the other hand, lay down in connection with proof such propositions, exclusively, as might have an official prohibition adduced against them — serves as a further confirmation of our notion. — A purely irenical composition of this kind will, for the most part, prove so meagre and indefinite, that there will be everywhere a want, not only of the middle terms which are necessary to effect a proof, but also of that precision in the definition of notions, which is necessary to procure for the delineation the confidence of the reader.

198. The immediate use of dogmatic theology in connection with church-guidance is, to show in how many ways, and up to what point, the principle of the current period has developed itself on every side; and how the germs of improved configurations which belong to the future are related thereto. At the same time it furnishes the department of practice with the norm for the popular mode of expression; by way of guarding against the recurrence of old forms of confusion, and of preventing by anticipation the occurrence of new ones.

This practical interest is to be referred exclusively to the conservative function of church-guidance; and it was from this that the gradual formation of the system of dogmatics originally proceeded. The division enunciated in the former sentence of the paragraph is explained by what was said in general with regard to the contents of every individual momentum.

199. In every momentum which admits of a separate delineation, that which, in the system of doctrine, is derived from the last preceding epoch, bears in the most marked degree the character of having been ecclesiastically determined; and that, on the contrary, which serves rather to prepare the way for the succeeding epoch, presents itself as originating with individuals.

The former seems ecclesiastically defined, not only in a higher degree

153

than the latter, but also in a higher degree than that which has been derived by transmission from earlier periods. — There is the more reason for tracing back the latter to individuals merely, in proportion as we may be unable, for the present, distinctly to anticipate a new configuration.

200. All points of doctrine which are developed by the dominant principle of the period, must agree amongst themselves; whereas, on the contrary, all others, so long as we can but say of them that they have not this for their point of departure, appear as forming an unconnected plurality.

The dominant principle itself, however, may be variously apprehended, and this may give rise to a number of dogmatic delineations, connected in themselves, respectively, but differing from one another, and all laying claim, perhaps not without reason, to a like degree of ecclesiasticality. — When the heterogenous, isolated elements become connected, they either present themselves to view as constituting a new apprehension of the principle already dominant, or else they announce the development of a new principle.

201. As a complete acquaintance with the state of doctrine embraces not merely that which is essentially interwoven with the further development, but also that which, although as a personal theory it was not unimportant, yet, as such, again disappears; so also must a comprehensive dogmatic method of treatment give a proper degree of attention to everything that has a contemporaneous existence in the Church community with which it is connected.

A place will always, of necessity, be found for this, if, in the attempt to establish the connection laid down [that is, as being the true inward connection of the system of doctrine] comparisons and parallels are not neglected.

202. A dogmatic delineation is perfect in proportion to the degree in which it possesses, along with the assertory character, a divinatory character also.

In the former is manifested the author's confidence in his own theory; in the latter, the clearness with which he apprehends the existing state of things upon the whole.

203. Every element of doctrine that is constructed in the spirit of a desire to hold fast that which is already matter of general acknowledgment, along with the natural inferences therefrom — is of an orthodox character; every element constructed with a tendency to keep the system of doctrine in a state of mobility, and to make room for other modes of apprehension, is heterodox.

It seems to be too great a limitation of these terms, when they are applied exclusively to the relation which doctrinal opinions bear to a certain norm that has been set up; the same antagonism may also be found where there is no such norm in existence. Rather may we say that, according to the explanation given above, it is possible for the symbol to have its own origin from the orthodox tendency; and so it has happened, often enough. What, on the other hand, may appear strange in our explanation, is, that it does not refer at all to the contents of the propositions, in and for themselves; and yet this, also, is easily justified upon a closer reflection.

204. Both classes of elements are alike important, as in relation to the historical progress of Christianity in general, so also in relation to every important momentum as such.

As, notwithstanding any degree of uniformity which might exist, there would still be no true unity without the former class of elements; so, notwithstanding any measure of diversity, there would still be no conscious, free mobility without the latter.

205. It is false orthodoxy, to wish for a continued retention, in the system of dogmatic treatment, of that also, which, in so far as the public communications of the Church are concerned, is already completely antiquated; and which, moreover, does not, by its scientific expression, exert any determinate influence upon other particulars of doctrine.

It is evidently necessary that a doctrinal definition to which these remarks become applicable, should be rendered moveable again, and that the inquiry should be conducted back to the point at which it stood previously.

206. It is false heterodoxy, to manifest hostility, in the system of dogmatic treatment, to such formulae as have their well-grounded point of support in the communications of the Church; and the scientific expression of which, too, does not create any confusion as it respects their relation to other particulars of Christian doctrine.

This principle, therefore, does not by any means extend to justify that servile spirit of accommodation, which would allow the retention of all that happens to be used by a number of persons for the purpose of edification, even though it may not be in accordance with the fundamental doctrines of our faith.

207. A dogmatic delineation [of the system of doctrine] intended for the Evangelical Church, will avoid both these forms of irregularity: and notwithstanding that mobility of the letter which we sought to vindicate, will still find it possible to be orthodox in regard to all the chief particu-

lars of doctrine; but it will also be compelled — notwithstanding that it confines itself exclusively to that which has currency — to give a start, in particular places, to some things which are heterodox, also.

The natural relation of the two elements will — if this discipline is symmetrically developed from its proper notion — always be that which is here laid down; and a change in this respect will become necessary, only when one of the two extremes has been for a long time predominant.

208. Every dogmatic theologian who either innovates, or cries up what is old, in a one-sided manner, is but an imperfect organ of the Church: and if occupying a falsely heterodox stand-point, he will declare even the most strictly proper orthodoxy to be false; and if a falsely orthodox standpoint, he will combat even the mildest and most inevitable heterodoxy as a destructive innovation.

These fluctuations have been the principal cause which has hitherto almost continually prevented the dogmatic theology of the Evangelical Church from developing itself in a peaceful progress.

Brief Outline of the Study of Theology, pp. 162-7

4

HERMENEUTICS:
CONVERSATION WITH HISTORY[*]

Schleiermacher's decisive contribution to the modern study of the interpre-
tation of written texts was made through his lecturing, which began at Halle
and continued throughout his time in Berlin. Apart, however, from a few
paragraphs in the Brief Outline of the Study of Theology *Schleiermacher*
published virtually nothing on the subject, and subsequent scholars have
been dependent upon the manuscript notes of his lectures, and some taken
by students. Attempting to reconstruct the scope and development of Schlei-
ermacher's thought on hermeneutics has itself therefore provided an intri-
cate hermeneutical task for students! There has also been some controversy
since H. Kimmerle, who in 1959 produced the most comprehensive critical
edition of Schleiermacher's notes, suggested that taken as a whole Schleier-
macher's lectures do not justify the 'subjectivist' emphasis in his hermeneu-
tics to the extent which Wilhelm Dilthey saw as his characteristic insight.
The 'psychological' element in Schleiermacher emerged particularly in his
later lectures, according to Kimmerle. Those of the earlier and middle peri-
ods are at least equally concerned with the objective, linguistic nature of the
text, and only later does Schleiermacher concentrate more on the 'thought'
as some ideal, inner reality which can exist apart from the language. The
main text selected here comes from the middle period of Schleiermacher's
Berlin years, a series of notes for lectures begun in 1819. In the critical
edition, these are supplemented by marginal notes dating from 1828.

MANUSCRIPT 3

HERMENEUTICS: THE COMPENDIUM OF 1819

Begun on April 19, 1819 with four lectures per week

I. 1. At present there is no general hermeneutics as the art of understanding but only a variety of specialized hermeneutics. Ast's explanation,
p. 172; Wolf, p. 37.

    1. Hermeneutics deals only with the art of understanding, not with the
presentation of what has been understood. The presentation of what

[*] See also pp. 46ff. above.

157

has been understood would be only one special part of the art of speaking and writing, and that part could be done only by relying upon general principles.

2. Nor is hermeneutics concerned exclusively with difficult passages of texts written in foreign languages. To the contrary, it presupposes a familiarity with both the contents and the language of a text. Assuming such familiarity, difficulties with particular passages of a text arise only because the easier ones have not been understood. Only an artistically sound understanding can follow what is being said and written.

3. It is commonly believed that by following general principles one can trust one's common sense. But if that is so, by following special principles, one can trust one's natural instincts.

2. It is very difficult to assign general hermeneutics its proper place among the sciences.

1. For a long time it was treated as an appendix to Logic, but since Logic is no longer seen as dealing with applied matters, this can no longer be done. The philosopher *per se* has no interest in developing hermeneutical theory. He seldom works at understanding, because he believes that it occurs by necessity.

2. Moreover, philology has become positivistic. Thus its way of treating hermeneutics results in a mere aggregate of observations.

3. Since the art of speaking and the art of understanding stand in relation to each other, speaking being only the outer side of thinking, hermeneutics is a part of the art of thinking, and is therefore philosophical.

1. Yet these two are to be related in such a way that the art of interpretation at once depends upon and presupposes composition. They are parallel in the sense that artless speaking does not require any art to be understood.

II. 4. Speaking is the medium for the communality of thought, and for this reason rhetoric and hermeneutics belong together and both are related to dialectics.

1. Indeed, a person thinks by means of speaking. Thinking matures by means of internal speech, and to that extent speaking is only developed thought. But whenever the thinker finds it necessary to fix what he has thought, there arises the art of speaking, that is, the transformation of original internal speaking, and interpretation becomes necessary.

2. Hermeneutics and rhetoric are intimately related in that every act of understanding is the reverse side of an act of speaking, and one must grasp the thinking that underlies a given statement.

3. Dialectics relies on hermeneutics and rhetoric because the development of all knowledge depends on both speaking and understanding.

5. Just as every act of speaking is related to both the totality of the language and the totality of the speaker's thoughts, so understanding a speech always involves two moments: to understand what is said in the context of the language with its possibilities, and to understand it as a fact in the thinking of the speaker.

1. Every act of speaking presupposes a given language. This statement could also be reversed, not only for the absolutely first act of speaking in a language, but also for its entire history, because language develops through speaking. In every case communication presupposes a shared language and therefore some knowledge of the language. Whenever something comes between the internal speaking and its communication, one must turn to the art of speaking. So the art of speaking is due in part to a speaker's anxiety that something in his use of language may be unfamiliar to the hearer.

2. Every act of speaking is based on something having been thought. This statement, too, could be reversed, but with respect to communication the first formulation holds because the art of understanding deals only with an advanced stage of thinking.

3. Accordingly, each person represents one locus where a given language takes shape in a particular way, and his speech can be understood only in the context of the totality of the language. But then too he is a person who is constantly developing spirit, and his speaking can be understood as only one moment in this development in relation to all others.

6. Understanding takes place only in the coinherence of these two moments.

1. An act of speaking cannot even be understood as a moment in a person's development unless it is also understood in relation to the language. This is because the linguistic heritage [*Angeborenheit der Sprache*] modifies the spirit.

2. Nor can an act of speaking be understood as a modification of the language unless it is also understood as a moment in the development of the person (later addition: because an individual is able to influence a language by speaking, which is how a language develops.)

III. 7. These two hermeneutical tasks are completely equal, and it would be incorrect to label grammatical interpretation the 'lower' and psychological interpretation the 'higher' task.

159

1. Psychological interpretation is higher when one regards the language exclusively as a means by which a person communicates his thoughts. Then grammatical interpretation is employed only to clear away initial difficulties.

2. Grammatical interpretation and language, because it conditions the thinking of every person, are higher only when one regards the person and his speaking exclusively as occasions for the language to reveal itself. Then psychological interpretation and the life of the individual become subordinate considerations.

3. From this dual relation it is evident that the two tasks are completely equal.

8. The task is finally resolved when either side could be replaced by the other, though both must be treated, that is to say, when each side is treated in such a way that the treatment of the other side produces no change in the result.

1. Both grammatical and psychological interpretation must be treated, even though either can substitute for the other, in accordance with II, 6.

2. Each side is complete only when it makes the other superfluous and contributes to its work. This is because language can be learned only by understanding what is spoken, and because the inner make-up of a person, as well as the way in which external objects affect him, can only be understood from his speaking.

9. Interpretation is an art.

1. Each side is itself an art. For each side constructs something finite and definite from something infinite and indefinite. Language is infinite because every element is determinable in a special way by the other elements.

This statement also applies to psychological interpretation, for every intuition of a person is itself infinite. Moreover, external influences on a person will have ramifications which trail off into infinity. Such a construction, however, cannot be made by means of rules which may be applied with self-evident certainty.

2. In order to complete the grammatical side of interpretation it would be necessary to have a complete knowledge of the language. In order to complete the psychological side it would be necessary to have a complete knowledge of the person. Since in both cases such complete knowledge is impossible, it is necessary to move back and forth between the grammatical and psychological sides, and no rules can stipulate exactly how to do this.

10. The success of the art of interpretation depends on one's linguistic competence and on one's ability for knowing people.

1. By 'linguistic competence' I am not referring to a facility for learning foreign languages. The distinction between one's mother tongue and a foreign language is not at issue here. Rather, I refer to one's command of language, one's sensitivity to its similarities and differences, etc. — It could be claimed that in this respect rhetoric and hermeneutics must always belong together. But hermeneutics requires one kind of competence, rhetoric requires another, and the two are not the same. To be sure, both hermeneutics and rhetoric require linguistic competence, but hermeneutics makes use of that competence in a different way.

2. One's ability to know people refers especially to a knowledge of the subjective element determining the composition of thoughts. Thus, just as with hermeneutics and rhetoric, so with hermeneutics and the artful description of persons, there is no permanent connection. Nonetheless, many errors in hermeneutics are due to a lack of this talent or to a flaw in its application.

3. Insofar as these abilities are universal gifts of nature, hermeneutics is everybody's concern. To the extent that a person is deficient in one of these talents, he is hampered, and the other gift can do no more than help him choose wisely from the suggestions made by others.

IV. 11. The art of interpretation is not equally interested in every act of speaking. Some instances fail to spark its interest at all, while others engage it completely. Most, however, fall somewhere between these two extremes.

1. A statement may be regarded to be of no interest when it is neither important as a human act nor significant for the language. It is said because the language maintains itself only by constant repetition. But that which is only already available and repeated is itself of no significance. Conversations about the weather. But these statements are not absolutely devoid of significance, since they may be said to be 'minimally significant', in that they are constructed in the same way as more profound statements.

2. A statement may be of maximum significance for one side of interpretation or the other. It is maximally significant for the grammatical side when it is linguistically creative to an exceptional degree and minimally repetitive: classical texts. A statement is maximally significant for the psychological side when it is highly individualized and minimally commonplace: original texts. The term 'absolute' is reserved for

statements that achieve a maximum of both linguistic creativity and individuality: works of genius [*das Genialische*].

3. 'Classical' and 'original' statements cannot be transitory, but must be definitive for later productions. Indeed, even absolute texts are influenced to some degree by earlier and more common ones.

12. Although both sides of interpretation should always be applied, they will always be weighted differently.

1. This is because a statement that is grammatically insignificant is not necessarily psychologically insignificant and *vice versa*. Thus, in dealing with a text that is in one respect insignificant, we cannot reach what is significant in it by applying both sides equally.

2. A minimum of psychological interpretation is appropriate when what is to be interpreted is predominately objective. Pure history, especially in its details, whereas the overall viewpoint requires more psychological interpretation since it is always subjectively affected. Epics. Commercial records that can be used as historical sources. Didactic treatments in the strict sense on every subject. In such cases the subjective is not applied as a moment of interpretation, but results from the interpretation. A minimum of grammatical interpretation in conjunction with a maximum of psychological is appropriate in dealing with letters, especially personal letters. There is a point of transition along the continuum from historical and didactic pieces to personal letters. Lyric poetry. Polemics?

13. There are no methods of interpretation other than those discussed above.

1. For example, in the dispute over the historical interpretation of the New Testament there emerged the curious view that there are several different kinds of interpretation. To the contrary, only historical interpretation can do justice to the rootedness of the New Testament authors in their time and place. (Awkward expressions. Concepts of time.) But historical interpretation is wrong when it denies Christianity's power to create new concepts and attempts to explain it in terms of conditions which were already present in the time. It is proper to reject such a one-sided historical interpretation, but it is improper to reject historical interpretation altogether. The crux of the matter, then, lies in the relationship between grammatical and psychological interpretation, since new concepts developed from the distinctive manner in which the authors were affected.

V. 2. Historical interpretation is not to be limited to gathering historical data. That task should be done even before interpretation begins, since it is the means for re-creating the relationship between the speaker and the original audience, and interpretation cannot begin until that relationship has been established.

3. Allegorical interpretation does not deal with allegories where the figurative meaning is the only one intended, regardless of whether the stories are based on truth, as in the parable of the sower, or on fiction, as in the parable of the rich man, but to cases where the literal meaning, in its immediate context, gives rise to a second, figurative meaning. Such instances cannot be dismissed by citing the general principle that a given passage can have only one meaning, that is, its usual grammatical one. Allusions always involve a second meaning, and if a reader does not catch this second meaning along with the first, he misses one of the intended meanings, even though he may be able to follow the literal one. At the same time, to claim that there is an allusion where there actually is none is also an error. An allusion occurs when an additional meaning is so entwined with the main train of thought that the author believes it would be easily recognized by another person. These additional meanings are not merely occasional and unimportant, but just as the whole world is posited ideally in man, it is always considered real, although only as a dark shadow-image. There is a parallelism of different stages [*Reihen*] in the large and the small, and therefore there can occur in any one something from another: parallelism of the physical and the ethical of music and painting. But these parallelisms are to be noted only when figurative expressions indicate them. There is a special reason why parallelism occurs without clues, especially in Homer and in the Bible.

VI. This accounts for the singularity of Homer as a book for general education and of the Old Testament as a body of literature from which everything is to be drawn. To this it should be added that the mythical contents in both are developed into esoteric [*gnomische*] philosophy on the one hand and into history on the other. But there is no technical interpretation for myth because it cannot be traced back to a single person, and the shifting in ordinary understanding between the literal and figurative meanings draws out the double meaning most clearly. In the case of the New Testament, however, the situation was quite different, and a method based on two principles was developed. First, in keeping with the close connection between the two testaments, the type of explanation used in interpreting the Old Testament was applied to the New Testament as well, and this type of interpretation was carried over into scholarly interpretations. The second principle was the idea, more thoroughly applied to the New Testament than to the Old, that the Holy Spirit was the author. Since the Holy Spirit could not be conceived as an individual consciousness that changed in time, there arose a tendency to find everything in each part. Universal truths or particular instructions satisfy this inclination, but the results which are produced are in the main unconnected and, taken in isolation, insignificant.

4. Incidentally, the question arises whether on account of the Holy Spirit the Scriptures must be treated in a special way. This question cannot be answered by a dogmatic decision about inspiration, because such a decision itself depends upon interpretation.

1. We must not make a distinction between what the apostles spoke and what they wrote, for the Church had to be built on their speeches.

2. But for this reason we must not suppose that their writings were addressed to all of Christendom, for in fact each text was addressed to specific people, and their writings could not be properly understood in the future unless these first readers could understand them. But these first readers would have looked for what was specifically related to their own situations, and from this material they had to derive the whole truth of Christianity. Our interpretation must take this fact into account, and we must assume that even if the authors had been merely passive tools of the Holy Spirit, the Holy Spirit could have spoken through them only as they themselves would have spoken.

VII. 5. The worst offender in this respect is cabalistic interpretation which labours to find everything in the particular elements and their signs. — One sees that whatever efforts can be legitimately called interpretation, there are no other types except those based on the different relationships between the two sides we have noted.

14. The distinction between artful and artless interpretation is not based on the difference between what is familiar to us and what is unfamiliar, or between what is spoken and what is written. Rather, it is based on the fact that we want to understand with precision some things and not others.

1. Were the art of interpretation needed only for foreign and ancient texts, then the original readers obviously would not have required it. Were this the case, then in effect the art of interpretation would be

based on the differences between the original readers and us. But historical and linguistic knowledge removes that obstacle, and so only after significant points of comparison between the first readers and us have been reached can interpretation begin. Therefore, the only difference between ancient and foreign texts and contemporary texts in our own language is that the comparisons necessary for interpreting the former cannot be completed prior to the interpretation but begins and is completed with the process of interpretation. As he works the interpreter should keep this fact in mind.

2. Nor do written texts alone call for the art of interpretation. Were that true, the art would be necessary only because of the difference between written and spoken words, that is, because of the loss of the living voice and the absence of supplementary personal impressions. But the latter must themselves be interpreted, and that interpretation is never certain. To be sure, the living voice facilitates understanding, and a writer must take this fact into consideration. Were he to do so, then, on the assumption that the art of interpretation is not necessary for oral statements, the art would not be necessary for his written text. But that simply is not the case. Therefore, even if an author did not consider the effects of the living voice, the necessity for the art of interpretation is not based on the difference between oral and written statements.

3. Given this relationship between speaking and writing, the distinction between artful and artless interpretation must be based on nothing else than the principle stated above, and it follows that artistic interpretation has the same aim as we do in ordinary listening.

VIII. 15. There is a less rigorous practice of this art which is based on the assumption that understanding occurs as a matter of course. The aim of this practice may be expressed in negative form as: 'misunderstanding should be avoided'.

1. This less rigorous practice presupposes that it deals mainly with insignificant matters or that it has a quite specific interest, and so it establishes limited, easily realizable goals.

2. Even here, however, difficulties may necessitate recourse to artful interpretation. In this way hermeneutics originated from artless practice. But because it was applied only to difficult cases, it produced merely a collection of observations. At the same time this practice gave rise to special hermeneutics, since difficult passages could be more easily worked out within a delimited framework. Both theological and juristic hermeneutics arose in this way, and even the philologists have pursued only specialized aims.

3. In short, the less rigorous practice is based on the fact that the speaker and hearer share a common language and a common way of formulating thoughts.

16. There is a more rigorous practice of the art of interpretation that is based on the assumption that misunderstanding occurs as a matter of course, and so understanding must be willed and sought at every point.

1. This more rigorous practice consists in grasping the text precisely with the understanding and in viewing it from the standpoint of both grammatical and psychological interpretation.

(Note: It is common experience that one notices no distinction until . . . [the] beginning of a misunderstanding.)

2. Therefore, this more rigorous practice presupposes that the speaker and hearer differ in their use of language and in their ways of formulating thoughts, although to be sure there is an underlying unity between them. This is one of the less significant matters overlooked by artless interpretation.

17. Both qualitative misunderstanding of the contents of a work and quantitative misunderstanding of its tone are to be avoided.

1. Objective qualitative misunderstanding occurs when one part of speech in the language is confused with another, as for example, when the meanings of two words are confused. Subjective qualitative misunderstanding occurs when the reference of an expression is confused.

2. Subjective quantitative misunderstanding occurs when one misses the potential power of development of a part of speech or the value given it by the speaker. Analogous to this, objective quantitative misunderstanding occurs when one mistakes the degree of importance which a part of speech has.

3. From quantitative misunderstanding, which usually receives less consideration, qualitative always develops.

4. This thesis (17) encompasses the full task of interpretation, but because it is stated negatively we cannot develop rules from it. In order to develop rules we must work from a positive thesis, but we must constantly be oriented to this negative formulation.

5. We must also distinguish between passive and active misunderstanding. The latter occurs when one reads something into a text because of one's own bias. In such a case the author's meaning cannot possibly emerge.

IX. 18. The rules for the art of interpretation must be developed from a positive formula, and this is: 'the historical and divinatory, objective and subjective reconstruction of a given statement'.

1. 'Objective-historical' means to consider the statement in [its] relation to the language as a whole, and to consider the knowledge it contains as a product of the language. — 'Objective-prophetic' means to sense how the statement itself will stimulate further developments in the language. Only by taking both of these aspects into account can qualitative and quantitative misunderstanding be avoided.

2. 'Subjective-historical' means to know how the statement, as a fact in the person's mind, has emerged. 'Subjective-prophetic' means to sense how the thoughts contained in the statement will exercise further influence on and in the author. Here, again, unless both of these aspects are taken into account, qualitative and quantitative misunderstandings are unavoidable.

3. The task is to be formulated as follows: 'To understand the text at first as well as and then even better than its author.' Since we have no direct knowledge of what was in the author's mind, we must try to become aware of many things of which he himself may have been unconscious, except insofar as he reflects on his own work and becomes his own reader. Moreover, with respect to the objective aspects, the author had no data other than we have.

4. So formulated, the task is infinite, because in a statement we want to trace a past and a future which stretch into infinity. Consequently, inspiration is as much a part of this art as of any other. Inasmuch as a text does not evoke such inspiration, it is insignificant. — The question of how far and in which directions interpretation will be pressed must be decided in each case on practical grounds. Specialized hermeneutics and not general hermeneutics must deal with these questions.

19. Before the art of hermeneutics can be practised, the interpreter must put himself both objectively and subjectively in the position of the author.

1. On the objective side this requires knowing the language as the author knew it. But this is a more specific task than putting oneself in the position of the original readers, for they, too, had to identify with the author. On the subjective side this requires knowing the inner and the outer aspects of the author's life.

2. These two sides can be completed only in the interpretation itself. For only from a person's writings can one learn his vocabulary, and so, too, his character and his circumstances.

20. The vocabulary and the history of an author's age together form a whole from which his writings must be understood as a part, and *vice versa*.

1. Complete knowledge always involves an apparent circle, that each part can be understood only out of the whole to which it belongs, and *vice versa*. All knowledge which is scientific must be constructed in this way.

2. To put oneself in the position of an author means to follow through with this relationship between the whole and the parts. Thus it follows, first, that the more we learn about an author, the better equipped we are for interpretation, but, second, that a text can never be understood right away. On the contrary, every reading puts us in a better position to understand because it increases our knowledge. Only in the case of insignificant texts are we satisfied with what we understand on first reading.

X. 21. An interpreter who gains all his knowledge of an author's vocabulary from lexical aids and disconnected observations can never reach an independent interpretation.

1. The only source independent of interpretation for knowing an author's vocabulary is the immediate, living heritage of the language. With Greek and Latin that source is incomplete. This is why the first lexicographical works, which searched the whole literature in order to learn about the language, were put together. Consequently, these dictionaries must be constantly emended by interpretation itself, and every artful interpretation must contribute to that end.

2. By the 'vocabulary' of an author I include the dialect, sentence structure, and type of language characteristic of a given genre, the latter beginning with the distinction between poetry and prose.

3. Various aids may be indispensable for a beginner's first steps, but an independent interpretation demands that the interpreter acquire his background knowledge through independent research. All of the information about a language which dictionaries and other resource works supply represents the product of particular and often questionable interpretations.

4. In New Testament studies, especially, it can be said that the questionableness and arbitrariness of interpretation is due in large measure to this failure. For references to particular observations can lead to contradictory results — the road to comprehending the language of the New Testament leads one from classical antiquity through (a) Macedonian Greek, (b) the Jewish secular writers (Josephus and Philo), (c) the deuterocanonical writings, and (d) the Septuagint, which is closest to Hebrew.

22. An interpreter who gains his historical knowledge solely from prolegomena cannot reach an independent interpretation.

1. Any editor who wants to be helpful should provide such prolegomena, in addition to the usual critical aids. Preparing such prolegomena requires a knowledge of the whole circle of literature to which a writing belongs and of everything that has been written about a given author. For this reason these prolegomena themselves depends on interpretation, and . . . at the same time how they were compiled may be irrelevant to the aim of the reader. The precise interpreter, however, must gradually derive all of his conclusions from the sources themselves. Thus he must proceed from the easier to the more difficult passages. A dependence on prolegomena is most damaging when one takes conclusions from them that should have been derived from the original sources.

2. In New Testament studies a separate discipline has been created to deal with this background information, the Introduction. The Introduction is not truly an organic part of the theological sciences, but it does serve a practical purpose for both the beginner and the master, because it is helpful to have all the previous research on a given topic collected in one place. But the interpreter must contribute to extending and verifying this information.

The various ways of arranging and using this fragmentary background information have given rise to different, but also one-sided, schools of interpretation, which can easily be branded as fads [als manier].

XI. 23. Also within each given text, its parts can only be understood in terms of the whole, and so the interpreter must gain an overview of the work by a cursory reading before undertaking a more careful interpretation.

1. Here, too, there seems to be a circle. This provisional understanding requires only that knowledge of the particulars which comes from a general knowledge of the language.

2. Synopses provided by the author are too sparse to serve the purpose of even technical interpretation and the summaries which editors customarily give in prolegomena bring the reader under the power of their own interpretations.

3. The interpreter should seek to identify the leading ideas by which all the others are to be assessed. Likewise, in technical interpretation, one should try to identify the basic train of thought by reference to which

particular ideas may be more readily recognized. That these tasks are indispensable for both technical and grammatical interpretation can be easily seen from the various types of misunderstanding.

4. It is not necessary to gain an overview of insignificant texts, and although an overview seems to offer little help in dealing with difficult texts, it is nonetheless indispensable. It is characteristic of difficult authors that an overview is of little help.

Whenever we are actually engaged in the interpretation of a particular text, we must always hold the two sides of interpretation together. But in setting forth the theory of hermeneutics we must separate them and discuss the two separately. Nonetheless, each side of interpretation must be developed so thoroughly that the other becomes dispensable, or, better, that the results of the two coincide. Grammatical interpretation comes first.   *Hermeneutics: The Handwritten Manuscripts*, pp. 95-117

*

ACADEMY ADDRESS, 1829

ON THE CONCEPT OF HERMENEUTICS

Nor is the hermeneutical task restricted to a foreign language. Even in our native language, and without considering the various dialects of the language or the peculiarities of a person's speech, the thoughts and expressions of another person, whether written or spoken, contain strange elements. Indeed, I readily acknowledge that I consider the practice of hermeneutics occurring in immediate communication in one's native language very essential for our cultured life, apart from all philological or theological studies. Who could move in the company of exceptionally gifted persons without endeavouring to hear 'between' their words, just as we read between the lines of original and tightly written books? Who does not try in a meaningful conversation, which may in certain respects be an important act, to lift out its main points, to try to grasp its internal coherence, to pursue all its subtle intimations further? Wolf — especially Wolf, who was such an artist in conversation, but who said more by intimation than by explicit statement, and even more by innuendo — would not deny that these were being understood by his listeners in an artistic way, so that he could count on the audience always knowing what he meant. Should the way we observe and interpret experienced, worldly-wise and politically shrewd persons really differ from the procedure we use with books? Should it be so different that it would depend on entirely different principles and be incapable of a comparably developed and orderly presentation? That I do not believe. On the contrary, I see two different applications of the same art. In the one application certain motives are more prominent, while others remain in the background; and in the other the relationship is just the reverse. In fact, I would go even further and assert that the two applications are so closely related that neither can be practised without the other. To be specific, however, and to deal with matters which are most similar to the interpretation of written works, I would strongly recommend diligence in interpreting significant conversations. The immediate presence of the speaker, the living expression that proclaims that his whole being is involved, the way the thoughts in a conversation develop from our shared life, such factors stimulate us far more than some solitary observation of an isolated text to understand a series of thoughts as a moment of life which is breaking forth, as one moment set in the context of many others. And this dimension of understanding is often slighted, in fact, almost completely neglected, in interpreting authors. When we compare the two, it would be better to say that we see two parts rather than two forms of the task. To be sure, when something strange in a language blocks our understanding, we must try to overcome the difficulty. But even if we do come to understand this strange element, we may still find ourselves blocked because we cannot grasp the coherence of what someone is saying. And if neither approach is able to overcome the difficulty, the problem may well go unsolved. *Hermeneutics: The Handwritten Manuscripts*, pp. 182-3

5

GOD AND THE WORLD[*]

The doctrines of creation and providence are those most immediately fraught with difficulty when the modern scientific world-view meets the traditional formulation of such beliefs. Schleiermacher refused to allow science and faith to compete over what he saw as the wrong ground. Each could maintain its integrity — the one based on observation and analysis of the natural world, the other based on immediate feeling of utter dependence. Neither contradicts the other, and indeed, argues Schleiermacher, an increase of natural knowledge supports instead of subverting the religious sense. Schleiermacher was preparing post-Enlightenment Germany for the full reception of natural science, in a way which no English-speaking theologian was ready so to do until Darwinism made such a controversial impact over a generation later.

SECOND DOCTRINE: PRESERVATION (CONSERVATION)

The religious self-consciousness, by means of which we place all that affects or influences us in absolute dependence on God, coincides entirely with the view that all such things are conditioned and determined by the interdependence of Nature.

1. It is not in the least meant that the pious self-consciousness is realized with every stimulation of the sensuous consciousness, any more than every perception causes us actually to visualize the interrelatedness of nature. But whenever objective consciousness reaches this degree of clarity we assume afresh the interdependence of nature as universal and as determining everything which has not led to our consciousness of it; and in the same way we recognize in the moments when the pious self-consciousness is present that those in which it is lacking are really imperfect states, and we postulate the feeling of absolute dependence as valid for everything without exception, because we apply it to our own existence in so far as we are a part of the world.

But neither is our proposition meant to fall short of the conception of

* See also pp. 50ff. above.

172

preservation, although in accordance with the nature of self-consciousness it is limited to what affects us; and, indeed, only the movements and changes of things stimulate us directly, not the things themselves or their inner being. For every impulse directed towards perception and knowledge which yet has the qualities, essence, and being of things as its object, begins with a stimulation of self-consciousness which thus accompanies the process of apprehending; and, consequently, the being and nature of things belongs to that which affects us. Within this range our proposition admits no distinction; in each and every situation we ought to be conscious of, and sympathetically experience, absolute dependence on God just as we conceive each and every thing as completely conditioned by the interdependence of nature.

But we find the opposite idea to this very widely spread. Namely, the idea that these two views do not coincide, but that each excludes the other as its contradictory. It is said that the more clearly we conceive anything to be entirely conditioned by the interdependence of nature, the less can we arrive at the feeling of its absolute dependence upon God; and, conversely, the more vivid this latter feeling is the more indefinitely must we leave its interrelatedness with nature an open question. But it is obvious that, from our standpoint and in consistency with what we have already said, we cannot admit such a contradiction between the two ideas. For otherwise (since everything would present itself to us as always in the system of nature), as our knowledge of the world grew perfect, the development of the pious self-consciousness in ordinary life would cease; which is quite contrary to our presupposition that piety is of the essence of human nature. And on the other hand, conversely, the love of religion would be opposed to all love of research and all widening of our knowledge of nature; which would entirely contradict the principle that the observation of creation leads to the consciousness of God. And besides, prior to the completion of both tendencies the most competent naturalist would have to be the least religious of men, and *vice versa*. Now, as the human soul is just as necessarily predisposed towards a knowledge of the world as towards a consciousness of God, it can only be a false wisdom which would put religion aside, and a misconceived religion for love of which the progress of knowledge is to be arrested.

The only apparent ground for this assertion is the fact that, as a rule, the more strongly the objective consciousness predominates at any given moment, the more at that identical moment the consciousness of self is repressed and *vice versa*, because in the one case, through absorption in ourselves, we lose consciousness of the object affecting us, just as in the other case we are entirely merged in the object. But this in no way prevents the one activity, after having satisfied itself, from stimulating and passing over into the other. We are clearly quite wrong if we allege, as a general experience, that the incomprehensible as such is more conducive to the awakening of the religious feeling than that which is understood. The favourite example is the great natural phenomena, produced by elementary forces; but in point of fact the religious feeling is not destroyed even by the completest confidence with which we accept this or that hypothetical explanation of these phenomena. The reason why these manifestations so readily arouse religious feeling lies rather in the immensity of their operations both in the promotion and destruction of human life and works of skill, and thus in the awakening of the consciousness of the limitation of our activity by universal forces. But this precisely is the most complete recognition of the universal interrelatedness of nature, and thus it turns out in fact to be the other way round, a support for our thesis. It is certainly, however, an expedient often adopted by human indolence to attribute what is not understood to the supernatural immediately; but this does not at all belong to the tendency to piety. Since the supreme being here takes the place of the system of nature, we find ourselves tending rather to knowledge; besides, in that case not everything but only the incomprehensible would be placed in absolute dependence upon God. Starting from this men have imagined evil and destructive supernatural powers in the same way as they have gone back to a highest good Power; which makes it immediately evident that this kind of linking up (with the supernatural) has not arisen in the interests of religion, for such a setting of one over against the other would inevitably destroy the unity and completeness of the relation of dependence.

As furthermore we regard everything stimulating us as an object of the pious consciousness, it follows that not even the least and most unimportant thing should be excluded from the relation of absolute dependence. But here it should be remarked that frequently, on the one hand, an undue value is placed on expressly tracing back the least detail to this relation; while on the other hand, with no greater justice, we often oppose such a relation. The first mistake appears in the view that, because the greatest events often arise from small, the smallest detail must be expressly ordained by God. For it appears to be only an empty, and by no means trustworthy, play of the fantasy, when we so often hear people describing great events as arising from small causes, and thereby drawing away our attention from the universal relatedness in which the true causes really lie hidden. A clear judgment can only be formed on the principle of the similarity of cause and effect in the domain of history or of nature, and it is only under definite conditions that individual changes with their causes can be severed from the universal interrelatedness and taken separately. But as soon as the pious feeling combines with such a view, thought has no choice but to recur to the universal interdependence of nature; otherwise an isolated and separate activity would be ascribed in too human fashion to God. The second point, *i.e.* that the application of absolute dependence to the smallest matters is felt to be objectionable, has its origins in the fear that religion might be drawn into blasphemy, if, say, our free choices in little things were to be traced back to divine appointment: for instance, the point which foot shall be put forward first, or chance in matters of no serious importance such as winning or losing in sports and contests. Still, the incongruity here does not lie in the object, but in our way of thinking about it: that is, in the isolation of single events, because in cases of the first kind the apparent free choice is sometimes only an individual instance of a general situation, from which many similar events follow, and sometimes it is the expression of a more general law by which many similar events are controlled; while in cases of the second kind, the issue can always be regarded as submission to a universal will. Neither of these can be regarded as insignificant, and thus no reason can be found against treating both as subsumed under absolute dependence on God.

2. If now we examine our proposition purely in itself, it must be directly evident in its wider scope to everyone who accepts it as a general principle of experience that the feeling of absolute dependence can be aroused through stimulations of our sensuous self-consciousness. For that feeling is most complete when we identify ourselves in our self-consciousness with the whole world and feel ourselves in the same way as not less dependent. This identification can only succeed in so far as in thought we unite everything that in appearance is scattered and isolated, and by means of this unifying association conceive of everything as one. For the most complete and universal interdependence of nature is posited in this 'all-one' of finite being, and if we also feel ourselves to be absolutely dependent, then there will be a complete coincidence of the two ideas — namely, the unqualified conviction that everything is grounded and established in the universality of the nature-system, and the inner certainty of the absolute dependence of all finite being on God. From this follows, on the one hand, the possibility of pious self-consciousness in every moment of the objective consciousness, and on the other the possibility of complete world-consciousness in every moment of pious self-con-

sciousness. For with regard to the latter, where a pious feeling is actually existent, there the interdependence of nature is always posited; and therefore the effort to extend the idea of the latter and perfect it in a world-representation will not be detrimental to the former, but can be effected just in so far as the tendency towards knowledge is predominant. And as regards the former, wherever there is an objective idea, there is always a stimulated self-consciousness; and from this the pious self-consciousness can develop without prejudice to the objective idea (with its world-conception, which is more or less clearly co-posited), in proportion as the tendency in each towards feeling is dominant. Now if we conceive both tendencies as fully developed in a given man, then each would with perfect ease call forth the other, so that every thought, as part of the whole world-conception, would become in him the purest religious feeling, and every pious feeling, as evoked by a part of the world, would become a complete world-conception. On the contrary, if the one did not call forth the other, but in some way limited it, then the more completely the one developed, the more would it destroy the other. It has been always acknowledged by the strictest dogmaticians that divine preservation, as the absolute dependence of all events and changes on God, and natural causation, as the complete determination of all events by the universal nexus, are one and the same thing simply from different points of view, the one being neither separated from the other nor limited by it. If anyone should detect in this an appearance of Pantheism, he ought to bear in mind that so long as philosophy does not put forward a generally accepted formula to express the relation of God and the world, even in the province of dogmatics, directly we begin to speak not of the origin of the world but of its co-existence with God and its relatedness to God, we cannot avoid an oscillation between formulae, on the one hand, which approach to the identification of the two, and formulae, on the other, which go near to putting them in opposition to one another. Moreover, in order not to confuse ourselves in this way, we ought to observe more carefully the difference between a universal and an individual cause. For in the totality of finite being only a particular and partial causality is given to each individual, since each is dependent not on one other but on all the others; the universal causality attaches only to that on which the totality of this partial causality is itself dependent.

Postscript. — In dogmatics the analytical method originating with the scholastics has led to a division of our simple proposition in a number of different ways into many elements and sections, and it will not make much difference which of these divisions we select in order to show its relation to our statement. Some have divided the conception of preservation, which is expressed in our proposition as referring both to the whole and the parts, into the following: the *general,* which is related to the whole world as a unity; the *special,* which is concerned with species; and the *most special,* which is concerned with individuals (*generalis, specialis et specialissima*). This classification does not appear to be made in the interest of religion (from which here everything should start), for the simple reason that it leads to a question which is purely one for natural science, *i.e.* whether there is anything in the world which cannot be brought under the idea of a species. But supposing this question must be answered in the affirmative and the division be made complete, nevertheless universal preservation must include everything, and the division thus becomes quite superfluous to us, since our fundamental feeling rests solely on the finiteness of being as such. But a further purpose of this division may be surmised, if we take into account the addition usually made to the third member of it — namely, that God sustains individual things in their existence and their powers as long as he wills. For in that case the species, as reproductions of individual things, are in a sense immortal, but the individual is mortal; and the wish arose to establish a difference between the preservation of what endures and of what is mortal.

For those, however, who accept a beginning and an end of the world there is absolutely no reason to differentiate between the world and individual things. But in any case the proposition must cover equally the beginning and the end; and we know fairly certainly of our earth that there have been species on it which are no longer extant and that the present species have not always existed; so that our proposition must be stretched to embrace these also. It really affirms nothing except that the temporality or the duration of the finite is to be conceived solely in absolute dependence upon God. But since the duration of individual as well as of universal things is simply an expression for the degree of their power as each co-exists with all the rest, it follows that the addition taken in itself contains nothing which our statement had not expressed already. But the way in which the addition is framed might easily give rise to the idea that the sustaining will of God began or ended at some particular time, and in anticipation of this it must be said that God, in sustaining as in creating, must remain apart from all means and occasions of time.

Another similar version is to discriminate between the work of God as *preserving* and as *co-operating,* but the distinction is not made in the same way by all teachers of doctrine, for some connect the expression 'preservation' only with matter and form, and 'co-operation' with powers and actions; others again connect preservation with the existence and powers of things, and co-operation only with activity. The fact, however, that the expression 'co-operation' contains a hidden meaning should not be overlooked, as if there were in the finite an activity in and for itself and thus independent of the sustaining divine activity. This tendency must be entirely avoided and not merely covered over by indefiniteness. If, however, such a distinction ought not to be drawn, and if the powers of things are something as little separated from the divine sustaining activity as their being itself (the latter we only divide into matter and form by an abstraction which has no place here), then the difference between preservation and co-operation rests also on a similar abstraction. For being posited for itself can only exist where there is also power, just as power always exists only in activity; thus a preservation which did not include the placing of all the activities of any finite being in absolute dependence on God would be just as empty as creation without preservation. And in the same way, if we conceived co-operation without conceiving that the existence of a thing in its whole duration was dependent on God, then this thing might be independent of God even at its first moment of existence, and this would be equivalent to conceiving preservation in such a way that it did not include creation and positing it without creation. It should be added here that even theologians who have treated the subject quite correctly on the whole have allowed themselves to be led into describing co-operation as something more immediate than preservation, so that deeds, as distinct from the preservation of powers, proceed from a divine activity. The result of this would be, if we took it seriously, to reduce the preservation of power to nothing, for in the system of nature power is always dependent on the activity of the rest of things. Thus we can only say that, in the region of absolute dependence on God, everything is equally direct and equally indirect, some in one relation and some in another.

Some combine the idea of divine *government* immediately with these two ideas. But if by that is meant the fulfilment of divine decrees or the guidance of all things to divine ends, and if it be taken as signifying anything else than that everything can happen and has happened only as God originally willed and always wills, by means of the powers distributed and preserved in the world — this is already included in our proposition, and we cannot consider it here. For here we are concerned in general with the description of the feeling of absolute dependence, and must set completely aside a view which is based upon the distinction between means and end without reference to the question whether this distinction can exist for God. On the one hand, for our Christian consciousness it could only be the Kingdom of God, established by means of redemption (*i.e.* something quite foreign to our present purpose), to which everything else is related as its goal: and on the other, if our self-consciousness is to represent finite existence in general, and end and means are related to one another as that which is posited for its own sake and that not posited for its own sake, or more exactly as what is willed by God and what is not willed by God, then we must take up into our religious self-consciousness an antithesis of which our present discussion knows nothing. The only thing then that this conception [divine government] could suggest to us at this point would be that so far as the divine preservation relates, as co-operation, to powers and activities taken separately, we require a counterpart to it to cover the passive state of finite things; but since these are just as essential parts for the attainment of the divine purpose, their absolute dependence is included in the conception of government. Even this is, however, superfluous so far as we are concerned. For since preservation has as its object the being of things, and in this, so far as they are centres of power the antithesis of self-activity and susceptibility is included, the passive states are already subsumed under absolute dependence; and particularly when they also belong to that which affects our self-consciousness, whether in the form of perception or of sympathy, they are included in our general proposition. But, in addition, the passive states of one thing are only the result of the active states of others; while, on the other hand, the way in which the active states emerge successively and the strength which they display depends not only on each thing's peculiar mode of existence, but also on its concurrence with other things, hence on the influence of others and on its own passive states. From this we may think that perhaps we should differentiate better if we said that what proceeds from the intrinsic characteristics of each individual thing and what proceeds from its co-existence with all other things are both alike to be placed in absolute dependence upon God. But even this would be an abstraction without importance for our religious self-consciousness, for which the two are not distinguished from one another as stimulating objects; and thus we should do better to include everything which stimulates our consciousness together in the idea of finite being which is only relatively individual and is conditioned in its individuality by the universal co-existence. And this is wholly identical with what our proposition denotes by the term interdependence of nature.

It can never be necessary in the interest of religion so to interpret a fact that its dependence on God absolutely excludes its being conditioned by the system of Nature.

1. This proposition is so much a direct consequence of what went before that there would be no reason to make an express statement of it, but that ideas which have still a circulation in the Christian Church must be considered in their appropriate place in any dogmatic. Now there is a general idea that the miracles which are interwoven with the beginnings of Christianity or at least in some form are reported in the Scriptures, should be regarded as events of the kind described: and yet if the idea itself is inadmissible, it cannot be applied to this or that particular fact. It is in this way that theologians from of old have generally treated the question. We have not to pass judgment here on its inherent possibility, but only on the relation of the theory to the feeling of absolute dependence. If, then, this relation is what our proposition declares it to be, we must in our field try, as far as possible, to interpret every event with reference to the interdependence of nature and without detriment to that principle.

Now some have represented miracle in this sense as essential to the perfect manifestation of the divine omnipotence. But it is difficult to conceive, on the one side, how omnipotence is shown to be greater in the suspension of the interdependence of nature than in its original immutable course which was no less divinely ordered. For, indeed, the capacity to make a change in what has been ordained is only a merit in the ordainer, if a change is necessary, which again can only be the result of some imperfection in him or in his work. If such an interference be postulated as one of the privileges of the supreme being, it would first have to be assumed that there is something not ordained by him which could offer him resistance and thus invade him and his work; and such an idea would entirely destroy our fundamental feeling. We must remember, on the other hand, that where such a conception of miracles is commonly found, namely, in conditions where there is least knowledge of nature, there, too, the fundamental feeling appears to be weakest and most ineffectual. But where a knowledge of nature is most widely spread, and therefore this conception seldom occurs, more is found of that reverence for God which is the expression of our fundamental feeling. It follows from this that the most perfect representation of omnipotence would be a view of the world which made no use of such an idea.

Other teachers defend the conception in a more acute but scarcely more tenable way, by saying that God was partly in need of miracles that he might compensate for the effects of free causes in the course of nature, and partly that he might generally have reasons for remaining in direct contact with the world. The latter argument presupposes, for one thing, a wholly lifeless view of the divine preservation, and for another, an opposition in general between the mediate and immediate activities of God which cannot be conceived without bringing the supreme being within the sphere of limitation. The former sounds almost as if free causes were not themselves objects of divine preservation, and (since preservation includes in itself the idea of creation) had not come into being and been maintained in absolute dependence upon God. But if, on the contrary, they are in this condition there can be just as little necessity for God to counteract their influences as to counteract the influences which a blind natural force exercises in the domain of another natural force. But none of us understands by 'the world' which is the object of the divine preservation a nature-mechanism alone, but rather the interaction of the nature-mechanism and of free agents, so that in the former the latter are taken into account just as in the latter the former is reckoned.

Moreover, the biblical miracles, on account of which the whole theory has been devised, are much too isolated and too restricted in content for any theory to be based on them which should assign them the function of restoring in the nature-mechanism what free agents had altered. That one great miracle, the mission of Christ, has, of course, the aim of restoration, but it is the restoration of what free causes have altered in their own province, not in that of the nature-mechanism or in the course of things originally ordained by God. Nor does the interest of religion require that the free cause which performs the function of restoration in the sphere of phenomena should have a different relation to the order of nature from that of other free causes.

Two other reasons may be put forward why an absolute suspension of the interrelatedness of nature by miracles may be held to be in the interests of religion. And it cannot be denied that it is mostly for these reasons, even though they may never have been formulated as actual Church doctrine, that this conception of miracle has maintained its practical hold over many Christians. The first is that of answer to prayer; for prayer seems really to be heard only when because of it an event happens which would not otherwise have happened: thus there seems to be the suspension of an effect which, according to the interrelatedness of nature, should have followed. The other is that of regeneration, which, represented as a new creation, in part requires some such suspension and in part introduces a principle not comprised in the system of nature.

Neither subject can be discussed in this place; but it may suffice to remark in relation to the first, which more concerns piety in general, that our statement places prayer, too, under divine preservation, so that prayer and its fulfilment or refusal are only part of the original divine plan, and consequently the idea that otherwise something else might have happened is wholly meaningless. With regard to the second we need only refer here to what was said above. If the revelation of God in Christ is not necessarily something absolutely supernatural, Christian piety cannot be held bound in advance to regard as absolutely supernatural anything that goes along with this revelation or flows from it.

2. The more accurate definitions by which the acceptance of such miracles is brought into connection with the propositions and concepts which indicate the complete dependence of the system of nature on God show very clearly how little that idea is demanded by our religious emotions. For the more they try definitely to fix an absolute miracle, the further off they are from making it the expression of a religious emotion, and, instead of genuine dogmatic material, something of quite a different character comes in. Speaking generally, the question can most easily be considered if we start from the point that the event in which a miracle occurs is connected with all finite causes, and therefore every absolute miracle would destroy the whole system of nature. There are, therefore, two ways of looking at such a miracle — a positive way when we consider the whole future, and a negative way when we consider it as affecting in some sense the whole of the past. Since, that is, that which would have happened by reason of the totality of finite causes in accordance with the natural order does not happen, an effect has been hindered from happening, and certainly not through the influence of other normally counteracting finite causes given in the natural order, but in spite of the fact that all active causes are combining to produce that very effect. Everything, therefore, which had ever contributed to this will, to a certain degree, be annihilated, and instead of introducing a single supernatural power into the system of nature as we intended, we must completely abrogate the conception of nature.

From the positive point of view we must consider that some event follows which is not to be explained by the totality of finite causes. But as this event now enters into the interrelatedness of nature as an active member, throughout the whole future everything will be different from what it would have been had this single miracle not occurred. Thus every miracle not only suspends the entire continuity of the original order for all future time, but every later miracle annuls all earlier ones, in so far as they have become part of the continuity of active causes. But now, in order to describe the origin of the effect, we have to allow for the entrance of a divine activity apart from natural causes. Yet at whatever point we admit the entrance of this particular divine activity, which must always seem like magic, in each case there will always appear a number of possibilities according to which the same result could have been attained by natural causes if they had been opportunely directed towards this end. In this way we shall be driven to hold either that miracles have a purely epideictic tendency in view of which God purposely did not so order the system of nature that his whole will should be accomplished in it (a view against which we directed our earlier discussion of the relation between omnipotence and this conception of miracle), or if the totality of finite causes could not have been so directed, then what can be explained by the order of nature can never rightly evoke in us the feeling of the absolute dependence of all finite being.

Now, if others think it would be easier to establish this conception of miracles by first dividing the divine co-operation into ordinary and extraordinary (which, however, is only ostensibly different from the unordered), and then attributing the former to the natural and the latter to the supernatural, so that the negative aspect of a miracle would be the withdrawal of the ordinary co-operation, but the positive aspect the entrance of the extraordinary, this means, on the one hand, that the ordinary co-operation is no longer ordinary if it can be withdrawn, and is not to be definitely distinguished from the extraordinary; only that we call that which occurs more frequently the ordinary, and what seldom occurs, the extraordinary, a relation which might equally well be reversed. On the other hand, the miracle is effected in the first instance by finite causes, even if by means of extraordinary divine co-operation; but since thereby something comes into existence which according to its natural character would not have come into existence, it follows that in this case either they are not causes, and the expression 'co-operation' is inaccurate, or they have become something different from what they were formerly. In that case, every such extraordinary co-operation is really a creation, on which afterwards the re-establishment of actual things in their original state must follow as a further creation cancelling the former one. Moreover, it should be recognized with regard to these explanations that the one corresponds more closely to the one class of biblical miracle and the other to the other class, and therefore the different characteristics of these events have had an important influence on the development of these different formulae. If, however, anyone finds it difficult to accept this view, yet it must be admitted that although the older theologians on the whole still maintain this conception of miracle, the younger ones do not maintain its exclusive validity, but also admit the legitimacy of another hypothesis — namely, that God has prepared miracles in nature itself in some way incomprehensible to us; and this, in the interests of religion itself, we must admit to be pure gain.

3. On the whole, therefore, as regards the miraculous, the general interests of science, more particularly of natural science, and the interests of religion seem to meet at the same point, *i.e.* that we should abandon the idea of the absolutely supernatural because no single instance of it can be known by us, and we are nowhere required to recognize it. Moreover, we should admit, in general, that since our knowledge of created nature is continually growing, we have not the least right to maintain that anything is impossible, and also we should allow, in particular (by far the greater number of New Testament miracles being of this kind), that we can neither define the limits of the reciprocal relations of the body and mind nor assert that they are, always and everywhere, entirely the same without the possibility of extension or deviation. In this way, everything — even the most wonderful thing that happens or has happened — is a problem for scientific research; but, at the same time, when it in any way stimulates the pious feeling, whether through its purpose or in some other way, that is not in the least prejudiced by the conceivable possibility of its being understood in the future. Moreover, we free ourselves entirely from a difficult and highly precarious task which dogmatics has so long laboured in vain, *i.e.* the discovery of definite signs which shall enable us to distinguish between the false and diabolical miracle and the divine and true.   *The Christian Faith*, pp. 170–184

*

Schleiermacher as pastor and preacher was aware that the doctrine of God's activity in the world and in human affairs, far from being an academic game, was of the most pressing concern to all people seeking to interpret their actual experience of life in the light of faith. He was a powerful preacher, usually delivering his discourse in extempore form and only afterwards writing it out in full. His sermon 'The Power of Prayer in Relation to Outward Circumstances' is a fine example of preaching which, in his own terms, is as theological as it is pastorally oriented.

THE POWER OF PRAYER IN RELATION TO OUTWARD CIRCUMSTANCES

Text: Matt. 26:36-46

To be a religious man and to pray are really one and the same thing. To join the thought of God with every thought of any importance that occurs to us; in all our admiration of external nature, to regard it as the work of his wisdom; to take counsel with God about all our plans, that we may be able to carry them out in his name; and even in our most mirthful hours to remember his all-seeing eye; this is the prayer without ceasing to which we are called, and which is really the essence of true religion.

As to the benefit of prayer there can be no question. Surely, surely we have all experienced it! If our joys have often remained innocent, while others strayed into ways of sin; if our judgments have been mixed with gentleness and modesty, where pride and arrogance might most easily have gained the day; if we have been guarded from the evil which the judgment of man all too willingly excuses; then we owe this beneficent protection to the power of prayer.

Whether prayer has another kind of power in the world besides this, is a question that may easily be raised, and on which, if we are not to have our minds needlessly disturbed, we must come to some fixed belief.

If we are to bring all our thoughts into harmony with the thought of God, then we may and shall direct our wishes to certain things that we desire may occur to, or be averted from ourselves or others. Now if we regard the fulfilment of those wishes as the aim of our prayers, and connect with this idea what is promised in answer to prayer — then, whether we consider this answer, as some do, as a distinct and infallible mark of the divine favour; or if we only believe, as very many do, that our prayers throw some additional weight into the scale; either way, what a narrowing of our mental condition accompanies such a belief; how it sets limits to the reasonableness of our wishes, and even to the humility of our hearts! For thus our minds are filled with hopes, the usually disappointing issues of which disturb our peace, and indeed may bring us into the most painful uncertainty as to our standing with God. Let us therefore consider together this aspect of prayer. The portion of the history of our Lord's passion which we take as our subject is specially suitable for this purpose, as it shows us our Lord himself engaged in the kind of prayer we are speaking of.

We will consider the nature of his prayer and its results: and you will certainly grant this beforehand, that the disciple is not above his master, and that we cannot expect more from our prayers than Christ obtained by his. For if the granting of our petitions is a token of God's favour, then it would certainly have been given above all to him in whom God was so supremely well-pleased. If it is only to be given when a man's own strength is not equal to what he seeks, and when there is need of special help, then let me remind you how utterly the Saviour denied himself all human succour, and what strict limits he set to himself by the laws which he followed in all his actions. If the success of the prayer depends on the importance, or on the innocence of the thing desired, then you know that no trifle ever occupied his mind, and that though in all points tempted like us, he was without sin.

If, then, we cannot beforehand come to the conclusion that what Christ's prayer effected ours can also effect, this at least is certain, that where his prayer could not prevail neither will ours succeed. This similarity of our position with his must be a soothing thought to us all, whatever may be the result of our inquiry; and therefore I ask the more confidently for your calm and unprejudiced attention.

We have here a direct view of the Saviour, before he fell into the hands of his enemies, in an agitated and anxious state of mind. He knew that there was a plot against his life, which was now on the point of being carried out; and plainly and calmly as he had before talked with his disciples of what was before him, now that he was to enter on the conflict — now that all, as it came nearer, looked darker and more certain — the various feelings that such a prospect could not but excite in his mind threw him into a state of stronger agitation than was at all usual with him. He sought solitude, and then fled from it; from prayer he went back to his disciples, who were in no condition to comfort or cheer him; and from them he went back again to prayer. In circumstances like these, even to those who are furthest from true piety, the old, half-forgotten memory of God comes back, and they turn to him for help and deliverance; in such circumstances even those whose spirit is bravest, and who are absolutely submissive to the divine will, are yet not quite without anxiety or without wishes; and therefore, in this instance, the prayer of the Saviour took the form of one of the ordinary petitions of men for a result according to their desires.

It is the value and the power of a prayer of this kind that we wish to consider. Let us first examine carefully the case before us, to see what it teaches us, and then, secondly, note any deductions to be drawn from it.

I. First, then, fix it firmly in your minds that you have the privilege of laying before God your wishes about the more important concerns of your lives. It cannot be superfluous, in these times, to strengthen our-selves in this belief. Those who would like to banish everything belong-ing to religion from the minds of men, by allowing no room for the exer-cise of it in daily life, do not fail to represent such a prayer as an offence against the Most High. It is irreverent, they say, to express a wish rising out of the narrowness of our intellect and heart, about something which his decree has long ago settled; it is an ill-timed curiosity to say, I wish it might be so and so, when we shall presently learn how he has willed it. Do not be perplexed by such words. Christ did it, therefore we, too, may do it. It is one of the privileges that belong to our position as children of God. That would be a slavish family in which the children were not at liberty to express their wishes in the presence of their wiser father. And is any one able all at once to suppress his desires? If we cannot do so, then let us always speak them out when our heart is moved to do so; for even if we do shut them up within us, they are not hidden from him. Do not listen to those who tell you that, before you approach God, you must have your mind composed and your heart at peace; that it is unseemly to appear before him in this agitated state, while the dread of pain and disappoint-ment, the clinging to some good thing which you are on the point of los-ing, still tosses your heart to and fro, and leaves no room for submission to the holy will of God. If you waited until submission had won the victory, you would feel neither the need nor the inclination for such a prayer, and the privilege of offering it would be useless to you. If the feelings that stir your heart are sinful emotions; if these emotions are kindled by the fire of passion; then the thought of God and prayer to him can have no place beside them. But that disquietude, so altogether natural to man as God has made him, which agitates us at the touch of loss and misfortune, or when threatened with a check being laid on our activities, or with separa-tion from those we love — such disquietude should not keep us back from God; for only thus will our hearts not condemn us, and we shall have con-fidence towards God (1 John 3:21). Christ himself, as you see here, used no other means to allay this so unusual agitation in his holy soul. Prayer alone was the means he took. In the very midst of his trouble he turned in supplication to his heavenly Father; just when his soul was sorrowful even unto death, he left his disciples to go and pray.

But while I most sincerely encourage you to do this, I just as earnestly entreat you, in the second place, by no means to feel sure that what you ask will of necessity take place because of your prayer. The words of Christ leave no room to doubt that he really and most earnestly prayed that the suffering before him might be averted: he uses the very same words which he always used in speaking of it; and we know only too well from the close of his history that the event was not according to his prayer. That which he had always foreseen and foretold befell him; he had the cup of suffering, just as he saw it set before him in his hour of sorrow and dread, to drain to the last drop. And a result which *his* prayer did not effect will not and cannot be effected by ours. Do not then infer, as many do, from the promises in certain passages of Scripture, that God always gives what is asked of him in true faith and out of a pure heart. You will not deny that Christ had a faith that might have been pre-eminently a reason for God's favour, and in his filial and submissive entreaty you will find nothing unbefitting to a pure heart. Such an answer then must have been given to him above all others; and the words spoken by himself, 'Ask, and ye shall receive', must therefore have some other meaning than that which we have indicated, since this was not the sense in which the promise was fulfilled to him, the author and finisher of our faith. And if not to him, how should it come to pass that God should fulfil *your* wishes because of your prayers? Do you think it might be more possible in your case than in his, because his suffering and death was a part of God's great plan for the restoration of the human race? But in reality everything is taken into account in God's plan, and it is all one plan. Whatever your heart may long for, sooner will heaven and earth pass away than the slightest tittle be changed of what has been decreed in the counsels of the Most High. Or is this your idea: it is true that the Eternal cannot change his purpose, but knowing all things beforehand, he knew when and what his pious and beloved children would ask from him, and has so arranged the chain of events that the issue shall accord with their wishes? That is to try at once to honour the wisdom of God and to flatter the childish fancies of men. God has not called us to so high a place as that our wishes should be prophecies; but certainly to something higher than that the granting of those wishes should be to us the most precious evidence of his favour. This is really among the most perverted of the devices with which people have tried to adorn religion; but it is only an invention of a warped understanding, not a conclusion drawn from the way in which God reveals himself in the world. It is dishonouring to Christ to think that he should not have been the first in this respect; and it is dishonouring to men that if God had arranged all this, we should so seldom meet with examples of answered prayer.

Let us see then, in the third place, what really is the effect of our prayers, if it is not to be sought in the agreement of the result with the expressed wish. Just the effect that it produced in Christ's own case. Consider, with me, what passed, on that occasion, in his mind. He began with the definite wish that his sufferings might pass away from him; but as soon as he fixed his thought on his father in heaven to whom he prayed, this wish was at once qualified by the humble, 'if it be possible'. When from the sleeping disciples, the sight of whom must have still more disheartened him and added fresh bitterness to his sense of desertion, he returned to prayer, he already bent his own wish before the thought that the will of the Father might be something different. To reconcile himself to this, and willingly to consent to it, was now his chief object; nor would he have wished that the will of God should not be done, had he been able by that means to gain all that the world could give.

And when he had prayed for the third time all anxiety and dread were gone. He had no longer any wish of his own. With words in which he sought to impart to them some of the courage he had gained, he awakened his friends from their sleep, and went with calm spirit and holy firmness to meet the traitor.

There you see the effect that such a prayer ought to have. It should make us cease from our eager longing for the possession of some earthly good, or the averting of some dreaded evil; it should bring us courage to want, or to suffer, if God has so appointed it; it should lift us up out of the helplessness into which we are brought by fear and passion, and bring us to the consciousness and full use of our powers; that so we may be able in all circumstances to conduct ourselves as it becomes those who remember that they are living and acting under the eye and the protection of the most high.

But prayer will more necessarily produce this effect if some point is not entirely lacking in our conception of the divine being. If we lay before God a wish that this or that may so happen in the world as it seems to be best for us, we must remember that we are laying it before the *Unchangeable*, in whose mind no new thought or purpose can arise since the day when he said, 'all is very good'. What was then decreed will take place; we must not lose sight of the indisputable certainty of this thought. Well, and suppose that which you fear has been decreed? Suppose you are to be torn away from your beloved field of labour, or to lose the friend to whom your heart cleaves, or that the undeserved calumny is still to rest on you? Inevitably our first impulse will be to thrust back those fears. It cannot be, we say; it will not be: it would be too hard; too unfatherly. But the thought, it cannot be, will perish in our hearts when we remember that it is the *unsearchable* whom our hope seeks to limit in this way. It may easily be — it may easily be, is the voice that reaches us from a thousand examples of unmerited and hardly endurable suffering. And if it should be so — we cannot bend *his* will; then what remains to us but to bring our will into accord with his?

And we are drawn to do this, and to do it from the heart, by the encouraging thought that he to whom we would present our petition is the *only wise.* You imagine something to be beneficial and good, and you wish that God may allow it to happen. Does not your wish as well as your judgment stand silent at the thought of him? How far can you see into the consequences and the connection of those events, even as regards your own well-being? He knows the best and the whole. If according to his appointment you must do without what you desire, you have compensation for that in all the good that you see in the world. And thus will be called forth in us distrust of our own wisdom; humility, that looks on ourselves as only a little part of the whole; benevolence, that will find its satisfaction more in consideration of the world than in our own prosperity.

But the wise is also the *kind.* He will not let thee suffer and lack thy desires merely for the sake of others; his will is that to the upright man everything shall serve to his own highest good. And so there comes to us the trust that, little part as we are, account has been taken of us among the whole; and from this comes repose of the spirit; for, whatever befalls us, good must come out of it; and thus, at last the quieted and soothed heart can cry, Father, thy will be done. If we once face the dreaded evil with calmness and submission, we shall readily see in the right light the intention of all that happens to us, and our chief attention will be directed to that. He who prays must remember that everything that befalls us has its end in ourselves, and is intended for our improvement and the increase of good in us. Then he will become conscious that this aim of the most high, which his excited feelings had for a little while pushed out of sight, is yet in reality his own aim also. And if everything can be, and ought to be, a means to this end, why should he shrink from anything that may come upon him? If both prosperity and adversity draw out and confirm good points of character; if in both he can act worthily and in a way well-pleasing to God; why should he not welcome both as coming from the hand of God and by his direction? When the heart has reached this point it has taken the right attitude. Now we are occupied with something else than our feelings; with the question, What will be required of me should this or that befall? What kind of powers shall I employ? What kind of stand shall I make against it? What acts of thoughtlessness must I avoid? And if we find that it always depends on those same qualities which we have often exercised and studied over; that the whole of what we may be able to accomplish consists of single acts which we have often before performed with good results; then the soul that had shrunk in fear comes back to the consciousness of its powers; then we feel ourselves strong enough to walk in the way that God has traced out for us, strong enough to comfort those who are sad on our account and more disheartened than ourselves; and if the hour comes when the evil does befall, we can say, with a mind composed and at peace, Let us rise and go to meet it.

According to the example of the Saviour, these are the right effects of such a prayer. I hope they will appear to you all great and important enough to make you willingly forget the impossible and wonderful which so many regard as the main point in prayer. If you count it a better thing to teach those whose training is in your hands to bear all kinds of trouble and hardships, than always to guard them from it, then praise the divine wisdom which, in giving us prayer, has put into our hands a powerful means to the former, but not to the latter.

In order to enable you still further to consider this important subject, let me add —

II. Some general inferences that may be drawn from what the example of Christ has taught us.

1. If nothing is changed on account of our prayers in the course of things ordained by God, we must not attach any special value to occasional apparent answers that we may receive. There seldom elapses any considerable time in which our health, or our outward prosperity, or our relations with those who are dearest to us in the world, are not threatened by various dangers; and I hope there are few among us who do not make such things subjects of prayer. But whatever may be the issue of these critical circumstances, beware of asking in your prayers for the reason of them, or seeking to know how far God has been pleased or displeased. Besides that this is dishonouring God, as we have already seen, it utterly corrupts your judgment of your own and of other men's merits, and teaches you to attach importance to things that have none whatever.

And yet on this judgment, if you are intelligent and consistent with yourself, depends your whole mode of life and action. And this holds good even as to the fulfilment of our purest and noblest wishes, that is, those which are concerned with the progress of good, whether in general or that in which we are instruments and fellow-labourers. Rejoice if your righteous undertakings are successful; rejoice if God makes use of you as direct instruments for the increase of good in the world; rejoice if at last you are specially successful in what has long been the chief object of your efforts, your anxieties and your prayers; but let not those things lead you to the proud belief that they are a distinctive sign of God's satisfaction with your spiritual condition. Many a one with whom nothing succeeds, and whose work in the world seems to be in vain, not only purposes as honestly, but certainly does his duty as zealously and is as thoroughly devout as you. To measure human merit by such things is a dangerous imperfection of faith, and one of those for which very specially Christ became the mediator between God and us. See how even he seemed to fail in everything, and yet how God made use of him in the noblest way! How his request was not granted, and yet he was at that moment, as always, the Son in whom the Father was well pleased.

2. You will now, I hope, admit that there is no true prayer but that which I described in the beginning of our meditation; that is to say, the prayer we offer when we have the living thought of God accompanying, purifying and sanctifying all other thoughts, feelings and purposes. All other forms which prayer may assume in isolated cases must, if you would really please God, resolve themselves into this one highest aspect, which takes in your whole manner of life. Our prayer of thanksgiving is just our thought of God united with our joy at what has taken place; and it will only be pleasing to him if it hallows and elevates this joy, if it is the means of raising our interest from earthly to higher things. If it is only thanks, mere joy in the new possession that God has lent us, our thankoffering has no value in his eyes.

And it is the same with our petitions, whether they concern our own circumstances, or are brotherly intercessions. If our prayer has not the effect of moderating the wish that it expressed, of replacing the eager desire with quiet submission, the anxious expectation with devout calmness; then it was no true prayer, and gives sure proof that we are not yet at all capable of this real kind of prayer.

3. In the third place, I will say to you frankly that it seems to me a mark of greater and more genuine piety when this entreating kind of prayer is only seldom used by us, and we do not allow our thoughts to be long occupied with it. For why is it, after all, that our prayer takes the form of entreaty? When we desire something that we ourselves cannot accomplish, and at the same time remember God; then occurs to us first of all the thought of his almighty power in contrast to our weakness, and we would like to try to make that power favourable to us. That is prayer as dictated by the weak human heart. But there lies at the bottom of this a defective idea of God. If we called to mind what should always come most readily to our thoughts — his holiness and wisdom — our wish would quickly take the form by which the prayers of pious men must always be

distinguished. And, no doubt, the more habitual real piety is with us, the oftener we think of all that we can learn about God, just so much the more quickly will this change take place.

Those who boast that they can persist in prayer, that they do not grow weary in beseeching God to bring about this or that, are still very far from the spirit of true godly fear. It is told us of Christ several times that he retired into solitude, and spent whole nights in prayer. But it was not the fear of anything that might occur, not interest in any event, that drew him to prayer; but the need of his heart to give himself up to devout meditation and to the undisturbed enjoyment of communion with his Father, without a definite wish or a special request. Whereas, when we find Jesus entreating, it is in exceptional and therefore only in rare instances. It needed, indeed, an occasion of strong emotion, such as is not likely to occur very frequently in our lives, to call forth in his holy soul so much that must tend to our comfort in the subject before us. Are you overtaken by such an occasion? Then entreat, until true prayer makes you forget entreaty.

As for those who boast that they often supplicate in this way; that they seek God's presence several times a day to ask about everything, either that has already happened or that they wish to obtain, and to thank him for every trifle connected with their daily life; it seems to me they have little to boast of. However much they may say of the devotion with which they offer these prayers, I really believe that in such prayers there is no *real* devotion. At stated times they lay their wants before God; their prayers belong, like other little pieces of business, to the order of the day; and from them they go at once to other employments or pleasures in which no trace of religion can be seen; and in the same way they come from the midst of cares and work and merriment to prayer, with their minds filled and pervaded with earthly things. Does that, to a heart whose intercourse with God is habitual, indicate a good state of things? He who is chiefly aroused to the thought of God by a sense of dependence certainly does not think really of him at all, and the true Christian spirit is utterly wanting in him. Whatever assurances such persons may give us of the blessings brought to their hearts by such prayer, these are certainly only incidental and passing emotions. Do they not always speak the same customary words? Do they not, for the most part, pray with their thoughts far away? We all know how little effect such prayer can have on one's inner life. It is in truth no loss to Christianity when such customs fall into disuse. No; with a light heart would I see all these forms and fixed hours of prayer disappear; free as they may be from any superstitious intention,

and whatever bearing they may be thought to have on morality and fulfilment of duty. A heart-stirring thought of the creator, when our eye rests
on his works, out of the quiet delight which we take in his creation; a
thought of the ruler of the world, checking our false estimates, amidst our
talk of the fortunes and undertakings of men; a sense of him whose image
becomes manifest in us when we feel ourselves overflowing with love and
good-will, amidst the social enjoyment of those noble human feelings; a
glad sense of his love when we are enjoying his gifts; when we succeed in
some good work, a thankful sense of his support; when we meditate on his
commandments, the great hope that he wishes to raise us to his own likeness; this is true prayer: the blessings of which I heartily desire we may all
abundantly enjoy.   *Selected Sermons*, pp. 38-51

6

THE PERSON AND WORK OF CHRIST[*]

For Schleiermacher, the person and work of Christ, like everything else in theology, were to be seen in relation to the fundamental datum of Christianity: the God-consciousness of members of the Christian community. His Jesus is the historical source of the present religious consciousness of Christians. In Christmas Eve. Dialogue on the Incarnation *Schleiermacher, then teaching at Halle, sets a discussion on the historicity of Jesus, and the orthodox doctrine of the incarnation, in the setting of a family Christmas gathering. The work probably represents Schleiermacher's own mind as it was then maturing towards a greater historical sense than in the relatively unqualified emphasis upon 'religion as feeling' of the* Speeches. *Christmas Eve, which appeared in 1806, is one of the most humanly charming pieces of serious theology ever written, as it vividly portrays young and old, men and women, sceptic and pietist, enjoying music and conversation and sharing their thoughts on the significance of the joy of the Christmas season. Schleiermacher's own thinking is probably best reflected in the thoughts of Ernst and Eduard, who are responding here to the questions placed by the rationalistic Leonhardt. Josef, who speaks last, returns the discussion to where, in Schleiermacher's heart of hearts, it really belongs, that is in the realm of feelings of pure joy. This work is an apt starting point for consideration of Schleiermacher's doctrine of the* necessity *for a redeemer to account for the unconditional sense of joy and freedom which is the present experience of Christanity.*

CHRISTMAS EVE. DIALOGUE ON THE INCARNATION

Ernst began: 'Before you spoke, Leonhardt, I should not have known whether what I want to say should be labelled "commending" or "honouring". But now I know that, in its own way it is a kind of honouring. For I too want to praise the Christmas festival as excellent in its kind. Unlike you, I shall not, however, leave up in the air whether the specific idea of the festival and its kind are to be commended as something good, but will

---

[*] See also pp. 53ff. above.

rather presuppose this. There is one qualification. Your definition of a festival does not suffice for me. It was one-sided, on the whole adapted only to your own requirements. My definition is different and proceeds from another direction. That is, while you only took the point of view that every festival is a commemoration of something, what concerns me is the question of what it commemorates. Accordingly I propose that a festival is founded only to commemorate that through the representation of which a certain mood and disposition can be aroused within men; and I propose, further, that the excellence of any festival consists in the fact that such an effect is realized within its entire scope, and vividly so.

'The mood which our festival is meant to incite is joy. That this mood is very widely and vividly aroused through the Christmas festival is so obvious that nothing more need be said on that score. Everyone can see for himself. Only there is one difficulty which might be mentioned, and I shall have to remove it. One might say that it is in no way distinctive of the Christmas festival or essential to it that it should produce this effect, which is only incidental like the particular presents that are given and received. Now this is plainly false, as I will try to show. Look, if you give children the same gifts at another time, you won't evoke even the semblance of Christmas delight — not unless you come to the corresponding point in their own lives, namely, the celebration of their birthdays. I believe I am right in calling this a corresponding point, and certainly no one will deny that the joy at a birthday has quite a different character from that at Christmas. One's mood on his birthday has all the intimacy of being confined within a particular set of personal circumstances, while that at Christmas-time bears all the fire, the rapid stirring of a widespread, general feeling. From this we see that it is not the presents in themselves which bring out the joy, but that they are given only because there is already great cause for rejoicing. And the distinctiveness of Christmas, which consists precisely in this great universality, also extends itself to the presents, so that throughout a great part of Christendom — as far as this fine old custom is still observed — everyone is occupied in preparing a gift, and in this awareness lies a great part of its all-pervasive charm.

'Think what it would be like if only a single family held to this observance while all the others in their area had given it up. The impression would no longer be the same — not by a long shot. But the fact that people are planning together for it, working to outdo each other in preparing for the special hours of celebration — and then out-of-doors the Christmas markets, open to all and intended for the whole populace, their lights reflecting off each gift just as sparkling little stars gleam from earth in the snowy winter night as if the reflection of heaven were cast upon it — all this gives the presents their special value.

'Nor can what is so all-inclusive have been arbitrarily devised or agreed upon. Some common inner cause must underlie it, otherwise it cannot have produced so similar an effect or survived as it has, as can be seen quite satisfactorily in contrast with many recent attempts which lacked these conditions. And this inner ground cannot be other than the appearance of the Redeemer as the source of all other joy in the Christian world; and for this reason nothing else can deserve to be so celebrated as this event.

'Some, to be sure, have attempted to transfer the widespread enjoyment of the Christmas season to the New Year, the day on which the changes and contrasts of time are pre-eminent. I cannot draw attention to this view without lodging a complaint against it, and for the reason I have just stated. Many people, of course, have followed this practice without thinking, and it would be unfair to claim that wherever gifts are exchanged at New Year's instead of at Christmas people are giving little place to the distinctively Christian element in their lives. Yet this divergent custom is connected plainly enough with just such a neglect. New Year's is devoted to the renewal of what is only transistory. Therefore is it especially appropriate that those who, lacking stability of character, live only from year to year should make a special holiday of it.

'All men are subject to the shifts of time. That goes without saying. But some of the rest of us do not desire to have our life in what is only transitory. For us the birth of the Redeemer is the uniquely universal festival of joy, precisely because we believe there is no other principle of joy than redemption. In its progress the birth of the divine Child is the first bright spot. We cannot postpone our joy by waiting for another. Thus, too, no other festival has such a kinship to this universal festival as that of baptism, through which the principle of joy in the divine Child is appropriated to the little ones. And this explains the particular fascination of Agnes' charming account, in which the two were conjoined.

'Yes, Leonhardt, look at it as we may there is no escaping the fact that that original, natural state of vitality and joy in which there are no opposites of appearance and being, time and eternity, is not ours to possess. And if we think these to exist in one person then we must think of him as Redeemer, and as one who must start out as a divine Child. By contrast, we ourselves begin with the cleavage between time and eternity, appearance and being; and we only attain to harmony through redemption, which is nothing other than the overcoming of these oppositions and which on this account can only proceed from one for whom they have not had to be overcome.

'Certainly no one can deny that. It is the distinctive nature of this festival that through it we should become conscious of an innermost ground out of which a new, untrammeled life emerges, and of its inexhaustible power, that in its very first germ we should already discern its finest maturity, even its highest perfection. However unconsciously it may reside in many people, our feeling of marvel can achieve resolution only in this concentrated vision of a new world, and in no other way. This vision may grip anyone, and he who brought it into being may thus be represented in a thousand images and in the most varied ways — as the rising, e'er returning sun, as the springtime of the spirit, as king of a better realm, as the most faithful emissary of the gods, as the prince of peace.

'And so I have come to the point of refuting you after all, Leonhardt, even in noting where we agree and in comparing the different viewpoints from which we have started. However unsatisfactory the historical traces of his life may be when one examines it critically — in a lower sense — nevertheless the festival does not depend on this. It rests on the necessity of a Redeemer, and hence upon the experience of a heightened existence, which can be derived from no other beginning than him. Often you yourself find less of a trace than I in particles upon which some crystallization of truth has been formed, but even the smallest elements have sufficed to convince you that a trace was present. So it is actually Christ to whose powers of attraction this new world owes its formation. And whoever acknowledges Christianity to be a powerful contemporary force, the great pattern of man's new life — as you are inclined to do — hallows this festival. He does so not as one who dares not impugn what he cannot understand, but in that he fully understands all its particulars — the gifts and the children, the night and the light.

'With this slight improvement, which I wish might also win your favour, I give your proposal for a toast once more. I trust, then, or rather prophesy, that the marvellous festival of Christmas will ever preserve the happy childlike mood with which it returns to us ever and again. And to all who celebrate it I wish and foresee that true joy in finding the higher life once more, from which alone all its blessings spring.'

'I must beg your pardon, Ernst', said Agnes. 'I had feared that I would not understand you at all; but this has not happened, and you have very nicely confirmed that the religious element is in truth the essence of the festival. Only it would certainly appear, from what has been said previously, as if we women should have less share in the joy because less of that disorder you spoke of is revealed in us. But I can account for that well enough for myself.'

'Very easily', Leonhardt jumped in. 'One could simply say right off – and it is as plain as can be – that women bear everything lightly regarding themselves and strive after little self-gratification, but that just as their innermost suffering is literally suffering-with, sympathy, so their joy too is shared joy. You must see to it, however, that you square accounts with the sacred authority of Scripture, to which you would ever remain faithful and which so clearly points to the women as the first cause of all cleavages and of all need of redemption! But if I were Friederike, I would declare war on Ernst for having so thoughtlessly, and without the slightest consideration of his situation, given baptism prominence over betrothal, which, I hope, is also to be regarded as a lovely and joyful sacrament.'

'Don't answer him, Ernst', piped Friederike. 'He has already answered himself.'

'How so?' inquired Leonhardt.

'Why obviously', countered Ernestine, 'in that you spoke of your own situation! But people like you never notice when you mix in your own dear egos. Ernst, however, has set up the distinction very well, and would no doubt say to you that a betrothal is closer to the enjoyment of a birthday than to the joy of Christmas.'

'Or', added Ernst, 'if you would have something specifically Christian at this point – that it is more like Good Friday and Easter than Christmas! Now, though, let's put aside all that has preceded and listen to what Eduard has to say to us.'

In response, Eduard began his discourse, as follows: 'It has already been remarked on a similar occasion, by a better man than I', he said, 'that the last one to speak on a topic this way, no matter what its nature, is in the worst position. That is the situation in which I find myself. For one thing, earlier speakers take the words out of one's mouth, and in this respect you two have certainly not taken much trouble to leave any particulars of the festival to me. The main difficulty, however, is that peculiar echoes continue to resound from each discourse in the minds of their listeners, and this forms an increasing resistance to new ideas, which the final speaker has the greatest difficulty in surpassing. Thus I must look about for aid, and let what I want to say rest on something you already know well and appreciate, so that my thoughts may find entrance into yours more easily.

'Now Leonhardt has mostly had the more external biographers of Christ in mind, seeking out the historical truth in them. In contrast, I shall turn to the more mystical among the four evangelists, whose account offers very little in the way of particular events. The Gospel according to John hasn't any Christmas even, recounted as an external event. But in his heart prevails an everlasting childlike Christmas joy. He gives us the higher, spiritual view of our festival. And so he begins, as you know: "In the beginning was the Word, and the Word was with God, and the Word was God. . . . In him was life, and the life was the light of men. . . . And the Word became flesh and dwelt among us . . . [and] we have beheld his glory, glory as of the only Son from the Father."

'This is how I prefer to regard the object of this festival: not a child of such and such an appearance, born of this or that parent, here or there, but the Word become flesh, which was God and was with God. The flesh, however, is, as we know, nothing other than our finite, limited, sensible nature, while the Word is thinking, coming to know; and the Word's becoming flesh is therefore the appearing of this original and divine wisdom in that form. Accordingly, what we celebrate is nothing other than ourselves as whole beings — that is, human nature, or whatever else you want to call it, viewed and known from the perspective of the divine. Why we must raise up one person alone in whom human nature permits of being represented in this way, and why this union of the divine and the earthly is placed in precisely this one person, and already even at his birth — all this can be clarified from this point of view.

'In himself what else is man than the very spirit of earth, or life's coming to know in its eternal being and in its ever-changing process of becoming? In such a state there is no corruption in man, no fall, and no need of redemption. But when the individual fastens upon other formations of his earthly environment and seeks his knowledge in them, for the process of coming to know them dwells in him alone: this is only a state of becoming. Then he exists in a fallen and corrupt condition, in discord and confusion, and he can find his redemption only through man-in-himself. He finds redemption, that is, in that the same union of eternal being and of the coming into being of the human spirit, such as it can be manifested on this planet, arises in each person and thus each contemplates and learns to love all becoming, including himself, only in eternal being. And insofar as he appears as a process of becoming, he wills to be nothing other than a thought of eternal being; nor will he have his foundations in any other expression of eternal being than in that which is united with the ever-changing, ever-recurrent process of becoming. In fact, the union of being and becoming is found in humanity not incidentally but eternally; and this is because that union exists and comes into being as man-in-himself does. In the individual person, however, this union — as it has reality in his own life — must come into being both as his own thinking and as the thinking which arises within a common life and activity with other men; for it is in community that that knowledge which is proper to our planet not only exists but develops. Only when a person sees humanity as a living community of individuals, cultivates humanity as a community, bears its spirit and consciousness in his life, and within that community both loses his isolated existence and finds it again in a new way — only then does that person have the higher life and peace of God within himself.

'Now this community, or fellowship, by which man-in-himself is thus exhibited or restored is the Church. The Church, by virtue of this relation, relates itself to all other human life around it and without, somewhat as the individual's own consciousness of humanity relates to what lacks consciousness. Everyone, therefore, in whom this genuine self-consciousness of humanity arises enters within the bounds of the Church. This is why no one can truly and vitally possess the fruits of science who is not himself within the Church, and why such an outsider can only externally deny the Church but not deep within himself. On the other hand, there may very well be those within the Church who do not possess science for themselves; for these can own that higher self-consciousness in immediate experience, if not in conceptual awareness as well. This is exactly the case with women, and likewise provides the reason why they are so much more fervently and unreservedly attached to the Church.

'This community, furthermore, is not only something which is coming into being but also something which has come into being. And it is also, as a community of individual persons, something which has come into being through communication of persons with each other. We also seek, therefore, for a single starting-point from which this communication can proceed — although we recognize that it must further proceed from each person out of his own self-activity — so that man-in-himself may also be born and formed in each one. But the man who is regarded as the starting-point of the Church, its originating conception, must already be the man-in-himself, the God-man, from birth — he must bear that self-knowledge in himself and be the light of men from the very beginning. Analogously one may as it were call the first free, spontaneous outbreak of fellowship at Pentecost, where people were joined in a common and immediate experience, the birth of the Church. For it is, in fact, through the Spirit of the Church that we are born again. The Spirit itself, however, proceeds only from the Son, and the Son needs no rebirth but is born of God originally. He is the Son of Man without qualification. Until he enters history, all else is presage: all human life is related to his life, and only through this relation does it partake of goodness and divinity. And now that he has come, in him we celebrate not only ourselves but all who are yet to come as well as all who have been before us, for they only were something insofar as he was in them and they in him.

'In Christ, then, we see the Spirit, according to the nature and means of our world, originating contact with us and forming his presence within the genuine self-consciousness of individual persons. In him, the Father and the brethren dwell in conformity and are one. Devotion and love are his essence. Thus it is that every mother who, profoundly feeling what she has done in bearing a human being, knows as it were by an annunciation from heaven that the Spirit of the Church, the Holy Spirit, dwells within her. As a result, she forthwith presents her child to the Church with all her heart, and claims this as her right. Such a woman also sees Christ in her child — and this is that inexpressible feeling a mother has which compensates for all else. And in like manner each one of us beholds in the birth of Christ his own higher birth whereby nothing lives in him but devotion and love; and in him too the eternal Son of God appears. Thus it is that the festival breaks forth like a heavenly light out of the darkness. Thus it is that a pulse of joy spreads out over the whole reborn world, a pulse which only those who are long ill or maimed of spirit do not feel. And this is the very glory of the festival, which you wished also to hear me praise.

'Ah! but I see I shall not be the last. For our long-awaited friend has come, and must have his say as well.'

Josef had come in while he was talking and, although he had very quietly entered and taken a seat, Eduard had noticed him. 'By no means', he replied when Eduard addressed him. 'You shall certainly be the last. I have not come to deliver a speech but to enjoy myself with you; and I must quite honestly say that it seems to me odd, almost folly even, that you should be carrying on with such exercises, however nicely you may have done them. Aha! but I already get the drift. Your evil principle is among you again: this Leonhardt, this contriving, reflective, dialectical, super-intellectual man. No doubt you have been addressing yourselves to him; for your own selves you would surely not have needed such goings on and wouldn't have fallen into them. Yet they couldn't have been to any avail with him! And the poor women must have had to go along with it. Now just think what lovely music they could have sung for you, in which all the piety of your discourse could have dwelt far more profoundly. Or think how charmingly they might have conversed with you, out of hearts full of love and joy. Such would have eased and refreshed you differently, and better too, than you could possibly have been affected by these celebratory addresses of yours!

'For my part, today I am of no use for such things at all. For me, all forms are too rigid, all speech-making too tedious and cold. Itself unbounded by speech, the subject of Christmas claims, indeed creates in me a speechless joy, and I cannot but laugh and exult like a child. Today all men are children to me, and are all the dearer on that account. The solemn wrinkles are for once smoothed away, the years and cares do not stand written on the brow. Eyes sparkle and dance again, the sign of a beautiful and serene existence within. To my good fortune, I too have become just like a child again. As a child stifles his childish pain, suppressing his sighs and holding back his tears, when something is done to arouse his childish joy, so it is with me today. The long, deep, irrepressible pain in my life is soothed as never before. I feel at home, as if born anew into the better world, in which pain and grieving have no meaning and no room any more. I look upon all things with a gladsome eye, even what has most deeply wounded me. As Christ had no bride but the Church, no children but his friends, no household but the temple and the world, and yet his heart was full of heavenly love and joy, so I too seem to be born to endeavour after such a life.

'And so I have roamed about the whole evening, everywhere taking part most heartily in every little happening and amusement I have come across. I have laughed, and I have loved it all. It was one long affectionate kiss which I have given to the world, and now my enjoyment with you shall be the last impress of my lips. For you know that you are the dearest of all to me.

'Come, then, and above all bring the child if she is not yet asleep, and let me see your glories, and let us be glad and sing something religious and joyful!'   *Christmas Eve. Dialogue on the Incarnation*, pp. 76-86

*

Schleiermacher, it is judged, was the first scholar to lecture publicly on the life of Jesus, beginning in 1819 with a series he repeated four times in succeeding years. The lectures reveal how deeply he was concerned with the historical nature of the biblical record, as well as with the dogmatic conception of the person of Christ. In addition, he was crucially aware of the immense problems which open up as soon as an attempt is made to study a historical figure from another social and cultural context. The same applies to our apprehension of the classic credal statements of the person of Christ, which Schleiermacher discussed in these lectures. The following text is from the notes of 1832 left by Schleiermacher, supplemented with notes taken by his students, edited by J.C. Verheyden and translated by S. Maclean Gilmour.

Lecture 13 (June 4). Therefore the actual reason for the discord in our theology is the practical necessity of conceiving Christ in purely human terms and the interest of faith in associating the divine with him. In view of the credal twofold nature it is impossible to bring them together. All artificial expedients fall short of their objective: the quiescing of the divine properties (the identity of essence and properties is lost), a double will, by which the same is intended (the divine will cannot will in temporal terms). From the practical viewpoint the impossibility occurs if Christ is to be completely conceived in the light of our imperfect circumstances, but the noble is not conceived by the ignoble, and consequently does not cease to be doctrine and example. Since every critical (or: uncritical?) theory necessarily becomes docetic, everything always comes back to the question, How can the divine be thought of in human terms in a human setting? However, we have not only the task of thinking this with respect to Christ, but [also] because of the Holy Spirit of doing the same with respect to ourselves, whether it be in personal or in common terms. Here, however, it has always been presupposed that the purely human existence and concept of existence are not therefore abandoned. The closer, then, we adhere to this analogy, the sooner we can achieve the solution.

We stopped at a point which is one of the most difficult. On the one hand one must conceive of something in Christ that specifically distinguishes him from other men, and on the other hand hold fast to the view of really human conditions of life. One cannot say that these two tasks would be carried out in mutual agreement in the course of the usual method of treatment, and one cannot hide the fact from himself that a sufficient reason exists for the division in contemporary theology, a division that has become the more apparent, the more these two tasks have been brought clearly into view. In connection with the customary credal formulae by which the superhuman, the divine, is ascribed to Christ, a concept of really human conditions of life on his part cannot be retained. The truth of the matter is that those who hold fast to the dogma in this way do not bother about the other, but it can easily be shown that they fall into a docetism which holds that Christ in his true life is no true man, and all artificial aids that have been employed do not achieve what they were intended to achieve. On the other hand it is clear that those who take their departure from the attempt to represent the life of Christ completely as a genuinely human life usually end up by conceiving Christ in such a way that no intelligible reason remains for making him in any way such an object of faith, a central point of the world (or: of mankind), and that is the division that characterizes contemporary theology.

If we begin with the dogmatic point in its usual understanding of a two-fold nature in the person of Christ and keep only in mind the disputes that raged in the earlier church, the difficulty of enlarging this doctrine into a clearly intelligible concept becomes already apparent, as well as the fact that the attempt has been unsuccessful. If we say that there is in Christ as a person a divine and human nature, then from each of these two points results must issue that cancel each other out. The human nature manifests itself everywhere as a definite, limited consciousness, but the divine nature excludes all that is limited. But therewith what is definite, as far as it exists in the man, is terminated. If I am now to think of the consciousness of Christ as a human consciousness, I think of it in every moment as fulfilled in a definite way, *but only in such a way that an infinite variety of consciousness is still possible outside fulfilment, and so one moment is included in the consciousness whereas another moment is not; but the divine nature must be omniscient and exclude such a distinction of the one moment in which one knows something and of the other that does not know it.* Consequently the artificial aid (or: way out) has been devised which asserts that the divine properties quiesced during the course of Christ's human life. But it became apparent that men in making use of this expedient are at the same time doing something wrong. What is regarded as the most essential in the knowledge of God ceases to be. It is thereby asserted that there is no relationship in God between essence and properties such as exists in finite things (or: in human nature), but both are the same. If one takes his departure from this and says that in Christ the divine properties are to quiesce, then the divine essence in him also quiesces, and the concept becomes an empty one. Other difficulties that have had to be encountered in a different fashion give rise to the same conclusion. It has been said, for example, that understanding and will belong to a spiritual nature (I do not wish to comment on the correctness of this distinction). Now the same thing is

205

said of God. Men speak of the divine will and understanding. If there is a twofold nature of Christ, then a divine understanding and a divine will are in him, and by reason of his human nature a human understanding and a human will are in him. Now you will recall that with respect to the one point, the will, there arose a well-known controversy within the Christian Church. One group declared that the unity of the person rests basically on the unity of the will. Accordingly, if there is to be a unity of person in Christ, he also must possess *only one* will. The other group maintained that with respect to the unity of the person it is not a question of the unity of the will so far as ability and power are concerned, but of the unity of the will in that it always wills only one thing. If several things are willed the unity of the sequence is destroyed. Therefore Christ can have two wills, but with both he wills only one and the same thing. However, how can a human will will the same thing as the divine will and yet remain a human will, and *vice versa*? All these expedients are inadequate.

Let us look at the matter from the other side. Those who predominantly take their departure from the other point of view are accustomed to say: If Christ is to have such a relationship to us that we regard him as the absolute teacher and the absolute model, then he must be capable of being conceived wholly in human terms. If his thoughts were not truly human (or: divine) we would not grasp them. They would exceed our power of comprehension. If they were truly human but were not his own, then he would always have been engaged in deceiving men and what was actually his own would be superfluous, for it would not contribute to our development. And on the other hand, if we regard him as an absolute model we must think of his action also as actually (or: wholly) human, for otherwise I cannot follow him. In this connection therefore the same situation emerges: If Christ because of his divine properties must have acted quite differently in order to be a model for men, then the divine properties had to quiesce. But then this being amounts to nothing and is superfluous, for he would accomplish the same without it. Since the theologians from the other side must maintain that Christ in just this sense is the perfect teacher and the perfect model, we now inquire what they do if he is to be understood wholly in human terms, with the divine in him, whether it quiesces or not, if no advantage accrues to us in our real relationship to Christ. So the whole theory reduces itself to one essential thing, namely, that this divine had to be in Christ in order to satisfy the divine righteousness, and that is the way and manner that, driven into a corner by the human demand, the theory which presupposes something divine in Christ centres on the doctrine of the representative reconciliation and the satisfaction of the divine righteousness achieved by the sufferings of Christ. This, however, is something quite worthless, for if it is asserted that the divine nature is *apathes* [incapable of suffering], the divine nature as a whole is bereft of meaning. On the other hand, it is not to be denied that the more strictly one undertakes to demonstrate that Christ must be perfectly comprehensible to us — otherwise he cannot be anything of that upon which his influence on the eternal being and life depends — the more easily one reaches the point of denying that specific dignity in its entirety.

But if I am to say what seems to me to be the easier — to be able to ascribe such a specific dignity to Christ from this point of view or, proceeding from that credal formula of a twofold nature in Christ, to be able to reach a human view of his life — I prefer to undertake the former task rather than the latter. If one believes that the former task results in the abrogation of everything that specifically distinguishes Christ, this belief rests on the fact that in undertaking to demonstrate that he is wholly conceivable one takes his departure at the same time from the imperfect state of our understanding, and this cannot possibly be regarded as an essential demand. The more incomplete the spiritual state of men, the less they are able (or: even?) to comprehend the perfect. If, for instance, we are concerned with how men of a low level of disposition explain to themselves what is noble in human action, we see that they do not comprehend the motives that lie outside their own range of thought. If, however, we were to undertake to show how all men of a higher range of disposition are to be understood by the others, we should abandon the task altogether. On the contrary, *men must gradually be led to become acquainted with the motives of others.* If they were also to comprehend the noble at the very moment it is given them, the task would be impossible. If we wish to apply the same reasoning to human nature, viewed in its development, we must say that, since it is apparent from time to time that individual phenomena lie in any respect far beyond the usual standard (or: standpoint) and that an enlargement of the concept of human nature (or: knowledge) takes place, this is applicable in any conceivable connection (or: area). We must recall, for example, that what is now usually performed in the area of the lordship of man over nature is something that could not have been conceived a number of centuries ago and which at that time lay wholly outside the idea of human nature. If one had said that a man could raise himself into the air, that would have been regarded as a fable (a phantom, Icarus). The same is true in every other area, and therefore we must not demand that every human phenomenon at any given point should be comprehensible, for that would have to cancel out all progress and we would not present human nature as involved in a progressive development. Consequently there is no possibility (or add: open to us?) of pursuing both tasks at the same time. The answer to the problem as it lies before us in symbolic form cannot be found in this way.

But the longer we reflect on it, the more we shall come to see that this rests on a way and manner of philosophizing which cannot any longer be retained. If we ask, for example, with what right these two concepts, the concept of the divine and the concept of nature, are combined, everyone will have to reply, if he reflects carefully on the matter, that the task is actually impossible. The expression 'divine nature' has its due and highly appropriate place in every polytheistic system, for it is implicit in such a system that the same one humanly (or: divinely) manifests itself in a variety of forms. However, since we can no longer accept this polytheistic idea, it is impossible for us to accept it in this instance. In another connection this implies a definiteness of being that excludes all else, but also in this connection no one can actually speak of a divine nature, and this is a combination that is wholly inadequate for a scientific presentation. It is probably possible to make use of it if one has been persuaded that it is intended in a figurative way, but in a theory it cannot be employed. The concept of the one, however, seems to involve a difficulty that cannot be removed. If we say that the interest of faith is the governing spirit in the Christian Church, as it is until now and also, if that impossibility is not to establish itself, hopefully will remain so, then the interest of faith is always to place something divine in Christ, something that exceeds the human. Anything that could be different, however, would in any case put an end to the human element. For instance, every Arian theory, carried to its logical conclusion, would necessarily be docetic. It would be impossible to assume anything truly human in Christ. As soon as one distinguishes what is higher in Christ from the divine and regards it as something created, it is a *nature*, and then the problem emerges in the truly definite sense that there are two natures in one person, and it is completely insoluble. One of the two must have been appearance. If we maintain the former proposition, we must face the question: Can we possibly conceive of the divine in the human? That is the point about which in the final analysis the matter revolves. If that were wholly inconceivable, we would reach the point at which that interest of faith would have to be abandoned, for what would be positively unthinkable could also possess no reality for us. It could exert no conscious influence except by self-deception, and then there would be no other choice than to go over to the other side (or: than to become rationalists).

In connection with that interest of faith, however, we are also expected to reflect on the divine in mankind in general, not only in Christ, for the concept of the Holy Spirit is nothing else than that. The divine becomes located in human beings, among whom we ourselves are included. We are also to have this element of the divine in our self-consciousness. We shall therefore have to admit that to do justice to the interest of faith with reference to Christ by a theory that does not at the same time do justice to the interest of faith in this respect would be a fragmentation of the Christian doctrine that could be of no help to us (or: would be entirely unsatisfactory). Both ideas, then, must be mutually compatible. And if we ask whether the idea can ever have existed that to assume the activity of the Holy Spirit as something truly divine in the compass of Christianity would in any way put an end to or limit the connection and the truth of what is human, the answer is that no such assertion has ever been made and that virtually no dispute about that has ever arisen. And if I ask someone, Well then, since you assume the activity in yourself of the Holy Spirit, explain what the divine nature in you effects and what the human nature? it necessarily follows that the same questions arise. Consequently it has always been tacitly admitted that it is possible for both the divine and the human to exist in an individual Christian, and the question resolves itself into the problem of accounting for the same conjunction in the instance of the person of Christ and in so doing to postulate nothing that has no bearing on the interest of faith.   *The Life of Jesus*, pp. 81-87

*

Schleiermacher's doctrine of Christ centres on the perfect God-consciousness of Jesus — 'a veritable existence of God in him'. But as the following extract from the crucial passages in The Christian Faith *shows, Schleiermacher, as well as seeking a revision of the traditional formulae, sought to reclaim the whole biblical scope of terminology to express the significance of Christ as the one in whom humanity is created anew. He is the new creation, the Second Adam, the Redeemer of the whole human race. Once more it is seen how Schleiermacher's journey 'inwards' does not result in an individualistic emphasis upon experience. In dwelling in Jesus, God dwells in the whole world.*

FIRST DOCTRINE: THE PERSON OF CHRIST

If the spontaneity of the new corporate life is original in the Redeemer and proceeds from him alone, then as an historical individual he must have been at the

same time ideal (i.e. the ideal must have become completely historical in him),
and each historical moment of his experience must at the same time have borne
within it the ideal.

1. If the peculiar dignity of the Redeemer can be measured only by his total activity as resting upon that dignity, while this activity can be seen in its completeness only in the corporate life he founded; if, further, on the one hand, all other religious communities are destined to pass over into this one, so that all religious life existing apart from this is imperfect, whereas in this there is perfection; if, on the other hand, this life itself, at all times and even in its highest development, has no other relation to the Redeemer than that which has been indicated above, so that it can be all that it is only in virtue of its susceptibility to his influence: then the dignity of the Redeemer must be thought of in such a way that he is capable of achieving this. But inasmuch as his activity, so far as we can relate it directly and exclusively to his person, is to be considered in the first place in his public life, but in this life there are no conspicuous isolated acts which definitely stood out in separation from the rest of it, the true manifestation of his dignity, which is identical with his activity in the founding of a community, lies not in isolated moments, but in the whole course of his life. These are the two truths which, in our proposition, are not simply laid down but are also fully and at every point related to each other.

2. Now, if we live in the Christian fellowship, with the conviction which is common to all Christians, that no more perfect form of the God-consciousness lies in front of the human race, and that any new form would simply be a retrograde step; and, further, that every increase in the activity of the God-consciousness within the Christian fellowship proceeds, not from any newly-added power, but always and only from an ever-active susceptibility to his influence, clearly every given state of this corporate life must remain no more than an approximation to that which exists in the Redeemer himself; and just this is what we understand by his ideal dignity. But this corporate life is not concerned with the multifarious relationships of human life — as though Christ must have been ideal for all knowledge or all art and skill which have been developed in human society — but only with the capacity of the God-consciousness to give the impulse to all life's experiences and to determine them. Hence we do not make the ideality of the Redeemer cover more than this. To this, it is true, it might still be objected that, since the potency of the God-consciousness in the corporate life itself remains always imperfect at best, we must certainly attribute an *exemplary (vorbildliche)* dignity to the Redeemer, but

ideality (Urbildlichkeit) (which, properly, asserts the existence of the concept itself), that is, absolute perfection, is not necessarily to be attributed to him, not even according to the principle laid down above, for it is not necessary to explain the result, which always remains imperfect. Rather, it might be argued, this is the fundamental exaggeration into which believers fall when they regard Christ in the mirror of their own imperfection; and this exaggeration continually perpetuates itself in the same manner, since believers in all ages read into Jesus whatever they are able to conceive as ideal in this sphere. But in this connection there are two things to be observed. First, that on this view (if clearly realized) there must be developed at least a wish — for the absolutely perfect is always at least an object of aspiration — the more the individual subordinates his personal consciousness to the God-consciousness, even a hope, that some day the human race, if only in its noblest and best, will pass beyond Christ and leave him behind. But this clearly marks the end of Christian faith, which on the contrary knows no other way to a pure conception of the ideal than an ever-deepening understanding of Christ. If, on the other hand, this consequence is not consciously realized, or is definitely rejected, then this limitation of the ideal to the merely exemplary can only be a misunderstood rule of prudence, the apparent ground for which will reveal itself later. Second, we must reflect, on the one hand, that as soon as we grant the possibility of a continued progress in the potency of the God-consciousness, while denying that its perfection exists anywhere, we can also no longer maintain that the creation of man has been or will be completed, since undoubtedly in progress thus continual perfection remains always only a bare possibility. And this would be to assert less of man than of other creatures — for it may be said of all more limited kinds of being that their concept is perfectly realized in the totality of individuals, which complete each other. But this cannot hold of a species which develops itself freely, if the perfection of an essential vital function be posited in the concept but actually found in no individual; for perfection cannot be obtained by adding together things that are imperfect. And, on the other hand, it is to be considered how difficult it would necessarily be to indicate a difference between a true ideal and such an example in which there at the same time resides the power to produce every possible advance in the totality. For productivity belongs only to the concept of the ideal and not to that of the exemplary. We must conclude, then, that ideality is the only appropriate expression for the exclusive personal dignity of Christ.

With regard to the above statement, however, that the thought either of desire or of ability to go beyond Christ marks the end of the Christian faith, here, too, it is not easy to distinguish, among the various conceptions of it which leave room for the perfectibility of Christianity, between those which, although they do not seem so, nevertheless are still Christian, and those which are not, yet wish to pass as such. Everyone recognizes that there is a great difference between two classes. There are those who say it is not only possible but our duty to go beyond much of what Christ taught his disciples, because he himself (since human thought is impossible without words) was seriously hindered by the imperfection of language from giving real expression to the innermost content of his spiritual being in clearly defined thoughts; and the same, it may be held, is true in another sense of his actions also, in which the relations by which they were determined, and therefore imperfection, are always reflected. This, however, does not prevent us from attributing to him absolute ideality in his inner being, in the sense that that inner being may always transcend its manifestations, and what is manifested be only an ever more perfect presentation of it. But there is another class: those who are of opinion that Christ is no more even in his inner being than could be manifested of it, while the fellowship of doctrine and life which takes its origin from Christ, with the testimonies to him which it preserves, has in virtue of special divine guidance so fortunate an organization that both doctrine and life can easily be re-modelled in accordance with any more perfect ideal which later generations might conceive, without the fellowship needing to lose its historical identity, so that the necessity of founding new religious fellowships has been for all time done away. A single step more, and even the first presuppositions of the Christian faith will be removed; and that step may quite consistently be taken. For if Christ was so much under the constraint of what was necessarily involved in his appearance in history, then both he himself, and his whole achievement as well, must be capable of being explained simply by what was historically given him. That is, Christianity in its entirety can be explained by Judaism at the stage of development which it had then reached — the stage at which it was possible for a man like Jesus to be born of it. Accordingly, Christianity was nothing but a new development of Judaism, though a development saturated with foreign philosophies then current, and Jesus was nothing but a more or less original and revolutionary reformer of the Jewish law.

3. But however certain it may be that the source of such a corporate life, continually advancing in the power of its God-consciousness, can lie only in the ideal, it is not on that account any easier to understand just

how the ideal can have been revealed and manifested in a truly historically-conditioned individual. Even generally considered, we are compelled to keep the two ideas separate, and, whether we are speaking of works of art or of the forms of nature, we regard each separate one only as a complement of the rest and as requiring completion by them. But if sin is posited as a corporate act of the human race, what possibility then remains that an ideal individual could have developed out of this corporate life? The way of escape, which suggests that the ideal might be produced by human thought and transferred more or less arbitrarily to Jesus, is already cut off. In that case Christianity would be founded upon an imperfect ideal; it would therefore have to give up its claim to take up into itself all forms of faith and to develop out of itself more and more perfection and blessedness. But if our aim is to make room in human nature before Christ, and apart from him, for the power of producing within itself a pure and perfect ideal — then human nature, since there is a natural connexion between reason and will, cannot have been in a condition of universal sinfulness. Hence, if the man Jesus was really ideal, or if the ideal became historical and actual in him — the one expression means the same as the other — in order to establish a new corporate life within the old and out of it, then certainly he must have entered into the corporate life of sinfulness, but he cannot have come out of it, but must be recognized in it as a miraculous fact *(eine wunderbare Erscheinung)*, and yet (in harmony with the analogies established above) only in the meaning of the word 'miracle' which has here once for all been determined. His peculiar spiritual content, that is, cannot be explained by the content of the human environment to which he belonged, but only by the universal source of spiritual life in virtue of a creative divine act in which, as an absolute maximum, the conception of man as the subject of the God-consciousness comes to completion. But since we can never properly understand the beginnings of life, full justice is done to the demand for the perfect historicity of this perfect ideal, if, from then on, he developed in the same way as all others, so that from birth on his powers gradually unfolded, and, from the zero point of his appearance onwards, were developed to completeness in the order natural to the human race. This applies also to his God-consciousness, with which we are here specially concerned; which certainly, in the case of others as little as in his, is infused by education — the germ of it is found originally in all — but which in him too, as in all, had to develop gradually in human fashion into a really manifest consciousness, and antecedently was only present as a germ, although in a certain sense always present as an active power. So even during this period of development, after it had actually become a consciousness, it could exert its influence over the sensuous self-consciousness only in the measure in which the various functions of the latter had already emerged, and thus, even regarded from this side, it appeared as itself something that was only gradually unfolding to its full extent. If we make the mistake of thinking that, on account of his ideal nature, we must deny this and assume that from the very beginnings of his life he carried the God-consciousness as such within himself — then from the very outset he must have been conscious of himself as an Ego; indeed (the deduction is very simple), he must have been master of language from the first, at least so far as its more abstract part is concerned, and before he ever spoke; thus his whole earliest childhood must have been mere appearance. This excludes the thought of a true human life and quite definitely adopts the error of docetism; and on these terms we should have to separate in time that in which Christ is like all men from what in him is ideal, allotting to the former the whole period of development up to the beginning of mature manhood, and only then allowing the ideal to come in over and above. But this latter is then inconceivable without an absolute miracle. Nay more, sin too would then, at that earlier stage, be at least possible in him, and therefore also certainly actually present, even if only in the faintest degree; and thus Jesus would be Redeemer and redeemed in one person — with all the further consequence of that.

The pure historicity of the person of the Redeemer, however, involves also this fact, that he could develop only in a certain similarity with his surroundings, that is, in general after the manner of his people. For since mind and understanding drew their nourishment solely from this surrounding world, and his free self-activity too had in this world its determined place, even his God-consciousness, however original its higher powers, could only express or communicate itself in ideas which he had appropriated from this sphere, and in actions which as to their possibility were predetermined in it. If we wished to deny this dependence of development upon surroundings, we should logically have to assume an empirical omniscience in Christ, in virtue of which all human forms of thought, as well as languages, would have been equally familiar to him, so that he would have lived in whatever is true and right in each of these just as much as in that of his native land. We should also have to add the same omniscience relatively to the various human relationships and their management. And this, too, would mean the loss of true humanity.

4. Further, whatever is involved in the ideality of the contents of his personal spiritual life must also be compatible with this purely human

conception of his historical existence. Thus, in the first place, his development must be thought of as wholly free from everything which we have to conceive as conflict. For it is not possible that, where an inner conflict has ever at any time taken place, the traces of it should ever disapear completely. Just as little could the ideal have been recognized as present where even the slightest traces of this conflict betrayed themselves. The power with which the God-consciousness, so far as it was developed at each particular moment, determined that moment could never have been in doubt, or disturbed by the memory of an earlier conflict. Nor could he ever have found himself in a condition through which a conflict could have been occasioned in the future, that is, there could have been in him, even from the beginning, no inequality in the relation of the various functions of sensuous human nature to the God-consciousness. Thus at every moment even of his period of development he must have been free from everything by which the rise of sin in the individual is conditioned. Two things, further, are quite well possible together: first, that all powers, both the lower ones which were to be mastered and the controlling higher ones, emerged only in gradual development, so that the latter were able to dominate the former only in the measure of their development; and, secondly, that the domination itself was nevertheless at each moment complete in the sense that nothing was ever able to find a place in the sense-nature which did not instantly take its place as an instrument of the spirit, so that no impression was taken up merely sensuously into the innermost consciousness and elaborated apart from God-consciousness into an element of life, nor did any action, that can really be regarded as such, and as a real whole, ever proceed solely from the sense-nature and not from the God-consciousness. What we could lay down above only as a possibility, namely, a sinless development of a human individual life, must have become actual in the person of the Redeemer in virtue of this undisturbed identity of the relationship, so that we can represent the growth of his personality from earliest childhood on to the fulness of manhood as a continuous transition from the condition of purest innocence to one of purely spiritual fulness of power, which is far removed from anything which we call virtue. For in the condition of innocence there is an activity of the God-consciousness, but only an indirect one, which, though still latently, restrains every movement in the sense-experience which must develop into opposition. The nearest approximation to this, which not seldom occurs in our experience, we usually call 'a happy childlike nature'. The adult fulness of power, on the other hand, although its growth is gradual and the result of practice, is distinguished from virtue in this respect, that it is not the result of a conflict, inasmuch as it does not need to be worked out either through error or through sin, nor even through an inclination to either. And this purity must on no account be regarded as a consequence of outward protection, but must have its ground in the man himself, that is, in the higher God-consciousness implanted in him originally. Otherwise, since such outward protection depends upon the actions of others, the ideal in him would be produced rather than productive, and he himself would be just as much the first from the totality redeemed, as afterwards himself the Redeemer.

Secondly, so far as what is conditioned by race in his person is concerned, Christ could hardly be a complete man if his personality were not determined by this factor; but such determination in no way concerns the real principle of his life but only the organism. Racial peculiarity is in no way the type of his self-activity; it is only the type of his receptivity for the self-activity of the spirit; nor can it have been like a repelling or exclusive principle in him, but must have been united with the freest and most unclouded appreciation of everything human, and with the recognition of the identity of nature and also of spirit in all human forms; also it must have been without any effort to extend what in him was racial beyond its appointed limits. And it is only when we have guarded ourselves thus that we can say that the racial too in him is ideally determined, both in itself and in its relation to the whole of human nature.

5. Here we can only call attention in passing and by anticipation to the influence which this conception of the ideality of the Redeemer in the perfectly natural historicity of his career exercises on all the Christian doctrines current in the Church, all of which must be formulated differently if that conception more or less is given up. To begin with, the fact that all doctrines and precepts developed in the Christian Church have universal authority only through their being traced back to Christ, has no other ground than his perfect ideality in everything connected with the power of the God-consciousness. Insofar as this is set aside, there must be conceded a possibility of doctrines and precepts arising in the sphere of piety which goes beyond the utterances of Christ. Similarly, the preaching of the written word, in so far as it contains only glorification of Christ, and the sacrament of the altar, can be regarded as permanent institutions in the Christian Church only if we premise that the whole development and maintenance of Christian piety must always proceed from vital fellowship with Christ. Nor could Christ be presented as a universal example unless his relation to all original differences in individ-

uals were uniform — for otherwise he would necessarily be more of an example for some than for others. This only becomes possible through his ideality. But just as little could he be a universal example, unless every moment of his life were ideal. Otherwise it would be necessary first to distinguish the ideal from the non-ideal, which could only be done according to an external law, which (it follows) would be superior to him. That law would come in, unless (as his ideality implies) what is racially determined in him had been limited; otherwise we should have to consent to adopt into the Christian norm of life all that is simply Jewish in his life. Moreover, these points, cardinal for the Christian fellowship, are not doctrines which became current only through later developments; they are the original doctrines of his disciples, closely bound up with the way in which they applied to Jesus the idea of the Messiah, and such as are easily brought into connection with his own utterances, so far as these are accessible to us.

The Redeemer, then, is like all men in virtue of the identity of human nature, but distinguished from them all by the constant potency of his God-consciousness, which was a veritable existence of God in him.

1. That the Redeemer should be entirely free from all sinfulness is no objection to all to the complete identity of human nature in him and others, for we have already laid down that sin is so little an essential part of the being of man that we can never regard it as anything else than a disturbance of nature. It follows that the possibility of a sinless development is in itself not incongruous with the idea of human nature; indeed, this possibility is involved, and recognized, in the consciousness of sin as guilt, as that is universally understood. This likeness, however, is to be understood in such a general sense that even the first man before the first sin stood no nearer the Redeemer, and was like him in no higher sense, than all other men. For if even in the life of the first man we must assume a time when sin had not yet appeared, yet every first appearance of sin leads back to a sinful preparation. But the Redeemer too shared in the same vicissitudes of life, without which we can hardly imagine the entrance of sin at a definite moment even in Adam, for they are essential to human nature. Furthermore, the first man was originally free from all the contagious influences of a sinful society, while the Redeemer had to enter into the corporate life when it had already advanced far in deterioration, so that it would hardly be possible to attribute his sinlessness to external protection — which we certainly must somehow admit in the case of the first man, if we would not involve ourselves in contradictions. Of the

Redeemer, on the contrary, we must hold that the ground of his sinlessness was not external to himself, but that it was a sinlessness essentially grounded in himself, if he was to take away, through what he was in himself, the sinfulness of the corporate life. Therefore, so far as sin is concerned, Christ differs no less from the first man than from all others.

The identity of human nature further involves this, that the manner in which Christ differs from all others also has its place in this identity. This would not be the case if it were not involved in human nature that individuals, so far as the measure of the different functions is concerned, are originally different from each other, so that to every separate corporate life (regarded in space as well as in time) there belong those who are more and less gifted; and we only arrive at the truth of life when we thus correlate those who differ from each other. In the same way, therefore, all those who in any respect give character to an age or a district are bound up with those over whom (as being defective in that particular respect) they extend an educative influence, even as Christ is bound up with those whom his preponderatingly powerful God-consciousness links to the corporate life thus indicated. The greater the difference, and the more specific the activity, the more must these also have established themselves against the hindering influences of a worthless environment, and they can be understood only by reference to this self-differentiating quality of human nature, not by reference to the group in which they stand; although by divine right they belong to it, as the Redeemer does to the whole race.

2. But in admitting that what is peculiar in the Redeemer's kind of activity belongs to a general aspect of human nature, we by no means wish to reduce this activity, and the personal dignity by which it is conditioned, to the same measure as that of others. The simple fact that faith in Christ postulates a relation on his part to the whole race, while everything analogous is valid only for definite individual times and places, is sufficient to prove this. For no one has yet succeeded, in any sphere of science or art, and no one will ever succeed, in establishing himself as head, universally animating and sufficient for the whole human race.

For this peculiar dignity of Christ, however, in the sense in which we have already referred back the ideality of his person to this spiritual function of the God-consciousness implanted in the self-consciousness, the terms of our proposition alone are adequate; for to ascribe to Christ an absolutely powerful God-consciousness, and to attribute to him an existence of God in him, are exactly the same thing. The expression, 'the existence of God in anyone', can only express the relation of the omnipresence of God to this one. Now since God's existence can only be apprehended as pure activity, while every individualized existence is merely an intermingling of activity and passivity — the activity being always found apportioned to this passivity in every other individualized existence — there is, so far, no existence of God in any individual thing, but only an existence of God in the world. And only if the passive conditions are not purely passive, but mediated through vital receptivity, and this receptivity confronts the totality of finite existence (so far, *i.e.*, as we can say of the individual as a living creature that, in virtue of the universal reciprocity, it in itself presents the world), could we suppose an existence of God in it. Hence this clearly does not hold of what is individualized as an unconscious thing; for since an unconscious thing brings no living receptivity to meet all the forces of consciousness it cannot represent these forces in itself. But just as little and for the same reason can what is conscious but not intelligent represent them, so that it is only in the rational individual that an existence of God can be admitted. How far this is also true similarly and without distinction if we regard reason as functioning in objective consciousness lies outside our investigation. But so far as the rational self-consciousness is concerned, it is certain that the God-consciousness which (along with the self-consciousness) belongs to human nature originally, before the Redeemer and apart from all connexion with him, cannot fittingly be called an existence of God in us, not only because it was not a pure God-consciousness (either in polytheism or even in Jewish monotheism, which was everywhere tinctured with materialistic conceptions, whether cruder or finer), but also because, such as it was, it did not assert itself as activity, but in these religions was always dominated by the sensuous self-consciousness. If, then, it was able neither to portray God purely and with real adequacy in thought, nor yet to exhibit itself as pure activity, it cannot be represented as an existence of God in us. But just as the unconscious forces of nature and non-rational life become a revelation of God to us only so far as we bring that conception with us, so also that darkened and imperfect God-consciousness by itself is not an existence of God in human nature, but only insofar as we bring Christ with us in thought and relate it to him. So that originally it is found nowhere but in him, and he is the only 'other' in which there is an existence of God in the proper sense, so far, that is, as we posit the God-consciousness in his self-consciousness as continually and exclusively determining every moment, and consequently also this perfect indwelling of the Supreme Being as his peculiar being and his inmost self. Indeed, working backwards we must now say, if it is only through him that the human God-consciousness becomes an existence of God in human nature, and only through the rational nature that the totality of finite powers can become an existence of God in the world, that in truth he alone mediates all existence of God in the world and all revelation of God through the world, in so far as he bears within himself the whole new creation which contains and develops the potency of the God-consciousness.

3. But if as a person of this kind he needs to have the whole human development in common with us, so that even this existence of God must in him have had a development in time, and as the most spiritual element in his personality could only emerge into manifestation after the lower functions; yet he cannot have entered life as one for whom the foundations of sin had already been laid before his being began to be manifested. We have envisaged this earlier establishment of sin for all of us, without entering upon natural-scientific investigations into the origin of the individual life, and the coming together in us (if we may use the phrase) of soul and body, but simply by holding to the general facts of experience; so here, too, we seek to combine with these facts only the relatively supernatural, which we have already admitted in general for the entrance of the Redeemer into the world.

The origin of every human life may be regarded in a twofold manner, as issuing from the narrow circle of descent and society to which it immediately belongs, and as a fact of human nature in general. The more definitely the weaknesses of that narrow circle repeat themselves in an individual, the more valid becomes the first point of view. The more the individual by the kind and degree of his gifts transcends that circle, and the more he exhibits what is new within it, the more we are thrown back upon the other explanation. This means that the beginning of Jesus' life cannot in any way be explained by the first factor, but only and exclusively by the second; so that from the beginning he must have been free from every influence from earlier generations which disseminated sin and disturbed the inner God-consciousness, and he can only be understood as an original act of human nature, *i.e.* as an act of human nature as not affected by sin. The beginning of his life was also a new implanting of the God-consciousness which creates receptivity in human nature; hence this content and that manner of origin are in such a close relation that they mutually condition and explain each other. That new implanting came to be through the beginning of his life, and therefore that beginning must have transcended every detrimental influence of his immediate circle; and because it was such an original and sin-free act of nature, a filling of his nature with God-consciousness became possible as its result. So that upon this relation too the fullest light is thrown if we regard the beginning of the life of Jesus as the completed creation of human nature. The appearance of the first man constituted at the same time the physical life of the human race; the appearance of the Second Adam constituted for this nature a new spiritual life, which communicates and develops itself by spiritual fecundation. And as in the former its originality (which is the condition of the appearance of human nature) and its having emerged from creative divine activity are the same thing, so also in the Redeemer both are the same — his spiritual originality, set free from every prejudicial influence of natural descent, and that existence of God in him which also proves itself creative. If the impartation of the Spirit to human nature which was made in the first Adam was insufficient, in that the spirit remained sunk in sensuousness and barely glanced forth clearly at moments as a presentiment of something better, and if the work of creation has only been completed through the second and equally original impartation to the Second Adam, yet both events go back to one undivided eternal divine decree and form, even in a higher sense, only one and the same natural system, though one unattainable by us.

The Christian Faith, pp. 377-89

*

The work of Christ in redemption is, for Schleiermacher, essentially his graciousness in enabling believers to participate in his God-consciousness, resulting in a dominance of the 'pious emotions' over sensuous and self-centred motivations. It is thus a highly experiential soteriology based on communion with the Redeemer, rather than an 'objective' transactional theory of atonement. Schleiermacher himself sees it as a 'mystical' concept of redemption. The suffering of the cross is not as such the means of redemption, but such suffering is the token of the Redeemer's willingness to enter into 'sympathy with misery', and hence a sign of his willingness to share his blessedness. It is, one could say, an incarnational theory rather than a theology of the cross as such.

SECOND DOCTRINE: THE WORK OF CHRIST

The Redeemer assumes believers into the power of his God-consciousness, and this is his redemptive activity.

1. In virtue of the teleological character of Christian piety, both the imperfect stage of the higher life, as also the challenge of it, appear in our self-consciousness as facts due to our own individual action — though we

221

do not feel responsible for the latter in the same way as for the former. In virtue, however, of the peculiar character of Christianity this challenge is also apprehended in our self-consciousness as the act of the Redeemer. These two points of view can be reconciled only by supposing that this challenge is the act of the Redeemer become our own act. And this, accordingly, is the best way of expressing the common element in the Christian consciousness of the divine grace. Hence, from this point of view, the peculiar work of the Redeemer would first be to evoke this act in us. But if we regard the matter more closely, it is clear that what we have thus described is in every case an act both of the Redeemer and of the redeemed. The original activity of the Redeemer, therefore, which belongs to him alone, and which precedes all activity of our own in this challenge, would be that by means of which he assumes us into this fellowship of his activity and his life. The continuance of that fellowship, accordingly, constitutes the essence of the state of grace; the new corporate life is the sphere within which Christ produces this act; in it is revealed the continuous activity of his sinless perfection.

But his act in us can never be anything but the act of his sinlessness and perfection as conditioned by the being of God in him. And so these too in addition must become ours, because otherwise it would not be his act that became ours. Now the individual life of each one of us is passed in the consciousness of sin and imperfection. Hence we can know the fellowship of the Redeemer only in so far as we are not conscious of our own individual life; as impulses flow to us from him, we find that in him from which everything proceeds to be the source of our activity also — a common possession, as it were. This too is the meaning of all those passages in Scripture which speak of Christ being and living in us, of being dead to sin, of putting off the old and putting on the new man. But Christ can only direct his God-consciousness against sin in so far as he enters into the corporate life of man and sympathetically shares the consciousness of sin, but shares it as something he is to overcome. This very consciousness of sin as something to be overcome becomes the principle of our activity in the action which he evokes in us. But our own immediate experience in being thus assumed into the fellowship of Christ will be explained in the first doctrine of the second main division, which deals with forgiveness. And the further development of this fellowship in time, through a series of common actions, is the subject of the second doctrine, dealing with sanctification. Here we have only to explain more exactly what the Redeemer does and how he accomplishes it.

2. All Christ's activity, then, proceeds from the being of God in him.

And we know no divine activity except that of creation, which includes that of preservation, or, conversely, that of preservation, which includes that of creation. So we shall have to regard Christ's activity too in the same way. We do not, however, exclude the soul of man from creation, in spite of the fact that the creation of such a free agent and the continued freedom of a being created in the context of a greater whole is something which we cannot expect to understand; all that we can do is to recognize the fact. The same is true of the creative activity of Christ, which is entirely concerned with the sphere of freedom. For his assumptive activity is a creative one, yet what it produces is altogether free. Now the being of God in him as an active principle is timeless and eternal, yet its expressions are all conditioned by the form of human life. It follows that he can influence what is free only in accordance with the manner in which it enters into his sphere of living influence, and only in accordance with the nature of the free. The activity by which he assumes us into fellowship with him is, therefore, a creative production in us of the will to assume him into ourselves, or rather — since it is only receptiveness for his activity as involved in the impartation — only our assent to the influence of his activity. But it is a condition of that activity of the Redeemer that the individuals should enter the sphere of his historical influence, where they become aware of him in his self-revelation. Now this assent can only be conceived as conditioned by the consciousness of sin; yet it is not necessary that this should precede entrance into the sphere of the Redeemer. Rather it may just as well arise within that sphere as the effect of the Redeemer's self-revelation, as indeed it certainly does come to full clarity only as we contemplate his sinless perfection. Accordingly, the original activity of the Redeemer is best conceived as a pervasive influence which is received by its object in virtue of the free movement with which he turns himself to its attraction, just as we ascribe an attractive power to everyone to whose educative intellectual influence we gladly submit ourselves. Now, if every activity of the Redeemer proceeds from the being of God in him, and if in the formation of the Redeemer's Person the only active power was the creative divine activity which established itself as the being of God in him, then also his every activity may be regarded as a continuation of that person-forming divine influence upon human nature. For the pervasive activity of Christ cannot establish itself in an individual without becoming person-forming in him too, for now all his activities are differently determined through the working of Christ in him, and even all impressions are differently received — which means that the personal self-consciousness too becomes altogether different. And just as creation is not concerned simply with individuals (as if each creation of an individual had been a special act), but it is the world that was created, and every individual as such was created only in and with the whole, for the rest not less than for itself, in the same way the activity of the Redeemer too is world-forming, and its object is human nature, in the totality of which the powerful God-consciousness is to be implanted as a new vital principle. He takes possession of the individuals relatively to the whole, wherever he finds those in whom his activity does not merely remain, but for whom, moving on, it can work upon others through the revelation of his life. And thus the total effective influence of Christ is only the continuation of the creative divine activity out of which the Person of Christ arose. For this, too, was directed towards human nature as a whole, in which that being of God was to exist, but in such a way that its effects are mediated through the life of Christ, as its most original organ, for all human nature that has already become personal in the natural sense, in proportion as it allows itself to be brought into spiritual touch with that life and its self-perpetuating organism. And this in order that the former personality may be slain and human nature, in vital fellowship with Christ be formed into persons in the totality of that higher life.

Let us now look at the corporate life, or at the fellowship of the individual with the Redeemer. We may best describe its beginning, since it is conditioned by a free acceptance, by the term *calling* — the whole official activity of Christ began with just such a call. But the share of the Redeemer in the common life, viewed as continuing, we are fully justified in calling *soul-bestowal* (*Beseelung*), primarily with reference to the corporate life — as indeed the Church is called his Body. In just the same way Christ is to be the soul also in the individual fellowship, and each individual the organism through which the soul works. The two things are related as in Christ the divine activity present in the act of union is related to that activity in the state of union, and as in God the activity of creation is related to that of preservation. Only that here it is still clearer how each moment of a common activity can be regarded also as a calling, and likewise how the calling proper can be regarded as soul-bestowal. But this formula, too, we shall employ in another place.

3. This exposition is based entirely on the inner experience of the believer; its only purpose is to describe and elucidate that experience. Naturally, therefore, it can make no claim to be a proof that things must have been so; in the sphere of experience such proof is only possible where mathematics can be used, which is certainly not the case here. Our purpose is simply to show that the perfect satisfaction to which we aspire

can only be truly contained in the Christian's consciousness of his relation to Christ in so far as that consciousness expresses the kind of relation which has been described here. If this content be lacking in the Christian consciousness, then either the perfect satisfaction must come from some other quarter, or it does not exist at all, and we must be content with an indefinite appeasement of conscience, such as may be found without any Redeemer; and in that case there would be no special possession of divine grace in Christianity at all. Now these negations cannot be logically refuted; they can only be removed by actual facts: we must seek to bring doubters to the same experience as we have had.

Now such a presentation of the redeeming activity of Christ as has been given here, which exhibits it as the establishment of a new life common to him and us (original in him, in us new and derived), is usually called by those who have not had the experience, 'mystical'. This expression is so extremely vague that it seems better to avoid it. But if we are willing to keep so close to its original use as to understand by it what belongs to the circle of doctrines which only a few share, but for others are a mystery, then we may accept it. Provided that we recognize that no one can be received into this circle arbitrarily, because doctrines are only expressions of inward experiences — whoever has these experiences *ipso facto* belongs to the circle; whoever has not, cannot come in at all. But an analogy to this relation may be pointed out in a sphere which is universally familiar. As contrasted with the condition of things existing before there was any law, the civil community within a defined area is a higher vital potency. Let us now suppose that some person for the first time combines a naturally cohesive group into a civil community (legend tells of such cases in plenty); what happens is that the idea of the state first comes to consciousness in him, and takes possession of his personality as its immediate dwelling-place. Then he assumes the rest into the living fellowship of the idea. He does so by making them clearly conscious of the unsatisfactoriness of their present condition by effective speech. The power remains with the founder of forming in them the idea which is the innermost principle of his own life, and of assuming them into the fellowship of that life. The result is, not only that there arises among them a new corporate life, in complete contrast to the old, but also that each of them becomes in himself a new person — that is to say, a citizen. And everything resulting from this is the corporate life — developing variously with the process of time, yet remaining essentially the same — of this idea which emerged at that particular point of time, but was always predestined in the nature of that particular radical stock. The analogy might be pushed even further, to points of which we shall speak later. But even this presentation of it will seem mystical to those who admit only a meagre and inferior conception of the civic state.

Let us be content, then, that our view of the matter should be called mystical in this sense; naturally everything to be derived from this main point will be called mystical too. But just as this mystical view can substantiate its claim to be the original one, so too it claims to be the true mean between two others, of which I shall call the one the magical way, and the other the empirical. The former admits, of course, that the activity of Christ is redemptive, but denies that the communication of his perfection is dependent on the founding of a community; it results, they maintain, from his immediate influence upon the individual: and for this some take the written word to be a necessary means, others do not. The latter show themselves the more consistent, but the more completely they cut themselves loose from everything originating in the community the more obvious becomes the magical character of their view. This magical character lies in an influence not mediated by anything natural, yet attributed to a person. This is completely at variance with the maxim everywhere underlying our presentation, that the beginning of the Kingdom of God is a supernatural thing, which, however, becomes natural as soon as it emerges into manifestation; for this other view makes every significant moment a supernatural one. Further, this view is completely separatist in type, for it makes the corporate life a purely accidental thing; and it comes very near being docetic as well. For if Christ exerted influence in any such way as this — as a person, it is true, but only as a heavenly person without earthly presence, though in a truly personal way — then it would have been possible for him to work in just the same way at any time, and his real personal appearance in history was only a superfluous adjunct. But those who likewise assume an immediate personal influence, but mediate it through the word and the fellowship, are less magical only if they attribute to these the power of evoking a mood in which the individual becomes susceptible to that personal influence. They are more magical still, if these natural elements have the power of disposing Christ to exert his influence; for then their efficacy is exactly like that attributed to magic spells. The contrary empirical view also, it is true, admits a redemptive activity on the part of Christ, but one which is held to consist only in bringing about an increasing perfection in us; and this cannot properly occur otherwise than in the forms of teaching and example. These forms are general; there is nothing distinctive in them. Even suppose if admitted that Christ is distinguished from others who contribute in the same way to our improvement, by the pure perfection of his teaching and his example, yet if all that is achieved in us is something imperfect, there remains nothing but to forgo the idea of redemption in the proper sense — that is, as the removal of sin — and, in view of the consciousness of sin still remaining even in our growing perfection, to pacify ourselves with a general appeal to the divine compassion. Now, teaching and example effect no more than such a growing perfection, and this appeal to the divine compassion occurs even apart from Christ. It must therefore be admitted that his appearance, in so far as intended to be something special, would in that case be in vain. At most it might be said that by his teaching he brought men to the point of giving up the effort, previously universal, to offer God substitutes for the perfection they lacked. But since the uselessness of this effort can be demonstrated, already in our natural intelligence we have the divine certainty of this, and had no need to obtain it elsewhere. And probably this view is chiefly to blame for the claim of philosophy to set itself above faith and to treat faith as merely a transitional stage. But we cannot rest satisfied with the consciousness of growing perfection, for that belongs just as much to the consciousness of sin as to that of grace, and hence cannot contain what is peculiarly Christian. But, for the Christian, nothing belongs to the consciousness of grace unless it is traced to the Redeemer as its cause, and therefore it must always be a different thing in his case from what it is in the case of others — naturally, since it is bound up with something else, namely, the peculiar redemptive activity of Christ.

The Redeemer assumes the believers into the fellowship of his unclouded blessedness, and this is his reconciling activity.

1. If this assumption into the fellowship of Christ's blessedness were independent of the assumption into the power of his God-consciousness, or even if the former were to follow from the latter, the teleological nature of Christianity would be changed. But just as in God blessedness and omnipotence are balanced, mutually conditioned, and yet also independent of each other, so also in the person of Christ blessedness and the power of the God-consciousness must be balanced in the same way, one conditioning the other and each independent of the other. Accordingly we can say that it must be the same with the effective influence of Christ. Either this must be simply admitted, or else there must be two contrasted ways of regarding Christianity, complementary to each other, one of them presenting it as an effort after blessedness for the sake of the power

of the God-consciousness, the other *vice versa*. But since the effective influence of Christ arises only in so far as a receptivity or a longing for it pre-exists in its object, so the reconciling activity can only manifest itself as a consequence of the redemptive activity because the consciousness of sin, in itself and not as a source of evil, forms the necessary basis of that longing, inasmuch as in the case of the individual evil is not connected with sin. So if we think of the Redeemer's activity as an influence upon the individual, we are bound to make the reconciling factor follow upon the redemptive and issue from it. But we equate the two thus far, that the communication of blessedness no less than the communication of perfection is given immediately in the assumption into vital fellowship with Christ.

2. Now in view of the exact parallel between this proposition and the preceding one, so that regarded in and by themselves they might fittingly have been run together into one, this seems hardly to need explanation. On the one hand, every activity in Christ proceeded from the being of God in him, and this activity was never hindered by any resistance of his human nature. Similarly, the hindrances to his activity never determined any moment of his life until the perception of them had been taken up into his inmost self-consciousness, which was so completely one with his powerful God-consciousness that they could appear in it only as belonging to the temporal form of the perfect effectiveness of his being. On the other hand, it was still less possible that hindrances arising out of his own natural or social life could be taken up in this innermost consciousness as hindrances; they could be no more than indications of the direction set for his activity. Similarly, the redeemed man too, since he has been assumed into the vital fellowship of Christ, is never filled with the consciousness of any evil, for it cannot touch or hinder the life which he shares with Christ. All hindrances to life, natural and social, come to him even in this region only as indications. They are not taken away, as if he were to be, or could be, without pain and free from suffering, for Christ also knew pain and suffered in the same way. Only the pains and sufferings do not mean simple misery, for they do not as such penetrate into the inmost life. And this holds good also of his consciousness of the sin still occurring in his life. It cannot have its source in his new life; he refers it therefore only to the corporate life of general sinfulness, which still has a place in him. Not that it is not pain and suffering, so far as he clings to his own personality; but it reaches the life of Christ in him only as an indication of what he has to do; consequently there is in it no misery. The assumption into vital fellowship with Christ, therefore, dissolves the

connection between sin and evil, since morally the two are no longer related to each other, even if from the merely natural point of view the one is the consequence of the other. Morally, however, each of them, by itself is regarded solely in relation to the task of the new life. Hence, just as the redemptive activity of Christ brings about for all believers a corporate activity corresponding to the being of God in Christ, so the reconciling element, that is, the blessedness of the being of God in him, brings about for all believers, as for each separately, a corporate feeling of blessedness. Therein, too, their former personality dies, so far as it meant a self-enclosed life of feeling within a sensuous vital unity, to which all sympathetic feeling for others and for the whole was subordinated. But what remains as the self-identity of the person is the peculiar way of apprehending and perceiving, which as individualized intelligence so works itself into the new common life that relatively to this factor also the activity of Christ is person-forming, in that an old man is put off and a new man is put on. Here too, if we wish to note similarities between the activity of Christ in forming the new corporate life and the divine activity in forming the personality of Christ, we shall be able to distinguish a first moment, which corresponds to the act of union as first beginning, and as such can only look back to what preceded, and a second, which represents the state of union, and, as expressing continuance, also looks forward to the future. Now here the beginning is the disappearance of the old man, and so also of the old reference of all evil to sin, that is, disappearance of the consciousness of deserving punishment. Consequently the first thing in the reconciling aspect is the forgiveness of sins. For in the unity of life with Christ all relation to the law ceases, since the general movement contrary to sin, proceeding from him, begins. But the state of union is the real possession of blessedness in the consciousness that Christ in us is the centre of our life, and this in such a way that this possession exists solely as his gift, which, since we receive it simply by his will that we should have it, is his blessing and his peace. But the same thing is true here again, that each moment or aspect may at the same time be regarded in accordance with the formula of the other. For in the first moment the whole development is already implicitly contained, but at the same time in every later moment the first persists; for the fact that this possession of blessedness is pervaded throughout by sin (a fact which our recurrence to Christ makes it all the more impossible to overlook) always points on in turn to the forgiveness of sins.

3. Obviously our proposition is mystical in the same sense as the previous one, and its truth also can only be proved in experience. But in the

same sense it too stands intermediate between a magical view, which destroys all naturalness in the continuous activity of Christ, and an empirical, which reduces it altogether to the level of ordinary daily experience, and thus does not make its supernatural beginning and its distinctive peculiarity the fundamental things in it.

The latter view likewise starts from the connection between sin and evil, and rightly infers that when sin is taken away so also is evil. But since this connection principally holds good for social evil alone, and is exact even for this only if we consider a large corporate life as a rounded whole, whereas in every individual part of that life inward improvement may well be accompanied by increasing evil, because of its connection with the rest, the growing improvement of the individual can furnish no guarantee at all that he is being set free from evil and cannot form a basis of blessedness. Even along with increasing perfection the fact remains not only that he encounters hindrances to life, but that they are such as in the light of the sin still present in him have the aspect of punishment. It follows that this reconciliation only very accidentally takes the form of enjoyment and possession; in essence it can never be set forth as more than hope. But in either form it is not, so far as content is concerned, anything peculiarly Christian, nor can it as enjoyment have a greater strength, or as hope possess a higher degree of certainty, within Christianity than without. And how slight this is everywhere, history clearly shows. For, altogether apart from Christianity, the dispute is constantly recurring as to whether evil in the world is really growing less, or only changing its form while in sum remaining what it has ever been. Not only so, but within the Christian Church itself the same doubt constantly reappears, and this the more strongly the less experience there is of the enjoyment of the unclouded blessedness of Christ, and the more recourse is had to that general hope. And, quite contrary to Christ's own assurance, that blessedness is relegated to the life beyond time, and thus clearly declared to be independent of the gradual improvement. But in that case Christ has part in our blessedness or salvation only through his influence upon this progressive improvement, which means that a specific difference between him and other men is of little importance.

Only those views of Christ's reconciling activity appear to be magical which make the impartation of his blessedness independent of assumption into vital fellowship with him. This means that the forgiveness of sins is made to depend upon the punishment which Christ suffered, and the blessedness of men itself is presented as a reward which God offers to Christ for the suffering of that punishment. Not, of course, that the thought of our blessedness as a rewarding of Christ is altogether to be rejected — on the contrary, we shall have to speak of that later. Nor that all connection between the suffering of Christ and the forgiveness of sins is to be denied. But both ideas become magical when blessedness and forgiveness are not mediated through vital fellowship with Christ. For within this fellowship the impartation of blessedness, as explained above, is a natural one; whereas without this the rewarding of Christ is nothing but divine arbitrariness. And this in itself is always something magical, but it is especially so when something so absolutely inward as blessedness is supposed to have been brought about externally, without any inner basis. For if it is independent of life in Christ, then, since man does not have the source of blessedness in himself, it can only have been infused into each separate individual somehow or other from without. In no less magical a way is the forgiveness of sins achieved, if the consciousness of deserving punishment is supposed to cease because the punishment has been borne by another. That in this way the expectation of punishment might be taken away is conceivable; but this is merely the sensuous element in the forgiveness of sins. The properly ethical element, the consciousness of deserving punishment, would still remain. And this therefore would have to disappear as if conjured away, without any reason. And to what extent something even of this view has passed over into Church doctrine is a question we shall have to discuss below.

4. Now if we compare the connected view here set forth with the two alternative views which have just been cited, they certainly suggest the reflection that in our view, the suffering of Christ has nothing to say, so that there has not even been an opportunity to raise the question whether, and to what extent, it belongs to redemption or to reconciliation. But the only conclusion to be drawn from this postponement of the question is that no reason existed for adducing it as a primitive element either in the one place or in the other. And this is so far correct, that otherwise no complete assumption into vital fellowship with Christ, such as makes redemption and reconciliation completely intelligible, would have been possible before the suffering and death of Christ. As an element of secondary importance, however, it belongs to both; immediately to reconciliation, and to redemption only mediately. The activity of Christ in founding the new corporate life could really emerge in its perfect fulness — although belief in this perfection could exist even apart from this — only if it yielded to no opposition, not even to that which succeeded in destroying his person. Here, accordingly, the perfection does not lie properly and immediately in the suffering itself, but only in his giving up of himself

to it. And of this it is only, as it were, a magical caricature, if we isolate this climax, leave out of account the foundation of the corporate life, and regard this giving up of himself to suffering for suffering's sake as the real sum-total of Christ's redemptive activity. But so far as reconciliation is concerned, our exposition makes it obvious that, in order to effect assumption into the fellowship of his blessedness, the longing of those who were conscious of their misery must first be drawn to Christ through the impression they had received of his blessedness. And here too the situation is that belief in this blessedness might be present even apart from this, but that nonetheless his blessedness emerged in its perfect fulness only in that it was not overcome even by the full tide of suffering. The more so that this suffering arose out of the opposition of sin, and that therefore the Redeemer's sympathy with misery, ever present, though without disturbing his blessedness, from the time of his entrance into the corporate life of sin, had here to enter on its greatest phase. And here it is not the giving up of himself to suffering, as something that forms part of the redemptive activity, but the suffering itself which is the full confirmation of belief in the Redeemer's blessedness. But here again it is only a magical caricature of this which, completely overlooking the necessity of an imperturbable blessedness in Christ, finds the reconciling power of his suffering precisely in the fact that he willingly gave up even his blessedness, and experienced, even if only for moments, real misery. So far as Church doctrine is not wholly free from this idea either, we shall return to the matter below.

The climax of his suffering, we hold then, was sympathy with misery. This, however, at once involves the further conclusion that no suffering which is not bound up with the redemptive activity of Christ can be regarded as belonging to reconciliation, because suffering of that sort would also have no connection with the Redeemer's opposition to misery, and so it could belong to the reconciliation only in a magical way. Now Christ's sufferings can be thought of in this connection with his redemptive activity only when regarded as a whole and a unity; to separate out any particular element and ascribe to it a peculiar reconciling value, is not merely trifling allegory if done in teaching, and worthless sentimentality in poetry; probably it is also seldom free from a defining admixture of superstition. Least of all is it proper to ascribe such a special reconciling value to his physical sufferings; and that for two reasons. On the one hand, these sufferings in themselves have only the loosest connection with his reaction against sin. On the other hand, our own experience teaches us that an ordinary ethical development and robust piety have as their reward the almost complete overcoming of physical sufferings in the presence of a glad spiritual self-consciousness, whether personal or corporate. Certainly they can never suppress that consciousness, nor make a moment of blessedness any less blessed. But in order that the exposition just given may serve as an all-round test in scrutinizing Church formulae, it must be brought into relation to our general formula of the creation of human nature as completed through Christ, so as to convince ourselves that in this twofold activity of Christ such a creation is really fully accomplished. For whatever in human nature is assumed into vital fellowship with Christ is assumed into the fellowship of an activity solely determined by the power of the God-consciousness, therefore adequate to every new experience and extracting from it all it has to yield. It is at the same time assumed into the fellowship of a satisfaction which rests in that activity and which cannot be disturbed by any outside influence. Now that each assumption of this sort is simply a continuation of the same creative act which first manifested itself in time by the formation of Christ's Person; that each increase in the intensity of this new life relatively to the disappearing corporate life of sinfulness is also such a continuation, must now be clear; and that in this new life man achieves the destiny originally appointed for him, and that nothing beyond this can be conceived or attempted for a nature such as ours — all this requires no further exposition.

However exactly this presentation of the subject may correspond to the immediate consciousness of the Christian, so that it recognizes itself in it, still it is inevitable that, as it stands half-way between the empirical and the magical interpretations, it should be mistaken by each of these for the opposite one. For, on the one hand, since a spiritual thing like the foundation of a corporate life must be spiritually achieved, and there is no spiritual influence but the presentation of oneself in word and deed, the Redeemer could only enter into our corporate life by means of such self-presentation, thereby attracting men to himself and making them one with himself. Now to warn those who lean to the side of magic, this touchstone must be kept before them, whether their conception really agrees with the possibility of conceiving the effective influence of Christ under this historical natural form. And nothing is easier than for them to misunderstand this, and to imagine that Christ must work simply in the ordinary human way as teacher and example, the divine in him being altogether left out of account. But on the other hand, the distinction between such a Christ and Christ as we here understand him, can only be made plain by reference to 'Christ in us', whereas the relation of teacher and pupil, like that of pattern and imitation, must always remain an external one. If, however, those who lean to the empirical view were asked whether they too had a real experience of vital fellowship with Christ, they would only too easily misunderstand the question, and suppose that they were being asked to assent to the objectionable magic view. For that reason we shall leave wide room on both sides open, not only for the Christian Church as a whole, but also for the Protestant Church, in which all these differences are present, in order that, wherever there is a recognition of Christ — and the danger of letting this go is just as great as on the side of the magical extreme as on that of the empirical — and so long as such an extreme has not yet been reached, we may always be able to maintain fellowship, and by means of it bring all ever nearer to the centre.

The Christian Faith, pp. 425-438

7

NATION, CHURCH AND STATE[*]

Schleiermacher's patriotism was most eloquently communicated through his preaching in the Trinity Church, Berlin. 1813, the year of the great blow for freedom against Napoleon, produced some of his most vivid oratory, as this sermon shows. It also advocated a view of national character and destiny which was to affect profoundly the growth of German nationalistic feeling over the following century, especially in the idea of 'nation' as a human entity specifically created by God with its own individuality to be preserved by any means.

A NATION'S DUTY IN A WAR FOR FREEDOM

Preached 28 March 1813
Text: Jeremiah 17:5-8 and 18:7-10

My devout hearers! Through an extraordinary occurrence we find the order of our discourses on the suffering Saviour interrupted, and our today's meeting devoted to a very different subject. How deeply have we all been moved by the events of the last weeks! We saw march forth from our gates the army of a people nominally allied to us, but our feeling was not that of parting with friends; with thankful joy did we feel at last the long, heavy pressure removed from us. Immediately after that came the troops of another nation, nominally at war with us; but with the most joyful enthusiasm were they received when they made themselves known as the friends of the king and the people. And when, not long after them, we saw our own warriors also returning, then no one could any longer doubt, and the word passed joyfully from mouth to mouth: Thanks for the heavenly, unmistakable tokens which God the Lord has given through the fearful turmoil of war in the North; thanks to the noble and brave military leaders who, disregarding the appearance of disobedience and the infraction of the letter, and acting really according to the mind and spirit of the king, dared to take the first decisive step towards freeing us from the intolerable bonds under which we had so long been held; thanks to the king, who when this favourable moment presented itself, could not do

---

[*] See also pp. 58ff. above.

otherwise than let his feeling, which was entirely the same as ours, bear sway; thanks to all this, the great change, the transition from bondage to freedom, is in preparation. But openly as we thanked God with joy among ourselves, it was not yet time to do so publicly; for the king had not yet spoken. At last sounded forth to us the long and impatiently expected royal word, which, although certainly the public papers have deeply impressed it on us all, we shall as certainly hear once more with joy and emotion when it is read today by the king's command from every pulpit in the city. It runs thus. [Here followed the summons of the king, To my people.]

Thus the king; and I count it only fair to abstain from speaking in laudation of this royal word. It is still fresh in all our hearts, the delight in the certainty of battle which this word gives us, in the high and noble spirit which here gives utterance to what all the best in the nation had long felt and thought. And now, hardly had we heard this glorious call when our ear was greeted by the triumphant shout of a city loved and revered by every German heart, which was the first to be freed from the direct yoke of the enemy; and, as the crown of all, we saw our beloved king himself come among us with a feeling — we may freely admit it to our-selves — that can never before have lifted up his heart, for he never before had an opportunity of feeling so deeply and truly that which is the source of the highest happiness and exaltation to a ruler, the purest harmony between his will and his people's wish; we saw him lead forth on the way to meet the enemy the army which, at his command, had been conse-crated and blessed for the battle by prayer. This then, the departure of our army to battle, to decisive battle for what is highest and noblest, is the subject which, as it assuredly fills and stirs all our hearts, is to occupy our attention at this hour, so that for us also this holy war may begin with humble, elevating thoughts of God, and that our hope and our joy may be sanctified to him.

I have taken these words of the prophet on which to found our medita-tion, not at all, as it may possibly appear, in order to institute a compar-ison between ourselves and that nation against whom we are going to war; but merely in order rightly to distinguish what is conflicting in our own history, that we may thus be led up to the essential part in the great change in which we are rejoicing. For, my friends, the joy that befits us in this place is not joy merely because the oppression and suffering under which we have long sighed are now at an end; not the joy which paints for us in anticipation bright pictures of future prosperity which we hope to attain; here this must be only second and last with us. And if, nevertheless, this contrast still presents itself to us, let us apply it to ourselves in this way, that we feel, as the prophet represents to us, that in the individual, but still more in the mass, changes in the lot depend on the rise and fall of intrinsic worth. Yes, let us here consider the great change entirely from this point of our worthiness before God. On two things included in this, these words give us light; first, what, in this aspect, is the exact significance and the real nature of the change; and second, what we must therefore feel called on to do.

1. In order to understand rightly what is the main point in the great change in our position as citizens which is begun by the present declaration of war, we must look back to a former time well known to us all, and through which many of us lived, when deep decay and fearful devastations had fallen on these lands. Then, through the efforts of several wise and strict rulers, through a judicious taking advantage of events, through successfully conducted wars, but most through the growing up of a noble and free aspiring spirit in the people themselves, we became a nation and kingdom regarding which the whole world saw that the Lord would build and plant it and had promised to do it good. And suddenly enough for all those to whom gradual growth is less perceptible, we found ourselves at this height. But gradually, and while dreaming of rising yet far higher, we slipped downwards, and then just as suddenly plunged to the bottom. For we began to boast of our strength, to rely on the fear with which we might inspire other nations, and thus the effects of our former fame were to carry us ever higher without the forth-putting of our own power, without works on our part pleasing to God. We became the man who makes flesh his arm and whose heart departeth from the Lord. Dishonest acquisitions enlarged our territory in a way more apparent than profitable; for we acquired but few true brethren who willingly obeyed the same laws and laboured for the same end. While other States put forth efforts and wore themselves out in constantly renewed wars, partly for the sake of the same great blessings for which we are now about to fight, we thought to become ever mightier and more formidable through repose. Thus our self-confident prudence was gradually followed by despondency, and we became in yet another way the man who trusts in man; for he also who flatters men and fears them trusts in man. And with our fame our very sense of honour became, more and more, as time went on, an empty name. And more and more our heart departed from the Lord. In a puffed-up, unnatural prosperity the old virtues were by degrees lost, a flood of vanity and dissipation laid waste the laborious works of long and better years; and plainly as the voice of the Lord made itself heard warning us to

repentance, we did not obey him; we did evil in his sight, and therefore he repented of the good that he had promised to do us. And suddenly, just as we seemed about to rouse up out of the long blindness and stupidity in which, however, the greater number were still wrapped, though not more deeply than before — suddenly the Lord spoke out against us as against a nation and kingdom which he would pluck up and pull down and destroy. Then there fell upon us that grievous, crushing disaster in war, and this sudden fall from the height into the abyss was followed by the ever more deeply and painfully suicidal calamity of peace. I am not speaking of the privations, of the distress, of the poverty, of the constantly increasing difficulty in all the external relations of life; I speak only of the inward spiritual corruption which was, one hardly knows whether to say, brought to light by this state of things, or actually created and formed by it. The wretched habit of continually bearing indignity, which we practised publicly and privately during those seven dismal years with the feeling that to let righteous indignation have free course could only increase the evil without any beneficial result — that habit and that feeling are the fruit of sluggishness, of enervation, of cowardice; but how did they in turn increase and spread cowardice, sluggishness and enervation, until all confidence in ourselves, every hope, except the foolish hope of a help that was to come merely from without — till even the wish to be able to help ourselves, nay, till even the sense of being worthy of a better condition disappeared; and the miserable idea took possession of men's minds that the living, mental energy of the nation was entirely exhausted, and the hour of utter ruin had come. This fear had power with not a few among us, who were day by day expecting the dissolution of our separate existence, and who, no longer hoping to see any comfort in the future, were only speculating how they could most comfortably accommodate themselves to the foreign yoke. The impossibility which we so often met, of escaping the danger of the moment without falsehood and fraud, the necessity to feign praise and approval, nay, even agreement and friendship, where we could only despise and detest; all this was no doubt the fruit of that loss of shame which for the sake of life ignored all life's noble aims; but how fearfully was this shamelessness developed by that condition of things, and what an amount of humiliation it took even to provoke public indignation! The insecurity of all property and all rights was no doubt in great part a consequence of the thoughtlessness with which, in times of calamity, people so often try to free themselves from the distress of the moment or to enjoy its fleeting pleasure, without remembering what they ruin or risk in the long run; but to what a degree did that insecure condition increase this thoughtlessness! How did we see luxury and extravagance as in the most prosperous times! how did we see usury and regardless violence sucking up the property of others and lavishing its own, as if all were indeed devoted to speedy ruin! This is the deep corruption into which, on the one hand, we had fallen; and if, on the other hand, our fall and these its effects opened the eyes of many for the first time, others made it more plainly visible than before what was wanting in us; if, in many, a noble ardour was kindled to cast off the indignity that oppressed us from without, and to banish what defiled us within, yet even these noble germs of better things, without definite form or connection, could only excite apprehensions of an irregular outbreak, behind which the cowardice and baseness of others would only the more impregnably intrench and fortify themselves.

Such was our condition, my friends, and no one could conceal from himself that if we continued in the same alliances and in the same state of dependence, we must become more and more like the heath in the desert. Now if I regard the renunciation of these alliances and the attitude of war which, on the contrary, we have assumed, and the beginning of which we are celebrating — if I regard these as the beginning for us all of being lifted up from this deep fall; if I hope that God will now repent of the evil that he purposed to do us; this is founded chiefly on the following things.

In the first place, and to begin with what every one must at moments have most deeply felt; this change is in itself the turning back to truth, the deliverance from the humiliating hypocrisy, which every one, the more he believed himself bound to represent in his talk not himself but the State, really carried to a dreadful perfection. Now, thank God, we can again say when we abhor, or when we love and respect; and as every man of honour must stand to his word with deeds, we must surely feel free and strong in this, we must feel that we have a right to hope; for he who yields himself to truth without reservation is trusting in the Lord. But just because the word alone is nothing, and because this word more than any other demands deeds, therefore this change is the return to free action and to independence. How long, my friends, have we really had no will about our common affairs, always accommodating ourselves to circumstances, and to the oppressive foreign force, so far as it chose to reach! Now we have once more a will; now the king, confiding in his people, has declared a determination in which (because after this no reconciliation can be hoped for) there is involved the resolution to enter on a course of brave deeds which can only end, as the royal word says, in glorious ruin or in the firm establishment of this precious blessing of liberty. And hence we found on this change the hope that we shall preserve for ourselves our own distinctive character, our laws, our constitution and our culture. Every nation, my friends, which has developed to a certain height is degraded by receiving into it a foreign element, even though that may be good in itself; for God has imparted to each its own nature, and has therefore marked out bounds and limits for the habitations of the different races of men on the face of the earth. And yet how the foreign element has lately been thrusting itself upon us! how it threatened the more as time went to drive out our good manners and ways! And *what* a foreign element! Half the product of the unbridled ferocity of those horrible internal disorders, half devised for the later tyranny. In rising up to cast this utterly off and to keep it away from us for the future, we become once more a kingdom that trusts in the Lord; for in him is that nation trusting which means to defend at any price the distinctive aims and spirit which God has implanted in it, and is thus fighting for God's work; and only in proportion as we succeed in this can we become as a tree planted by the waters, that fears not when heat cometh, and brings forth its own fruit without ceasing.

But a joyful hope of revival arises very specially from the way and manner in which the great work of which we are celebrating the commencement is developing. First of all, let us not pass unmentioned the gifts which we see offered by rich and poor, great and small, on the altar of the Fatherland. We do not wish to consider those according to their sufficiency for the purpose to which they are devoted — for willingly and abundantly as they are given, they yet meet but a small part of the need — but according to their inward significance and to the spirit of which they are the expression. In offering them we did not wait till a requisition was made and a command given, but as soon as we knew the need we hastened to offer. As it is death to any commonwealth if only the letter of the law prevails, and no one takes more interest in it, by act or feeling, than *that* prescribes; as this is a sure sign that the higher blessings of life are not produced by fixed regulations; so this loyal, living feeling about whatever is necessary for the commonwealth is a sure sign that the life-giving sap of true love has penetrated into the State, and that the leaves of this spiritual tree will remain green even in the heat and in the year of drought. And if many a one has devoted all that he had remaining of earthly jewels and treasures, let us regard this as the necessary avowal that in this war it is not a question of earthly but of spiritual possessions, and that we are ready, and will be so to the last, to do without and sacrifice all the former in order to gain the latter, and content although we should be obliged, after the successfully decisive battle, to begin the building up of our earthly prosperity from the very foundation. That is what it is to trust in the Lord, and to seek only after his kingdom.

But let us look particularly at the form which the defence of the Fatherland is to take. Among all the divisions that crippled our powers and impeded our progress, there was none more unhappy than that between soldier and citizen, resulting from the rooted opinion that he who was engaged in a peaceful trade or profession could have neither knowledge nor skill to defend his property and the common Fatherland in the time of danger. Hence the special privileges which were granted to those on whom alone the safety of the State depended, and still more to those who were exclusively appointed to command them; hence the jealousy of the citizen as to those privileges, and the general dislike to a class which in time of peace seemed only a burden to all the rest. Many commendable attempts were no doubt made to diminish this evil, but without results of any consequence. Now this separation is to be abolished; the difference is now to exist only between those who, constantly occupied with the proper arts of war, are, in the precision of their exercises and performances, an example to all others as well as the nucleus to which they gather, and those who, scantily instructed and drilled, only take up arms when it becomes necessary; but courage is to be expected from all, all are to know the use of their weapons, all are to take a growing share in the danger, the greater it becomes. We have been wisely led thus far step by step. The brave ardour of our young men was known whenever it became a question of this struggle; they were appealed to, and we saw them at the first call pour in from all ranks, from all nobler occupations to arms. Where a new good thing is to be quickly spread, the fathers must often be taught by the children; we have good reason to hope that it will be so at present, and that after that example of the young, for whom we should venture everything rather than they for us, every one will now be prepared to take part in the defence of the Fatherland according to his assigned order. For this reason the king is now instituting the *Landwehr*. And as this is also to be specially published today, hear what he says about it. [Here followed the summons to the *Landwehr*.]

What an exalted feeling this call must awaken in all of us! what a firm confidence in the strength thus united! what a happy foretaste of the harmony and love in which all ranks will be bound together, when they have all stood side by side to face with death for the Fatherland! what a happy anticipation of the united endeavour to lay in this way the foundation of a life that shall be worth such efforts, and in which unity and strength shall be equally seen!

Thus, my dear friends, we see in this glorious and spirited change in our condition the beginnings of a happy rising again from a deep fall, the returning favour of the Most High, who is again promising to do us good. Let us, then, also reflect how we are obeying his voice, let us further consider, in a few words, what we must in the first place feel called on to do, by this change of affairs. I shall be able to be the shorter about this, as your minds must already, by what has gone before, be directed to what I have to say.

2. I speak first of those who are called directly to the defence of the Fatherland, whether they belong to the armies that are already in motion, or whether, according to their own inclination or by the law of the lot, they are incorporated in that great bulwark which is still to be formed. I do not wish to do what is superfluous, by exhorting them to courage and bravery. He can never be wanting in courage whose mind is filled with the common aim, and who has made it entirely his own. For if, in that case, he finds himself in the great mass of conflicting powers which are organized into a noble whole; if he finds it impossible to think of himself singly, but must regard himself as only a little part of the whole; then his attention and his wishes can also only be directed to the movements of the whole. And that these movements may always accomplish the proposed aim — that alone is what he works for with all his strength; and thus whatever may befall himself in doing so, even were it the final human event, must appear to him only as an utterly insignificant casualty, which he himself regards as little as it can be regarded among the whole. This is the natural courage of him who loves the cause for which he is fighting. But I should like to warn you lest personal ambition weaken the high nobility and the true effectiveness of this courage. Let your emulation never be as to what each one brings to pass; let it be only as to the spirit that each manifests and the virtue he practises. He who strives to do this and that, and not just what always comes to him in his own place, is withdrawing from the natural arrangement of united work, to the injury of the whole. If public distinctions must certainly depend on success, then let every one strive, not to earn them, but to deserve them; let every one remember that all who did their duty faithfully helped to earn those things which others have received; and that the consciousness of having done all that it was possible for zeal and goodwill to do, and the recognition of those who know this, outweigh all other distinctions. I would caution you, moreover, not to let thoughtlessness weaken this natural courage. Not a few seem to think that everything is already done, that there is hardly need of the armies that have already gone forth and are doubtless about to begin the

pursuit of the scattered, terrified remnant of the enemy's ruined forces to the utmost bounds of the German Fatherland; and that if more men fit for arms were called out, it could only be, not so much for immediate need, as to make use of this splendid opportunity in forming a better and more powerful system of defence for the future. Let such people beware lest the unexpected, which is what oftenest casts men down, come upon them with its terrible force, and they then indeed fear, when the heat cometh. The king's message is very far from countenancing this light view; it does not conceal from us the power of the enemy, nor the greatness of his resources; and we ourselves have some idea of the embittered feeling that he must have against us. Let us secure our courage by being prepared for everything, even for each of us in person to defend or avenge home and hearth.

I speak in the next place of the rest of us in connection with those, the defenders of the common cause; of ourselves as their relatives and friends. The feeling which formerly, when the State was involved in war, was shared by only a few, and as to which they were sometimes pitied and sometimes envied by others — the seeing of their best-beloved ones exposed to the danger of death in battle and to the various disasters of war; this feeling will now become universal. For which of us is there that will not now see among the hosts of the army or of the *Landwehr*, at least relations, benefactors, pupils, heart-friends, if not father, husband, brother and son going to meet those very dangers? And let us then feel that we are not on this account to be pitied, but to be counted happy; that the more highly we value those connected with us, the more ought we to sympathize with and enter into all that is great and glorious in their calling. And the more we love them as ourselves, let us all the more offer and consecrate them to the Fatherland, just as we would yield up our own lives for it were we called on to do so. Much precious blood will flow, many a beloved head will fall; let us not embitter their glorious lot by mournful fears and weak sorrow, but to see to it that, worthy of the great cause, we remain green and fresh; let us remember how much happier it is to offer up life as a sacrifice in the noble struggle against this destructive power than in the impotent struggle of medical art against the unknown powers of nature. And the loving cares which, if we could, we would gladly bestow on our own when sick and wounded — let those cares make us entirely a joint community, as the cause is common; let us care for and serve all whom we can, in the firm confidence that in the same way there will be no lack of tender nursing and treatment of our loved ones from others who feel as we do. But, above all, let us take care that the well-deserved honour of those who have dedicated themselves to this sacred struggle be not lost. As we ourselves have been most deeply moved by the distress and humiliation of the past years, and the glorious resurrection of the Fatherland in these days, let us also impress all this most strongly on the rising generation; that this eternally memorable time may indeed be remembered, and that each descendant whom it concerns may say with just pride, There fought, or there fell, a relation of mine.

I speak further, on the other hand, of those who, while others have gone out to defend the Fatherland, are to regulate and direct its internal affairs, and discharge all the various offices which it requires. May this great decisive time arouse them all to redoubled faithfulness and solicitude, to redoubled abhorrence of all neglect at home through indolence or irregularity — for I will not say through self-interest or unfaithfulness — while in the field citizens are offering up their life-blood. May they abhor it as the most shameful treachery to this very blood and to all the virtues that offer it up. Let them remember that every power must be conscientiously applied, every department of the commonwealth faithfully administered, if the great work is to succeed. Above all, let them remember that if the courage of those who have gone to the war is to hold out, they wish to see, in the strength and wisdom of the constitution and government, a guarantee for the higher blessings for which they are fighting. Therefore be it far from any one among us to think himself wise when he is not so; let no one thrust himself, to the exceeding detriment of the commonwealth, into an office which he is not capable of filling; let no one allow himself to be so blinded by friendly partiality as to favour such presumptuous undertakings. But when one *is* wise, then let him strive to act, and to act vigorously and faithfully. Let those who administer justice remember that the sacred sense of the rights of nations and states, which lies at the foundation of this whole struggle, can only be a healthy state where the rights of the citizens are faithfully observed; let those who have the care of keeping order and security remember that very specially in the exercise of their occupation is to be shown most gloriously that noble and beautiful combination of liberty and obedience in which we have long prided ourselves, and by which, in days of repose as in times of war, we must chiefly mark our difference, both from the former licence and from the later servitude of the nation against which we are contending. Let those who are to elevate the sentiments of the people and to form the minds of the young remember that they, in their quiet work, are the guardians and keepers of the most sacred property; that on their faithfulness in duty and on the blessing resting on it, it depends whether there shall be faculties with which to fight, and above all whether there shall be anything to fight for — a faith, a hope, a love. Lastly, let those who manage the public taxes remember that under the poor earthly form of money and of goods there is offered to them in tribute the efforts of all the noble and intellectual faculties which have established the dominion of man over nature; that it is not the people's superfluity, not their savings which are to be disposed of, but what they have pinched themselves to give. Let all remember how greatly the importance of their work is increased in such times as these, so that, in the first place, they themselves, to whom obedience is to be given, may in their great calling obey the voice of the Lord.

And finally, in contrast with those who are directly at work for the Fatherland, I speak of those to whom this is not permitted, who dare not even wish that the necessity should arise that would call them also to arms. Well, if it is painful to them to devote this great time entirely to quiet work, although they would gladly be waging war, let them consider that we have an internal war to carry on, which is of equally decisive importance. If our real low condition consists in evil of many kinds, let us begin first by lifting ourselves out of that; there is still much to be rooted out, much to be fought against. Let us be brave in this war — it also requires courage; it has its dangers also. Let no one enjoy unshaken respect in society, who still by word or deed preaches despondency or indifference, and who seems inclined to prefer our former condition with quietness to the struggle for a better! Let every one be watched and unmasked who thinks that the more the eyes of all are turned to those at a distance, he may the more securely and secretly indulge in a now more than ever criminal and traitorous selfishness. Let no one remain unchecked, who perhaps in the foolish delusion of preparing for himself a more endurable fate in the event of an unsuccessful issue, seeks to exempt himself from, or in any way to obstruct, the vigorous measures which are indispensably necessary to making the issue successful. And even if narrow-mindedness and baseness of this kind should try in a greater or less degree to creep into the public administration, then, because the danger is doubled, let us also fight with double energy and take no rest until we conquer. Thus shall we also have our own part to sustain, we shall wage the same war as the others, only in a different way; and if those who are placed behind doubtful troops to intimidate those who might think of giving way prematurely, take credit to themselves for a part of the victory, though they have done no fighting, this may also be permitted to us.

These, my friends, are the demands which the present times make on us. Let each of us, then, stand to his post and not give way! let each of us keep fresh and green in the sense of the great holy powers that animate him! let each of us trust in God and call on him, as we are now about to do together!

Merciful God and Lord! Thou hast done great things for us in calling our Fatherland to fight for a free and honourable existence, in which we may be able to advance thy work. Grant us in addition, safety and grace. Victory comes from thee, and we know well that we do not always know what we are doing in asking of thee what seems good to us. But with greater confidence than ever, even with a strong faith, we entreat of thee prosperity and blessing on the arms of our king and his allies, because it seems to us almost as if thy kingdom and the noblest gifts that past centuries have won for us would be in danger, if these efforts were in vain. Protect the beloved head of our king, and all the princes of his house, who are now with the army. Grant wisdom and strength to the commanders, courage to the soldiers, faithful steadfastness to all. And grant also, as thou canst change and turn the fortune of war, that its blessings may not be lost to us; that each one may be purified and grow in the inner man; that each may do what he can, be it much or little; that we may grow stronger in confidence in thee, and in obedience to thy will, an obedience reaching even to death, like the obedience of thy Son. Amen. *Selected Sermons*, pp. 67-82

*

Schleiermacher, more Lutheran perhaps than Reformed at this point, distinguished sharply between Christian obedience to Christ in the Church, and civil obedience to the secular power. Christ does not yet have the kingdom of power which the Father reserves to himself, and so there are no direct, specifically Christian injunctions for ethical directives for the civil sphere, beyond those which operate for the maintenance of civil order. The following extract from The Christian Faith, *which includes criticism of both 'theocracy' and 'political religion', makes interesting reading in view of Schleiermacher's preparedness to risk the wrath of the state during 1810-13 for his subversively liberal and patriotic activities. At that time, did he consider 'patriotism' such a 'fleshly' motive? Here is focused one of the greatest problems modern Christianity has had to face — that of a secular loyalty which arouses an almost religious passion.*

*Third Theorem — The kingly office of Christ consists in the fact that every-
thing which the community of believers requires for its well-being continually
proceeds from him.*

1. The term 'king' has, and had in the time of Christ, many meanings; and
there is a great difference between its strict official use and its vague
polite use. It is, therefore, impossible to base our presentation upon an
exegetical decision on the questions in what sense Christ was asked
whether he was a king, and whether he answered in the same sense or
another. Rather we must keep to the recollection, not yet extinct, that the
conception of king was opposed on the one hand to that of a tyrant, whose
power was just as unlimited, but not natural; and on the other hand, to
that of the authorities of a society, who possessed only a limited and dele-
gated power, conferred on them by the governed themselves. A tyranny,
on the other hand, always involved the possibility, not to say the assumption, that the power which had been arbitrarily seized was also selfish,
and might have other aims than the free development and the natural
prosperity of those over whom it was exercised. In contrast with both, the
lordship of Christ is as unlimited as that of the animating principle
always is when it is neither outwardly hindered nor inwardly weakened.
Moreover, it is in the interest of those over whom it is exercised, as obviously follows from the facts that it is nothing but the lordship of that element whose weakness in themselves men deplore, and that submission to
his lordship must always be voluntary. But the kingly power has this in
common with the other two, that its object cannot be an individual as
such, but only a society, and the individual only in so far as he belongs to
the society. Individuals, then, submit voluntarily to the lordship of
Christ; but in so doing they at the same time enter a society to which they
did not previously belong. So that, in attributing a kingly dignity to
Christ, we are *eo ipso* declaring ourselves definitely opposed to the contention that Christ did not intend to found an organic community, but
that the society of believers came into being, or was formed, later, without
his injunction. But since, at the same time, no one enters this community
except by submitting himself to Christ's lordship, it follows that Christ
himself initiated this Kingdom, and is thus without any predecessor in
his kingly dignity.

Christ himself, however, indicates still another contrast, when he
describes his Kingdom as not of this world, and so distinguishes it in yet
another way from both those others. This negative description involves
in the first place that his kingly power is not immediately concerned with

247

the disposal and arrangement of the things of this world — which means that nothing remains as the immediate sphere of his kingship but the inner life of men individually and in their relation to each other. It involves further, that for the exercise of his lordship he makes use of no means which are dependent upon the things of this world, *i.e.* of no constraint which requires superiority in material forces, nor yet of enticements or threatenings of any kind which require support of that kind and make a merely sensuous appeal — for that, too, belongs to this world. But this is by no means to say that the kingly power of Christ began only after he had been raised above the earth, still less — as might be held — that it covers only his exalted life; he himself says, not that he will be a king, but that he is one; and not only did he prove himself a king during his earthly life — by giving laws for his community, by sending out his servants for its extension, by imposing rules of conduct and giving directions as to the way in which his commanding will should be carried out — but his kingly power is and remains everywhere and always the same. For those laws and directions do not grow old, but remain valid, with undiminished force, in the Church of Christ; and if for the future he refers his disciples to his spiritual presence, yet even that does not make a distinction between different times. For even his original influence was purely spiritual, and was mediated through his bodily appearance not otherwise than even now his spiritual presence is mediated through the written Word and the picture it contains of his being and influence — so that even now his directive control is not simply a mediate and derived one. So that, keeping in mind what was said above, we may say that his government of us bears the same relation to our activity in his name as his representation of us does to our prayer in his name. Indeed, it is also obvious that since he stands to the totality of believers in exactly the same relation as the divine nature in him does to the human, animating and taking it up into the fellowship of the original life, his lordship too is in the strictest sense a sole lordship, for no one else is in a position to share it. Thus, just as Christ has no predecessor in the society governed by him, but is its original founder, so too he has in it no successor and no representative. For he exercises his lordship through ordinances which he himself established, and has himself declared these to be sufficient, so that nothing is now necessary but the right application of these; and to apply them is the common task of those who are ruled by Christ, just because they are his subjects. Even if at any time they could transfer this task, either to one individual or to several — though of course they could not do so without giving up their vital relation to Christ — yet any such individual would be only their representative, and not a representative of Christ. So that among believers there is nowhere any lordship other than his alone.

2. The difficulty in regard to this part of the work of Christ consists especially in defining aright the kingly power of Christ in relation to the general divine government (a difficulty which cannot be overlooked once the subject is somewhat more closely scrutinized from a *theoretical* point of view), and further in defining it aright relatively to secular government (a difficulty which at once emerges in the *practical* treatment of the question).

The customary division of the Kingdom of Christ into the kingdom of power, the kingdom of grace, and the kingdom of glory helps us little. We have first to break it up so as to comprehend under the two latter the proper object of Christ's kingly activity, namely, the world which has become participant in redemption, while under the kingdom of power we understand the world as such, and in itself. But in taking this position, we seem to lend ourselves to the extravagant notion that there belonged to Christ a kingdom of power, as it were, before the kingdom of grace, and independent of it. Now, to say the least, such a kingdom could not possibly belong to his redemptive activity; and if the Apostles knew of such a kingdom belonging to the Word, it must have been a knowledge which, because unconnected with redemption, could not belong to Christian piety either. Anyone who thinks it necessary to interpret the expressions which they use with reference to Christ as the Word made flesh, the God-man and the Redeemer, or which Christ uses of himself, as if they attributed to him the governance of the whole world, involves himself in a contradiction, not only with all the passages in which Christ himself offers petitions to the Father and refers to what the Father has retained in his own power, but also with all passages which express his intention to establish an immediate relationship, both of petition and response, between believers and the Father. It is true that occasionally there is to be found even within the Protestant Church a form of doctrine, and here and there, in conjunction with it, even a type of Church service which leaves room (all the prayers being addressed solely to Christ) only for a relationship of believers to Christ, to the exclusion of the Father. But we must, with Scripture and very much more with the Church, pronounce this a dubious innovation. If, however, this rock is to be avoided, by the power of Christ we can understand only that power which begins with the kingdom of grace and is essentially included in it. And this itself is a power over the world only in so far as believers are taken out of the midst of the world, and the fellowship of believers or the kingdom of Christ can increase only as the world (as the antithesis of the Church) decreases, and its members are gradually transformed into members of the Church, so that evil is overcome and the sphere of redemption enlarged. But even this is a power of Christ over the world which proceeds only from the kingdom of grace, *i.e.* it exists in virtue of the influence of the command to preach given by Christ and perpetually valid in the Church. On the other hand, what part of the world, or what individual, becomes ripe for the fruitfulness of this preaching before other parts, or before other individuals, is a matter belonging to the kingdom of power, which the Father has retained for himself. Accordingly, the only things which remain subject to Christ's direct control are the forces of redemption implanted in the Church; and it would be a rather unfruitful distinction, and not even correctly described, if we called his Kingdom a kingdom of grace in so far as these forces show themselves effective in a purely inward way, for sanctification and edification, and a kingdom of power in so far as they are employed in the overcoming of the world; for these two things it is quite impossible to separate from each other. The distinction, however, between the kingdom of grace and the kingdom of glory is usually taken to be that the latter follows upon the former, so soon as all Christ's subjects have been placed in full possession of all the benefits won for them, and no longer have any contact with the world — an assumption which we shall consider more closely later. Here it need only be remarked, with reference to the kingly dignity of Christ, that if the assumption is taken strictly then there can be no other activity in this Kingdom than one of expressive representation, in which case the exercise of a general directive power is reduced to a minimum. Hence we can certainly regard it as a glory of Christ that he has no more to suffer, even in sympathy, with the whole body of believers, because it has been finished and perfected; but in no sense is this a condition which should be described as a Kingdom. Thus there remains only the one kingdom of grace as Christ's true kingdom, as indeed it is the only one a consciousness of which really emerges in our moods of devotion, the only one of which we require knowledge for our guidance, because our active faith must be directed towards it. The two other terms in the customary division we can use only to determine the scope of this very kingdom of grace. In calling it a kingdom of power we are asserting, not only that the extension of the influence of Christ over the human race knows no limits, and that no people is able to offer it a permanently effective opposition, but also that there is no stage of purity and perfection which does not belong to Christ's Kingdom. And in calling it a kingdom of glory we are confessing our belief — of course in connection with that highest purity and perfection, only approximately given in experience — in an unlimited approximation to the absolute blessedness to be found in Christ alone.

So far as the distinction between the kingly power of Christ and civil government is concerned, it would seem, after what has been said, that nothing is easier than to distinguish exactly between the two in conception. For civil government is unquestionably an institution which belongs to the general divine government of the world, and even by his own declaration is accordingly as such alien to Christ's Kingdom. On the other hand, civil government is a legal thing, and exists everywhere, even where there is no Christian religion. Hence, since it springs out of the corporate life of sinfulness, and everywhere presupposes this (for of course for the sanction of its laws it reckons upon the force of sensuous motives), it cannot as such have the slightest authority in the Kingdom of Christ. On this view the two powers seem to be held entirely apart from each other, so that the sole lordship of Christ in his Kingdom remains secure although his followers conduct themselves in wordly affairs in accordance with the regulations of the secular government, and regard everything that comes to them from it as coming from the divine government of the world. But how greatly the situation is altered as soon as we think of the secular government as exercised by Christians over Christians, is clearly to be seen in the fact that, on the one side, the Church has attempted to control the secular government in the name of Christ, while on the other, the Christian magistracy as such has claimed for itself the right to regulate the affairs of the society of believers. In order not to introduce at this point anything which belongs to Christian Ethics — from which even the theological principles of Church Law must be derived — the only question we shall here have to propound is whether the Kingdom of Christ is changed in extent through the entrance of this new material relationship. Now it is certainly true that Christ must completely control the society of believers, and consequently that every member of the society must show himself, wholly and in every part of his life, to be governed by Christ. But since this depends entirely upon the inner vital relationship in which each individual stands to Christ, and since there can be no representative who exercises the kingly office of Christ in his name, this simply means that everyone, whether magistrate or private citizen, has to seek in the directions given by Christ, not indeed right directions for his conduct under civil government (for this is always a matter of the art of politics), but certainly the right temper of mind even in this relationship. On the other hand, it also remains true that no one can exert influence upon the society of believers except in the measure in which he is a pre-eminent instrument of Christ's kingly power, since otherwise the sole lordship of Christ would be imperilled. And this does not at all depend on his outward vocation; one who is called as a bond-servant is not therefore a bond-servant in the society, but a freedman of the Lord, and similarly he who is called as a lord does not therefore become a lord in the society, but only a bond-servant of Christ like every-one else. So that the civil contrast between magistrate and private citizen loses all significance in the Church; it makes no difference to a man's relationship to the kingly power of Christ.

3. In this way, then, we have separated the kingly power of Christ, on the one hand, from the power which the Father has retained for himself, while on the other we have set it beyond all the resources of the civil power. The latter is undoubtedly the way in which what Luther called 'the two swords' should be kept separate from each other. We may there-fore say of this part also of the work of Christ, as of the former ones, that he is the climax and the end of all spiritual kingship; and this will hold true in and for itself as well as relatively to this separation. In and for itself we must compare his lordship with every other purely spiritual power, and all the relationships of master and scholars, pattern and imitators, law-giver and law-receivers, we must put far below it — they stand on a vastly lower level, and are only concerned with individual parts of the life of the human spirit. The same is true of the founders of other religions, who neither evoked a temper of mind opposed to former habits and customs, as Christ did (rather they accommodated themselves to these in various ways), nor, as Christ did, called the whole human race under their lord-ship. In the same way he is the end of all such kingship, for there is just as little possibility of a similar kingdom after his, as there is that a similar one should now exist or should ever have existed alongside of it. But he is both climax and end, only in so far as the above-mentioned separation is maintained. For it is part alike of the purity and of the perfection of his spiritual power that sensuous motives can have no share whatever in it. That is why Christianity is neither a political religion nor a religious state or a theocracy. The former are those religious fellowships which are regarded as the institutions of a particular civil society, and which rest upon the assumption that the religion is derived from civil legislation, or is related as a subordinate movement to the same higher impulse which first called the civil organization into being, so that for the sake of the civil society its members also unite in a religious fellowship, which therefore is animated by the common spirit of the society and by patriotism — these

being 'fleshly motives' in the Scriptural sense. Theocracies, on the other hand, are religious fellowships which as such have subordinated the civil society to themselves; in which consequently political ambition aims at pre-eminence within the religious fellowship, and there is the underlying assumption that the religious society, or the divine revelation upon which it rests, was able to call into being the civil society — which in this sense is possible only for religious fellowships which are nationally limited. To both, then, political religions as well as theocracies, Christ puts an end through the purely spiritual lordship of his God-consciousness; and the stronger and more extensive his Kingdom becomes, the more definite becomes the severance between Church and State, so that in the proper outward separation — which, of course, may take very different forms — their agreement is ever more perfectly worked out.

The Christian Faith, pp. 466-473

CHRISTIANITY AND THE RELIGIONS*

Schleiermacher's view of religion as always subsisting in a variety of specific ways, rather than a generalized 'natural religion', reads astonishingly fresh today. Schleiermacher's lively sense of individuality was conveyed into the religious as well as the personal and communal sphere. This informed his polemic against the Enlightenment's tendency to seek general truths and principles, and to look adversely on the 'positive' religions as actually existing. Each 'positive religion', according to Schleiermacher (not excepting Christianity) needs to be appreciated in its specific historical characteristics.

FIFTH SPEECH

THE RELIGIONS

. . . That no man can perfectly possess all religion is easy to see. Men are determined in one special way, religion is endlessly determinable. But it must be equally evident that religion is not dismembered and scattered in parts by random among men, but that it must organize itself in manifestations of varying degrees of resemblance. Recall the several stages of religion to which I drew your attention. I said that the religion of a person, to whom the world reveals itself as a living whole, is not a mere continuation of the view of the person who only sees the world in its apparently hostile elements. By no amount of regarding the Universe as chaotic and discrete can the higher view be attained. These differences you may call kinds or degrees of religion, but in either case you will have to admit that, as in every similar case, the forms in which an infinite force divides itself is usually characteristic and different.

Wherefore, plurality of religions is another thing than plurality of the Church. The essence of the Church is fellowship. Its limit, therefore, cannot be the uniformity of religious persons. It is just difference that should be brought into fellowship. You are manifestly right when you believe that the Church can never in actuality be completely and uniformly one. The only reason, however, is that every society existing in space and time is thereby limited and losing in depth what it gains in

---

* See also pp. 61ff. above.

breadth, falls to pieces. But religion, exactly by its multiplicity, assumes the utmost unity of the Church. This multiplicity is necessary for the complete manifestation of religion. It must seek for a definite character, not only in the individual but also in the society. Did the society not contain a principle to individualize itself, it could have no existence. Hence we must assume and we must search for an endless mass of distinct forms. Each separate religion claims to be such a distinct form revealing religion, and we must see whether it is agreeable to this principle. We must make clear to ourselves wherein it is peculiar. Though the difference be hidden under strange disguises, though it be distorted, not only by the unavoidable influence of the transitory to which the enduring has condescended, but also by the unholy hand of sacrilegious men, we must find it.

To be satisfied with a mere general idea of religion would not be worthy of you. Would you then understand it as it really exists and displays itself, would you comprehend it as an endlessly progressive work of the Spirit that reveals himself in all human history, you must abandon the vain and foolish wish that there should only be one religion; you must lay aside all repugnance to its multiplicity; as candidly as possible you must approach everything that has ever, in the changing shapes of humanity, been developed in its advancing career, from the ever fruitful bosom of the spiritual life.

The different existing manifestations of religion you call positive religions. Under this name they have long been the object of a quite pre-eminent hate. Despite of your repugnance to religion generally, you have always borne more easily with what for distinction is called natural religion. You have almost spoken of it with esteem.

I do not hesitate to say at once that from the heart I entirely deny this superiority. For all who have religion at all and profess to love it, it would be the vilest inconsequence to admit it. They would thereby fall into the openest self-contradiction. For my own part, if I only succeeded in recommending to you this natural religion, I would consider that I had lost my pains.

For you, indeed, to whom religion generally is offensive, I have always considered this preference natural. The so-called natural religion is usually so much refined away, and has such metaphysical and moral graces, that little of the peculiar character of religion appears. It understands so well to live in reserve, to restrain and to accommodate itself that it can be put up with anywhere. Every positive religion, on the contrary, has certain strong traits and a very marked physiognomy, so that its every movement, even to the careless glance, proclaims what it really is.

If this is the true ground of your dislike, you must now rid yourself of it. If you have now, as I hope, a better estimate of religion, it should be no longer necessary for me to contend against it. If you see that a peculiar and noble capacity of man underlies religion, a capacity which, of course, must be educated, it cannot be offensive to you to regard it in the most definite forms in which it has yet appeared. Rather you must the more willingly grant a form your attention the more there is developed in it the characteristic and distinctive elements of religion.

But you may not admit this argument. You may transfer all the reproaches you have formally been accustomed to bestow on religion in general to the single religions. You may maintain that there are always, just in this element that you call positive, the occasion and the justification of these reproaches, and that in consequence the positive religions cannot be as I have sought to represent, the natural manifestations of the true religion. You would show me how, without exception, they are full of what, according to my own statement, is not religion. Consequently, must not a principle of corruption lie deep in their constitution? You will remind me that each one proclaims that it alone is true, and that what is peculiar to it is absolutely the highest. Are they not distinguished from one another by elements they should as much as possible eliminate? In disproving and contending, be it with art and understanding, or with weapons stranger and more unworthy, do they not show themselves quite contrary to the nature of true religion? You would add that, exactly in proportion as you esteem religion and acknowledge its importance, you must take a lively interest in seeing that it everywhere enjoys the greatest freedom to cultivate itself on all sides. You must, therefore, hate keenly those definite religious forms, that hold all their adherents to the same type and the same word, withdraw the freedom to follow their own nature and compress them in unnatural limits. In contrast, you would praise mightily the superiority in all these points of the natural to the positive religions.

Once more I say, I do not deny that misunderstandings and perversions exist in all religions, and I raise no objections to the dislike with which they inspire you. Nay, I acknowledge there is in them all this much bewailed degeneration, this divergence into alien territory. The diviner religion itself is, the less would I embellish its corruptions, or admiringly cherish its excrescences. But forget for once this one-sided view and follow me to another. Consider how much of this corruption is due to those who have dragged forth religion from the depths of the heart into the civil world. Acknowledge that much of it is unavoidable as soon as the Infinite, by descending into the sphere of time and submitting to the general influence of finite things, takes to itself a narrow shell. And however deep-rooted this corruption may be, and however much the religions may have suffered thereby, consider this also: if the proper religious view of all things is to seek even in things apparently common and base every trace of the divine, the true and the eternal, and to reverence even the faintest, you cannot omit what has the justest claims to be judged religiously.

And you would find more than remote traces of the Deity. I invite you to study every faith professed by man, every religion that has a name and a character. Though it may long ago have degenerated into a long series of empty customs, into a system of abstract ideas and theories, will you not, when you examine the original elements at the source, find that this dead dross was once the molten outpourings of the inner fire? Is there not in all religions more or less of the true nature of religion, as I have presented it to you? Must not, therefore, each religion be one of the special forms which mankind, in some region of the earth and at some stage of development, has to accept?

I must take care not to attempt anything systematic or complete, for that would be the study of a life, and not the business of a discourse. Yet you must not be allowed to wander at hazard in this endless chaos. That you may not be misled by the false ideas that prevail; that you may estimate by a right standard the true content and essence of any religion; that you may have some definite and sure procedure for separating the inner from the outer, the native from the borrowed and extraneous, and the sacred from the profane, forget the characteristic attributes of single religion and seek, from the centre outwards, a general view of how the essence of a positive religioin is to be comprehended and determined.

You will then find that the positive religions are just the definite forms in which religion must exhibit itself — a thing to which your so-called natural religions have no claim. They are only a vague, sorry, poor thought that corresponds to no reality, and you will find that in the positive religions alone a true individual cultivation of the religious capacity is possible. Nor do they, by their nature, injure the freedom of their adherents.

Why have I assumed that religion can only be given fully in a great multitude of forms of the utmost definiteness? Only on grounds that naturally follow from what has been said of the nature of religion. The whole of religion is nothing but the sum of all relations of man to God, apprehended in all the possible ways in which any man can be immediately conscious in his life. In this sense there is but one religion, for it would be but a poverty-stricken and halting life, if all these relations did not exist wherever religion ought to be. Yet all men will not by any means apprehend them in the same way, but quite differently. Now this difference alone is felt and alone can be exhibited while the reduction of all differences is only thought.

You are wrong, therefore, with your universal religion that is natural to all, for no one will have his own true and right religion, if it is the same for all. As long as we occupy a place there must be in these relations of man to the whole a nearer and a farther, which will necessarily determine each feeling differently in each life. Again, as long as we are individuals, every man has greater receptiveness for some religious experiences and feelings than for others. In this way everything is different. Manifestly then, no single relation can accord to every feeling its due. It requires the sum of them. Hence, the whole of religion can be present only, when all those different views of every relation are actually given. This is not possible, except in an endless number of different forms. They must be determined adequately by a different principle of reference to the others, and in each the same religious element must be characteristically modified. In short, they must be true individuals.

What determines and distinguishes these individuals, and what, on the other hand, is common to all their component parts, holds them together, and is their principle of adhesion, whereby any given detail is to be adjudged to its own type of religion, are implied in what has been already said. But this view can only be verified by the existing historical religions, and of them it is maintained that all this is different, and that such is not their relation to one another. This we must now examine.

First, a definite quantity of religious matter is not necessarily, in the same degree, a definite form of religion.

This is an entire misunderstanding of the nature of the different religions. Even among their adherents it is general, and causes manifold opposite and false judgments. They suppose that because so many men acknowledge the same religion, they must have the same body of religious views and feelings. Their fellow-believers must have the same opinions and the same faith as they have, and this common possession must be the essence of their religion. The peculiarly characteristic and individual element in a religion is not easy to find with certainty from instances, but, however general the idea may be, if you believe that it consists in including a definite sum of religious intuitions and feelings, and that as a consequence the positive religions are prejudicial to the freedom of the individual in the development of his own religion, you are in error. Single perceptions and feelings are, as you know, the elements of religion, and it can never lead to the character of any one religion to regard them as a mere heap, tossed together without regard to number, kind or purpose.

If now, as I have sought to show, religion needs to be of many types because, of every relation different views are possible, according as it stands related to the rest, how would we be helped by such a compendium of some of them that could define none? If the positive religions were only distinguished by what they exclude, they could certainly not be the individual manifestations we seek. That this is not their character, however, appears from the impossibility of arriving from this point of view at a distinct idea of them.

As they continue to exist apart, such an idea must be possible, for only what commingles in fact is inseparable in idea. It is evident that the different religious perceptions and feelings are not, in a determinate way, awakened by one another or interdependent. Now, as each exists for itself, each can lead, by the most various combinations, to every other. Hence, different religions could not continue long beside one another, if they were not otherwise distinguished. Very soon each would supplement itself into uniformity with all others.

Even in the religion of any one man, as it is fashioned in the course of life, nothing is more accidental than the quantity of religious matter that may arrive at consciousness. Some views may set and others may rise and come to clearness, and his religion in this respect is ever in flux. Much less can the boundary, which in the individual is so changeable, be permanent and essential in the religion of several associated individuals. In the highest degree it must be an unusual and accidental occurrence that, even for a little time, several men remain in the same circle of perceptions and advance along the same path of feeling.

Hence, among those who determine their religion in this way, there is a standing quarrel about essentials and non-essentials. They do not know what is to be laid down as characteristic and necessary, and what to separate as free and accidental; they do not find the point from which the whole can be surveyed; they do not understand the religion in which they live and for which they presume to fight; and they contribute to its degeneration, for, while they are influenced by the whole, they consciously grasp only the detail. Fortunately the instinct they do not understand, guides them better than their understandings, and nature sustains what their false reflections and the doing and striving that flow from them would destroy.

If the character of any special religion is found in a definite quantity of perceptions and feelings, some subjective and objective connection, binding exactly these elements together and excluding all others, must be assumed. This false notion agrees well enough with the way of comparing religious conceptions that is common but is not agreeable to the spirit of religion. A whole of this type would not be what we seek, to give religion in its whole compass a determinate shape. It would not be a whole, but an arbitrary section of the whole; it would not be a religion, it would be a sect. Except by taking the religious experiences of one single person, and necessarily of only one short period of his life, as the norm for a society, it could hardly arise. But the forms which history has produced and which are now actually existing are not wholes of this sort. All sectarianism, be it speculative, for bringing single intuitions into a philosophical coherence, or ascetic, for reaching a system and a determinate series of feelings, labours for the utmost uniformity among all who would share the same fragment of religion. Those who are infected with this mania certainly do not lack activity, and if they have never succeeded in reducing any one positive religion to a sect, you will have to acknowledge that the positive religions must be formed on another principle and must have another character.

You will see this even more clearly by thinking of the times that gave them birth. You will recall how every positive religion, in its growth and bloom, when its peculiar vigour was most youthful, fresh and evident, did not concentrate and exclude, but expanded and pushed fresh shoots and acquired more religious matter to be wrought up in accordance with its own peculiar nature.

Therefore religions are not fashioned on this false principle. It is not one with their nature, it is a corruption that has crept in from the outside, as hostile to them as to the spirit of religion generally. Their relation to it which is a standing warfare, is another proof that they actually are constituted as individual manifestations of religion should be.

Just as little could the general differences of religion suffice to produce a thoroughly definite individual form. The three ways of being conscious of existence and of its totality, as chaos, system and elemental diversity, so often mentioned, are very far from being so many single and distinct religions. Divide an idea to infinity if you will, you cannot thereby reach an individual. You only get less general ideas which may, as genus and species, embrace a mass of very different individuals. To find the character of individual beings, there must be more than the idea and its attributes. But those three differences in religion are only the usual division according to the current scheme of unity, diversity and totality. They are types of religion but not religious individualities, and the need to seek for this individuality is by no means satisfied by the existence of religion in this threefold way. It is clear as day that there are many distinct manifestations of religion belonging to each type.

Just as little are the personal and the opposing pantheistic modes of conception two such individual forms. They go through all three types of religion and, for that reason alone, cannot be individualities. They are simply another principle of division. Only recently we agreed that this antithesis rests simply on a way of regarding the religious feeling, and of ascribing to its phenomena a common object. Hence the fact that any particular religion inclines more to one form of representation and expression than to the other, no more determines its individuality than it would its worth and the stage of its development. The individual elements of religion are as indefinite, and none of the various ways of regarding them are realized, because either the one or the other thought accompanies them. This may be seen in all purely deistic manifestations of religion. Though they desire to be considered quite definite, you will find everywhere that all religious feelings, and especially what is most dwelt on — all views of the movements of humanity in the individual, of the highest unity of mankind, of everything in the mutual relations of men that lies beyond each man's good pleasure, are utterly indefinite and ambiguous. The personal and the pantheistic conceptions, therefore, are only very general forms that may be further determined and individualized in various ways.

Perhaps you may seek this further determination by uniting the two modes of conception with the three modes of intuition. You would reach narrower sub-divisions, but not a thoroughly definite and individual whole. Neither naturalism — meaning perception of the world limited to elemental diversity, without the conception of a personal consciousness and will in the various elements — nor pantheism, nor polytheism, nor deism are single and definite religions, such as we seek. They are simply types within which there have been, and there will still be, very many genuine individualities developed.

Let me say then at once, that the only remaining way for a truly individual religion to arise is to select some one of the great relations of mankind in the world to the Highest Being, and, in a definite way, make it the centre and refer to it all the others. In respect of the idea of religion, this may appear a merely arbitrary proceeding, but, in respect of the peculiarity of the adherents, being the natural expression of their character, it is the purest necessity. Hereby a distinctive spirit and a common character enter the whole at the same time, and the ambiguous and vague reach firm ground. By every formation of this kind one of the endless number of different views and different arrangements of the single elements, which are all possible and all require to be exhibited, is fully realized. Single elements are all seen on the one side that is turned towards this central point, which makes all the feelings have a common tone and a livelier closer interaction.

The whole of religion can only be actually given in the sum of all the forms possible in this sense. It can, therefore, be exhibited only in an endless series of shapes that are gradually developed in different points of time and space, and nothing adds to its complete manifestation that is not found in one of those forms. Where religion is so moulded that everything is seen and felt in connection with one relation to the Deity that mediates it or embraces it, it matters not in what place or in what man it is formed or what relation is selected, it is a strictly positive religion. In respect of the sum of the religious elements — to use a word that should again be brought to honour — it is a heresy, for from many equals one is chosen to be head of the rest. In respect, however, of the fellowship of all participants and their relation to the founder of their religion who first raised this central point to clear consciousness, it is a school and a discipleship.

But if, as is to be hoped, we are agreed that religion can only be exhibited in and by such definite forms, only those who with their own religion pitch their camp in some such positive form, have any fixed abode, and, if I might so say, any well-earned right of citizenship in the religious world. They alone can boast of contributing to the existence and the progress of the whole, and they alone are in the full sense religious persons, on one side belonging by community of type to a kindred, on the other being distinguished by persistent and definite traits from everyone else.

But many perhaps who take an interest in the affairs of religion may ask with consternation, or some evil-disposed person may ask with guile, whether every pious person must connect himself with one of the existing forms of religion. Provisionally, I would say, by no means. It is only necessary that his religion be developed in himself characteristically and definitely. That it should resemble any great, largely accepted, existing form is not equally necessary. I would remind him that I have never spoken of two or three definite forms, and said that they are to be the only ones. Rather, they may evermore develop in countless numbers from all points. Whosoever does not find himself at home in an existing religion, I might almost say whosoever is not in a position to make it if he had not found it, must belong to none but should be held bound to produce a new one for himself. Is he alone in it and without disciples, it does not matter. Everywhere there are germs that cannot arrive at any more extended existence, and the religion of one person may have a definite form and organization, and be quite as genuinely a positive religion as if he had founded the greatest school.

In my opinion, then, you will see that the existing forms should not in themselves hinder any man from developing a religion suitable to his own nature and his own religious sense. The question of abiding in one of them or of constructing a religion of one's own, depends entirely on what relation develops in a man as fundamental feeling and middle-point of all religions.

This is my provisional answer, but if he will hear more I would add that, except by misunderstanding, it would be very difficult to find oneself in such a position. A new revelation is never trivial, and merely personal, but always rests on something great and common. Hence adherents and fellow-believers have never failed the man really called to institute a new religion. Most men, following their nature, will belong to an existing form, and there will be only few whom none suffices.

Yet — and this is my chief point — the authority being the same for all, the many are no less free than the few, and do no less fashion something of their own. If we follow any man's religious history, we find first dim presentiments which never quite stir the depths of the heart, and, being unrecognized, again disappear. Around every man, especially in earlier days, they doubtless hover. Some hint may awaken them, and they may again vanish without reaching any definite form and betraying aught charactersitic. Afterwards it first comes to pass that the sense for the Universe rises once for all into clear consciousness. One man discovers it in one relation, another in another. Hereafter all things are referred to this relation, and so group themselves around it. Such a moment, therefore, in the strictest sense, determines every man's religion. Now I hope you will not consider a man's religion less characteristic, less his own, because it lies in a region where already several are collected. In this similarity you are not to find a mechanical influence of custom or birth, but, as you do in other cases, you are to recognize a common determination by higher causes. This agreement is a guarantee of naturalness and truth, and cannot, whether one is first or last, be hurtful to individuality. Though thousands before him and after him referred their religious life to one relation, would it, therefore, be the same in all?

Remember that every definite form of religion is exhaustless for any one man. In its own way it should embrace the whole, a thing too great for any man. And not only so, but in itself there exist endless varieties of cultivation which are, as it were, subordinate types of religion. Is there not here work and scope enough for all? I, at least, am not aware that any religion had succeeded in so taking possession of its territory, and had so determined and exhibited everything therein, according to its own spirit, that, in any one professor of distinguished gifts and individuality of mind, nothing is wanting to perfection. Only to few of our historical religion has it been granted, even in the time of their freedom and higher life, to develop rightly and perfectly the neighbourhood of the middle-point, and, in even a few forms, to give individual impress to the common character. The harvest is great but the labourers are few. An infinite field is opened in each of those religions, wherein thousands may scatter themselves. Uncultivated regions enough present themselves to every one who is capable of making and producing something of his own.

The charge that everyone who allows himself to be embraced in a positive religion, can only be an imitator of those who have given it currency and cannot develop himself individually, is baseless. This judgment no more applies here, than it would to the state or to society. It seems to us morbid or quixotic for any one to maintain that he has no room in any existing intuition, and that he must exclude himself from society. We are convinced that every healthy person will, in common with many, have a great national character. Just because he is rooted in it and influenced by it, he can develop his individuality with the greatest precision and beauty. Similarly, in religion only morbid aberration so cuts off a man from a life in fellowship with those among whom nature has placed him, that he belongs to no great whole. Somewhere, on a great scale, everyone will find exhibited or will himself exhibit what for him is the middle-point of religion. To every such common sphere we ascribe a boundless activity that goes into detail, in virtue of which all individual characteristics issue from its bosom. Thus understood, the church is with right called the common mother of us all.

To take the nearest example, think of Christianity as a definite individual form of the highest order. First there is in our time the well known outward division, so definite and pronounced. Under each section there is then a mass of different views and schools. Each exhibits a characteristic development, and has a founder and adherents, yet the last and most personal development of religiousness remains for each individual, and so much is it one with his nature that no one can fully acquire it but himself. And the more a man, by his whole nature, has a claim to belong to you, ye cultured, the more religion must reach this stage in him, for his higher feeling, gradually developing and uniting with other educated capacities, must be a characteristic product.

Or if, after unknown conception and rapid birth-pangs of the spirit, the higher feelings develop, to all appearance suddenly, is not then a characteristic personality born with the religious life? There is a definite connection with a past, a present and a future. The whole subsequent religious life is linked in this way to that moment and that state in which this feeling surprised the soul. It thus maintains its connection with the earlier, poorer life, and has a natural uniform development. Nay more, in this initial consciousness there must already be a distinctive character. Only in a shape and only under circumstances thoroughly definite, could it so suddenly enter a life already developed. This distinctive character, then, every subsequent moment displays and is thus the purest expression of the whole nature. The living spirit of the earth, rending itself from itself as it were, links himself as a finite thing to one definite moment in the series of organic evolutions and a new man arises, a peculiar nature. His separate existence is independent of the mass and objective quality either of his circumstances or his actions. It consists in the peculiar unity of the abiding consciousness that is linked to that first moment, and in the peculiar relation to it which every later moment preserves. Wherefore, in that moment in which in any man a definite consciousness of his relation to the highest Being has, as it were, original birth, an individual religious life originates.

It is individual, not by an irreversible limitation to a particular number and selection of feelings and intuitions, not by the quality of the religious matter. This matter all who have the spiritual birth at the same time and in the same religious surroundings have in common. But it is individual by what he can have in common with no man, by the abiding influence of the peculiar circumstances in which his spirit was first greeted and embraced by the Universe, and by the peculiar way in which he conducts his observation and reflection on the same. This character and tone of the first childhood of his religion are borne by the whole subsequent course of his views and feelings, and are never lost, however far he may advance in fellowship with the Eternal Fountainhead.

Every intelligent finite being announces its spiritual nature and individuality by taking you back to what I may call a previous marriage in him of the Infinite with the finite, and your imagination refuses to explain it from any single prior factor, whether caprice or nature. In the same way you must regard as an individual everyone who can point to the birthday of his spiritual life and relate a wondrous tale of the rise of his religion as an immediate operation of the Deity, an influence of his spirit. He must be characteristic and special, for such an event does not happen to produce in the kingdom of religion vain repetition. Everything that originates organically and is self-contained can only be explained from itself. If its origin and individuality are not regarded as mutually explanatory and identical, it can never be quite understood. Thus you can only understand the religious person in so far as you know how to discover the whole in the notable moment that began his higher life, or from the developed manifestation can trace back this uniform character to the first, dimmest times of life.

All this being well considered, it will not be possible for you, I believe, to be in earnest with this complaint against the positive religions. If you still persist in it, it can only be from prejudice, for you are far too careless about the matter to be justified by your own observation. You have never felt the call to attach yourselves to the few religious men you might be able to discover. Though they are ever attractive and worthy enough of love, you have never tried by the microscope of friendship, or even of closer sympathy, to examine more accurately how they are organized both by and for the Universe.

For myself I have diligently considered them, I have sought out as patiently and studied them with the same reverent care that you devote to the curiosities of nature, and it has often occurred to me whether you would not be led to religion simply by giving heed to the almighty way in which the Deity builds up, from all that has otherwise been developed in man, that part of the soul in which he specially dwells, manifests his immediate operation, and mirrors himself, and thus makes his sanctuary quite peculiar and distinct, and if you only noticed how he glorifies himself in it by the exhaustless variety and opulence of forms. I, at least, am ever anew astonished at the many notable developments in a region so sparsely peopled as religion. Men are distinguished by all degrees of receptivity for the charm of the same object and by the greatest difference of effect, by the variety of tone produced by the preponderance of one or other type of feeling, by all sorts of idiosyncrasies of sensitiveness and peculiarity of temperament, and the religious view of things nevertheless is perpetually prominent. Again I see how the religious character of a man is often something quite peculiar in him, strongly marked off to the common eye from everything else shown in his other endowments. The most quiet and sober mind may be capable of the strongest, most passionate

266

emotions; a sense most dull to common and earthly things feels deeply even to sadness, and sees clearly even to rapture and prophecy; a heart most timid in all worldly matters testifies even by martyrdom to the world and to the age. And how wonderfully is this religious character itself fashioned and composed. Culture and crudeness, capacity and limitation, tenderness and hardness are in each, in a peculiar way, mixed and interwoven.

Where have I seen all this? In the peculiar sphere of religion, in its individual forms, in the positive religions which you decry as utterly wanting in variety. I have seen it among the heroes and martyrs of a definite faith in a way for which the friends of natural religion are too cold, among enthusiasts for living feeling, in a way they hold as too dangerous, among the worshippers of some new sprung light and individual revelation. There I will show you them, there at all times and among all peoples. Nowhere else are they to be met. No man as a mere single being can come to actual existence. By the very fact of existence he is set in a world, in a definite order of things, and becomes an object among other objects, and a religious man, by attaining his individual life, enters by this very fact into a common life, which is to say into some definite form of religion. The two things are simply one and the same divine act, and cannot be separated. If the original capacity of a man is too weak to reach this highest stage of consciousness, by fashioning itself in a definite way, the stimulus must also be too weak to initiate the process of a characteristic and robust religious life. *On Religion, Speeches . . .*, pp. 212-219, 228-280

*

The Speeches *were written primarily to counter Enlightenment dismissal of positive religion. By the time Schleiermacher wrote* The Christian Faith, *he was evidently more concerned to argue against the orthodox Christian tendency to separate Christianity from any affinity with the 'lower' religions. Schleiermacher sought to insist on the* uniqueness *of Christianity, but not its* discontinuity *with other religions. Unless there is continuity at some level, there could be no progress from one religion to Christianity. It was a position to be characteristic of liberal evangelicalism, to the present day.*

THE DIVERSITIES OF RELIGIOUS COMMUNIONS IN GENERAL: PROPOSITIONS BORROWED FROM THE PHILOSOPHY OF RELIGION

The various religious communions which have appeared in history with clearly defined limits are related to each other in two ways: as different stages of development, and as different kinds.

1. The religious communion which takes the form of household worship within a single family cannot fitly be regarded as an appearance in the realm of history, because it remains in the obscurity of an inner circle. Moreover, the transition from this to a really historical appearance is often very gradual. The beginning of it is seen in the large style of the patriarchal household, and the persisting association between families of sons and grandsons that live near each other; and it is out of these alone that the two fundamental forms previously mentioned (6, 4) can be developed. In these transitions, if several of them are placed beside each other, both kinds of difference can be found at least in germ.

Now in the first place, as regards the different stages of development: the historical appearance is in itself a higher stage, and stands above the mere isolated household worship, just as the civic condition, even in its most incomplete forms, stands above the formless association of the precivic condition. But this difference by no means relates only to the form or the compass of the fellowship itself, but also to the constitution of the underlying religious affections, according as they attain to clearness in conscious antithesis to the movements of the sensible self-consciousness. Now this development depends partly on the whole development of the mental powers, so that for that reason alone many a communion cannot continue longer in its own peculiar mode of existence; as, *e.g.* many forms of idol-worship, even though they might claim a high degree of mechanical skill are incompatible with even a moderate scientific and artistic education, and perish when confronted by it. Yet it is also partly true that the development takes its own course; and there is no contradiction in saying that, in one and the same whole, the piety may develop to its highest consummation, while other mental functions remain far behind.

But all differences are not to be thus regarded as distinct stages or levels. There are communal religions (Greek and Indian polytheism are good cases in point), of which one might well seem to be at the same point in the scale as the other, but which are yet very definitely different from each other. If, then, several such exist which belong to the same stage or level, the most natural course will be to call them different kinds or species. And indisputably it can be shown, even at the lowest stage, that most religious communions which are geographically separated from each other are also divided by inner differences.

2. But of course these two distinctions, into stages of development and into kinds (genera) or species, cannot in this realm, or indeed generally in the realm of history or of so-called moral 'persons', be maintained so definitely or carried through so surely as in the realm of Nature. For we are not here dealing with invariable forms which always reproduce themselves in the same way. Each individual communion is capable of a greater or lesser development within the character of its kind or genus. Let us, now, consider that in this way, just as the individual may pass from a more imperfect religious communion to a higher one, so a particular communion might without prejudice to its generic character, develop beyond its original level, and that this may happen equally to all. Then the idea of stages would naturally disappear, for the last phase of the lower and the first of the higher might be continuously connected, and it would then be more correct to say that each genus works itself up by a series of developments from the imperfect to the more perfect. But, on the other hand, we may take the fact that, just as we say an individual becomes in a certain sense a new man by passing to a higher form of religion, so the generic character of a communion must be lost when it rises to a higher level. Then even on any one level, if the inner development is to go on, the generic character would become uncertain and altogether unstable, while the levels or stages would be all the more sharply and definitely distinguished.

This variability, however, does not discredit the reality of our twofold distinction. For every religious communion which appears in history will be related to the others in this twofold way. It will be co-ordinate with some, and subordinate or superior to others; and thus it is distinguished from the former in the one manner and from the latter in the other. And if those who busy themselves most with the history and criticism of religions have given less attention to the task of fitting the different forms into this framework, this may be partly because they confine themselves almost exclusively to the individual, and partly also because it may be difficult in particular cases to lay bare these relationships and properly to distinguish and separate co-ordinates and subordinates. It may here suffice us to have established the twofold distinction in a general way, since our sole concern is to investigate how Christianity is related, in both respects, to other religious communions and forms of faith.

3. Our proposition does not assert, but it does tacitly presuppose the possibility, that there are other forms of piety which are related to Christianity as different forms on the same level of development, and thus so far similar. But this does not contradict the conviction, which we assume every Christian to possess, of the exclusive superiority of Christianity. In the realm of Nature also we distinguish perfect and imperfect animals as different stages of the development of animal life, and again on each of these stages different genera, which thus resemble each other as expressions of the same stage; but this does not mean that one genus of the lower stage may not be nearer to the higher, and thus more perfect, than the others. Similarly, though several kinds of piety belong to the same stage as Christianity, it may yet be more perfect than any of them.

Our proposition excludes only the idea, which indeed is often met with, that the Christian religion (piety) should adopt towards at least most other forms of piety the attitude of the true towards the false. For if the religions belonging to the same stage as Christianity were entirely false, how could they have so much similarity to Christianity as to make that classification requisite? And if the religions which belong to the lower stages contained nothing but error, how would it be possible for a man to pass from them to Christianity? Only the true, and not the false, can be a basis of receptivity for the higher truth of Christianity. The whole delineation which we are here introducing is based rather on the maxim that error never exists in and for itself, but always along with some truth, and that we have never fully understood it until we have discovered its connection with truth, and the true thing to which it is attached. With this agrees what the apostle says when he represents even polytheism as a perversion of the original consciousness of God which underlies it, and when, in this evidence of the longing which all these fancies have failed to satisfy, he finds an obscure presentiment of the true God.

Those forms of piety in which all religious affections express the dependence of everything finite upon one Supreme and Infinite Being, i.e. the mono-theistic forms, occupy the highest level; and all others are related to them as subordinate forms, from which men are destined to pass to those higher ones.

1. As such subordinate stages we set down, generally speaking, idol-wor-ship proper (also called fetishism) and polytheism; of which, again, the first stands far lower than the second. The idol-worshipper may quite well have only one idol, but this does not give such monolatry any resemblance to monotheism, for it ascribes to the idol an influence only over a limited field of objects or processes, beyond which its own interest and sympathy do not extend. The addition of several idols is merely an accident, usually caused by the experience of some incapacity in the orig-inal one, but not aiming at any kind of completeness. Indeed, the main reason why people remain on this level is that the sense of totality has not yet developed. The old εόava of the original Greek tribes were probably idols in the proper sense, each being something in itself alone. The unifi-cation of these different worships, by which one Being was substituted for several such idols, and the rise of several cycles of myths by which these creations were brought into connection with each other — this was the development through which the transition from idol-worship to polytheism proper took place. But the more the idea of a multiplicity of local habitations clung to the beings thus constituted, the more did polytheism continue to savour of idol-worship. Polytheism proper is present only when the local references quite disappear, and the gods, spiritually defined, form an organized and coherent plurality, which, if not exhibited as a totality, is nevertheless presupposed and striven after as such. The more, then, any single one of these beings is related to the whole system of them, and this system, in turn, to the whole of existence as it appears in consciousness, the more definitely is the dependence of everything finite, not indeed on a highest one, but on this highest totality, expressed in the religious self-consciousness. But in this state of reli-gious faith there cannot fail to be here and there at least a presentiment of one supreme being behind the plurality of higher beings; and then polytheism is already beginning to disappear, and the way to mono-theism is open.

2. As for this difference, of believing in one God on whom the religious man regards himself as being (along with the world of which he is a part) absolutely dependent, or in a group of gods to whom he stands in differ-ent relations according as they divide the government of the world among

them, or finally in particular idols which belong to the family or the locality or the particular occupation in which he lives: it seems at first, indeed, to be only a difference in the mode of representation, and therefore, from our point of view, only a derivative difference. And only a difference in the immediate self-consciousness can for us be a fit measure of the development of religion. But it is also very easy to show that these different representations depend on different states of self-consciousness. Idol-worship proper is based upon a confused state of the self-consciousness which marks the lowest condition of man, since in it the higher and lower are so little distinguished that even the feeling of absolute dependence is reflected as arising from a particular object to be apprehended by the senses. So, too, with polytheism: in its combination of the religious susceptibility with diverse affections of the sensible self-consciousness, it exhibits this diversity in such a very preponderant degree that the feelings of absolute dependence cannot appear in its complete unity and indifference to all that the sensible self-consciousness may contain; but, instead, a plurality is posited as its source. But when the higher self-consciousness, in distinction from the sensible, has been fully developed, then, in so far as we are open in general to sensible stimulation, *i.e.* in so far as we are constituent parts of the world, and therefore in so far as we take up the world into our self-consciousness and expand the latter into a general consciousness of finitude, we are conscious of ourselves as absolutely dependent. Now this self-consciousness can only be described in terms of monotheism, and indeed only as we have expressed it in our proposition. For if we are conscious of ourselves, as such and in our finitude, as absolutely dependent, the same holds true of all finite existence, and in this connection we take up the whole world along with ourselves into the unity of our self-consciousness. Thus the different ways of representing that existence outside of us to which the consciousness of absolute dependence refers, depend partly on the different degrees of extensiveness of the self-consciousness (for as long as a man identifies himself only with a small part of finite existence, his god will remain a fetish); and partly on the degree of clearness with which the higher self-consciousness is distinguished from the lower. Polytheism naturally represents in both respects an indeterminate middle stage, which sometimes is very little different from idol-worship, but sometimes, when in the handling of the plurality there appears a secret striving after unity, may border very closely on monotheism; whether it be that the gods rather represent the forces of nature, or that they symbolize the human qualities which are operative in social relationships, or that both these tendencies are united in the same cult. Otherwise it could not in itself be explained how the correlative term in the feeling of absolute dependence could be reflected as a plurality of beings. But if the higher consciousness has not become quite distinct from the lower, then the correlative can only be conceived in a sensible way, and then for that very reason it contains the germs of plurality. Thus it is only when the religious consciousness expresses itself as capable of being combined with all the states of the sensible self-consciousness without discrimination, but also as clearly distinct from the latter, in such a way that in the religious emotions themselves no sharper distinction appears than that between the joyful and depressing the tone — it is only then that man has successfully passed beyond those two stages, and can refer his feeling of absolute dependence solely to one supreme being.

3. It can therefore justly be said that as soon as piety has anywhere developed to the point of belief in one God over all, it may be predicted that man will not in any region of the earth remain stationary on one of the lower planes. For this belief is always and everywhere very particularly engaged, if not always in the best way, in the endeavour to propagate itself and disclose itself to the receptive faculties of mankind; and this succeeds eventually, as we can see, even among the rudest human races, and by a direct transition from fetishism without any intermediate passage through a stage of polytheism. On the other hand, there is nowhere any trace, so far as history reaches, of a relapse from monotheism, in the strict sense. In the case of most of those Christians who under persecution went back to heathenism, it was only an apparent return. Where it was a matter of real earnest, these people must, previously, at their conversion to Christianity, have been simply carried on by a general movement, without having appropriated the essence of this belief into their own personal consciousness. However, we must not, from all this, draw the conclusion that the existence of fetishism requires for its explanation the assumption of a still lower stage, in which religious emotion would be altogether lacking. Many have, indeed, described the original state of mankind as such a brute-existence; but, even if we cannot deny all trace of such a state, it can be neither proved historically nor imagined in a general way how of itself this state should have given rise to the development of something higher. No more can it be shown that polytheism has anywhere transformed itself, by a sheer process from within, into genuine monotheism; although this can at least be conceived as possible, as has been indicated above. In any case, we must secure ourselves against the demand that, since we have definitely exhibited such a gradation, we are bound also to

give a definite account of such an original state of religion; for in other connections also it is the case that we never get back to origins. If, then, we keep simply to our presuppositions, without resorting to any historical statements about a period which is altogether prehistoric, we are left with a choice between two ways of conceiving it. Either that quite obscure and confused form of religion was everywhere the original form, and advanced to polytheism through the concentration of several small tribes into one larger community; or a childish monotheism (which for that very reason was subject to a confused mingling of the higher and the lower) was the original stage, and among some people darkened completely into idol-worship, while among others it clarified into a pure belief in God.

4. On this highest plane, of monotheism, history exhibits only three great communions — the Jewish, the Christian, and the Mohammedan; the first being almost in process of extinction, the other two still contending for the mastery of the human race. Judaism, by its limitation of the love of Jehovah to the race of Abraham, betrays a lingering affinity with fetishism; and the numerous vacillations towards idol-worship prove that during the political heyday of the nation the monotheistic faith had not yet taken fast root, and was not fully and purely developed until after the Babylonian Exile. Islam, on the other hand, with its passionate character, and the strongly sensuous content of its ideas, betrays, in spite of its strict monotheism, a large measure of that influence of the sensible upon the character of the religious emotions which elsewhere keeps men on the level of polytheism. Thus Christianity, because it remains free from both these weaknesses, stands higher than either of those other two forms, and takes its place as the purest form of monotheism which has appeared in history. Hence there is strictly no such thing as a wholesale relapse from Christianity to either Judaism or Mohammedanism, any more than there is from any monotheistic religion to polytheism or idol-worship. Individual exceptions will always be connected with pathological states of mind; or, instead of religion, it will prove to be simply one form of irreligion that is exchanged for another, which indeed is what always happens in the case of renegades. And so this comparison of Christianity with other similar religions is in itself a sufficient warrant for saying that Christianity is, in fact, the most perfect of the most highly developed forms of religion.

Postscript 1. — The above account is at variance with the view which sees no real piety at all, but only superstition, in the religions of the lower levels, mainly because they are supposed to have had their source simply in fear. But the honour of Christianity does not at all demand such an assertion. For since Christianity itself affirms that only perfect love casts out all fear, it must admit that imperfect love is never entirely free from fear. And likewise it is always the case, even in idol-worship, if the idol is worshipped as a protector at all, and not as an evil being, that the fear is by no means quite without any impulses of love, but is rather an adaptation, corresponding to the imperfect love, of the feeling of absolute dependence. Moreover (quite apart from the fact that many of these religions are too cheerful to be explicable by fear), if we should set out to discover for them a quite different origin from that of true religion, it would be difficult to show what sort of tendency this is in the human soul, and what its inner aim is, which engenders idol-worship, and which must again be lost when the latter gives place to Religion. The truth is, rather, that we must never deny the homogeneity of all these products of the human spirit, but must acknowledge the same root even for the lower powers.

Postscript 2. — But for the assonance of the names there would scarcely be any occasion for us expressly to remark that it is not at all our present business to say anything about that way of thinking which is called pantheism. For it has never been the confession of a religious communion which actually appeared in history, and it is only with these that we are concerned. Moreover, this name was not originally used even by individuals to designate their own views, but crept in as a taunt and nickname; and in such cases it always remains difficult to hold consistently to any one meaning. The one thing concerning the subject which can be discussed in this place (and indeed *only* in such a place as this) is the question of the relation of this way of thinking to piety. It is admitted that it does not, like the three above-described theories, spring from the religious emotions, by direct reflection upon them. But it may be asked whether, having once arisen in some other way — by the way of speculation or simply of reasoning — it is yet compatible with piety. To this question an affirmative answer may be given without hesitation, provided that pantheism is taken as expressing some variety or form of theism, and that the word is not simply and solely a disguise for a materialistic negation of theism. If we look at idol-worship, and consider how it is always conjoined with a very limited knowledge of the world, and is also full of magic and sorcery of every sort, it is very easy to see that in very few cases can one speak of a clear distinction on this level between what is assigned to God and what is assigned to the world. And why could not a Hellenic polytheist, embarrassed by the entirely human shapes of the gods, have identified his great gods with the evolved gods of Plato, leaving out the God

275

whom Plato represents as addressing them, and positing only the enthroned Necessity? This would not imply any change in his piety, yet his representation of it would have become pantheistic. But let us think of the highest stage of religion, and let us accordingly hold pantheism fast to the usual formula of One and All: then God and world will remain distinct at least as regards function, and thus such a man, since he reckons himself as belonging to the world, can feel himself, along with this All, to be dependent on that which is the corresponding One. Such states of mind can scarcely be distinguished from the religious emotions of many a monotheist. At any rate, the distinction (always rather a curious one, and, if I may say so, roughly drawn) between a God who is outside of and above the world, and a God who is in the world, does not particularly meet the point, for nothing can strictly be said about God in terms of the antithesis between internal and external without imperilling in some way the divine omnipotence and omnipresence.   *The Christian Faith*, pp. 31-39

SELECT BIBLIOGRAPHY

A. WORKS OF SCHLEIERMACHER IN ENGLISH

The Life of Schleiermacher as Unfolded in his Autobiography and Letters 2 volumes. Translated by Frederica Rowan, London: Smith, Elder and Co, 1860. (Orig: *Aus Schleiermachers Leben in Briefen,* Berlin, 1860.)

On Religion. Speeches to Its Cultured Despisers. Translated by John Oman, London: Kegan Paul, Trench, Trubner and Co, 1893; also Harper Torchbook edition 1958. (Orig. *Über die Religion: Reden an die Gebildeten unter ihren Verächtern,* critical edition, Braunschweig, 1879.)

Selected Sermons of Schleiermacher. Translated by Mary F. Wilson, London: Hodder and Stoughton, 1890 (Foreign Biblical Library Series).

Brief Outline of the Study of Theology. Translated by W. Farrer, Edinburgh: T. and T. Clark, 1850; also an edition translated by T. Tice, John Knox Press, 1966. (Orig: *Kurze Darstellung des theologischen Studiums,* Berlin, 1810.)

Hermeneutics: The Handwritten Manuscripts. Edited by H. Kimmerle. Translated by J. Duke and J. Forstman, American Academy of Religion Texts and Translations Series, Missoula, Montana: Scholars Press, 1977. (Orig: *Hermeneutik: Nach den Handschriften,* ed H. Kimmerle, Heidelberg, 1959.)

The Life of Jesus. Translated by S. Maclean Gilmour. Edited by J.C. Verheyden, Philadelphia: Fortress Press, 1975. (Orig: *Das Leben Jesu. Vorlesungen an der Universität zu Berlin im Jahr 1832,* ed. K.A. Rutenik, Berlin 1864.)

The Christian Faith. Translation of the second edition by H.R. Mackintosh and J.S. Stewart, Edinburgh: T. and T. Clark, 1928. (Orig: *Der Christliche Glaube nach den Grundsatzen der evangelischen Kirche im Zusammenhange dargestellt,* Berlin, 1830.)

Christmas Eve: Dialogue on the Incarnation. Translated by T. Tice, Richmond, Virginia: John Knox Press, 1967. (Orig: *Schleiermachers Weihnachtsfeier: Ein Gesprach,* critical edition of H. Mulert, Leipzig, 1908.)

B. WORKS ON SCHLEIERMACHER IN ENGLISH

Barth, K. *The Theology of Schleiermacher. Lectures at Göttingen 1923-24.* Edinburgh: T. and T. Clark and Grand Rapids: Eerdmans, 1982.

Brandt, R.B. *The Philosophy of Schleiermacher. The Development of his Theory of Scientific and Religious Knowledge.* Westport, Connecticut: Greenwood Press, 1968 (originally published 1941 by Harper and Row).

Dawson, J.F. *Friedrich Schleiermacher. The Evolution of a Nationalist.* Austin, Texas and London: University of Texas Press, 1966.

Gerrish, B.A. *A Prince of the Church. Schleiermacher and the Beginnings of Modern Theology.* Philadelphia: Fortress Press and London: SCM Press, 1984.

Niebuhr, R.R. *Schleiermacher on Christ and Religion.* London: SCM Press, 1965.

Redeker, M. *Schleiermacher: Life and Thought.* Translated by J. Wallhauser. Philadelphia: Fortress Press, 1973. (Orig: *Friedrich Schleiermacher Leben und Werk,* Berlin, 1968.)

C. WORKS CONTAINING RELEVANT MATERIAL ON SCHLEIERMACHER

Barth, K. *From Rousseau to Ritschl.* London: SCM Press, 1959.

Reardon, B.M.G. *Religious Thought in the Nineteenth Century. Illustrated from Writers of the Period.* Cambridge: Cambridge University Press, 1966.

Reardon, B.M.G. *Religion in the Age of Romanticism. Studies in Early Nineteenth Century Thought.* Cambridge: Cambridge University Press, 1985.

Sykes, S. *The Identity of Christianity. Theologians and the Essence of Christianity from Schleiermacher to Bart.* London: SPCK, 1984.

NOTES

Abbreviations
LS — *The Life of Schleiermacher as Unfolded in his Autobiography and Letters.*
OR — *On Religion. Speeches to Its Cultured Despisers.*
CF — *The Christian Faith.*

[1] B.M.G. Reardon, *Religion in an Age of Romanticism* (Cambridge 1935), p. 4.
[2] LS Vol. II p. 125.
[3] ibid. p. 23.
[4] LS Vol. I p. 284.
[5] LS Vol. II p. 56 f.
[6] LS Vol. I p. 95.
[7] ibid. p. 159.
[8] ibid. p. 188.
[9] ibid. p. 318.
[10] ibid. p. 382.
[11] OR p. 12.
[12] Cf B.A. Gerrish, *A Prince of the Church: Schleiermacher and the Beginnings of Modern Theology* (London 1984), p. 20.
[13] LS Vol. II p. 203 f.
[14] *Brief Outline of the Study of Theology* p. 94.
[15] OR p. 36.
[16] ibid. p. 39.
[17] ibid. p. 148.
[18] See J. Macquarrie, *Twentieth Century Religious Thought* (London 1963), pp. 218-223.
[19] CF p. 52.
[20] ibid. p. 199.
[21] See B.M.G. Reardon, *Liberal Protestantism* (Cambridge 1968).
[22] J. Baillie, *Our Knowledge of God,* (Oxford 1939) p. 468.
[23] OR p. 35.
[24] CF p. 76.
[25] OR p. 101.
[26] CF p. 101.
[27] R.R. Niebuhr, *Schleiermacher on Christ and Religion* (London 1965) p. 148.
[28] ibid. p. 28.
[29] See e.g. R. Bultmann, *Jesus Christ and Mythology* (London 1960); F. Gogarten, *Demythologising and History* (London 1955).
[30] See e.g. G. Guttierez, *A Theology of Liberation* (London 1974); A. Fierro, *The Militant Gospel* (London 1977).
[31] LS Vol. II p. 27.

[32] *Hermeneutics* p. 101.
[33] LS Vol. I, p. 2 f.
[34] Cf H.A. Hodges, *Wilhelm Dilthey* (London 1944).
[35] M. Heidegger, *Being and Time* (London 1962).
[36] R.G. Collingwood, *The Idea of History* (Oxford 1946).
[37] H.-G. Gadamer, *Truth and Method* (London 1975).
[38] *Hermeneutics* p. 112.
[39] OR p. 45.
[40] ibid. p. 36.
[41] CF p. 170.
[42] ibid. p. 178.
[43] ibid. p. 171.
[44] *Selected Sermons* p. 46.
[45] Gerrish, op. cit. p. 23.
[46] CF p. 377.
[47] *The Life of Jesus* p. 11.
[48] CF p. 387.
[49] ibid. p. 388.
[50] See e.g. D. Bonhoeffer, *Letters and Papers from Prison* (London 1971); N. Pittenger, *The Lure of Divine Love* (Edinburgh 1979); J. Moltmann, *The Crucified God* (London 1973); E. Jüngel, *God as the Mystery of the World* (Edinburgh 1983).
[51] *Selected Sermons* p. 73.
[52] M. Redeker, *Schleiermacher: Life and Thought* (Philadelphia 1973), p. 89.
[53] *Selected Sermons* p. 74.
[54] See especially J.F. Dawson, *Schleiermacher: The Evolution of a Nationalist* (Texas 1966).
[55] CF p. 471.
[56] ibid. p. 38.
[57] ibid. p. 37.
[58] K. Barth, *The Theology of Schleiermacher* (Edinburgh 1982) p. 271 f, and also Chapter VIII in his *From Rousseau to Ritschl* (London 1959).
[59] *The Theology of Schleiermacher* p. 272.
[60] ibid. p. 278.

INDEX

Page numbers in *italics* denote references in the Schleiermacher texts, those in ordinary type denote pages in editorial sections.